2,00

# The Pursuit of the Kingfisher

CHRISTOPHER MIDDLETON

# The Pursuit
# of the Kingfisher *essays*

CARCANET PRESS/MANCHESTER

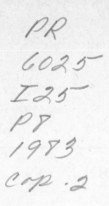

*First published in the UK in 1983*
*by Carcanet Press Ltd,*
*208 Corn Exchange Building, Manchester M4 3BQ*
*Copyright © Christopher Middleton 1983*

Middleton, Christopher
   The pursuit of the kingfisher & other essays.
   I. Title
   082      PR6063.I/

   ISBN 0-85635-473-2

The publisher acknowledges the financial assistance of the Arts
Council of Great Britain

Printed in England by SRP Ltd, Exeter

# Contents

# Introductory Afterthoughts

## 1

The essays in this book are reconnaissances around areas of experience which in blander times might have been called spiritual. Yet this assertion has to be taken with a grain of salt, as do most alibis. My main concerns have been the workings of imagination, specifically of lyrical imagination. The latter has a tendency to vanish the moment it is looked at and spoken of. Hence the book's title: by the title is meant not what the kingfisher pursues, but the writer's pursuit of the kingfisher.

Even then, how shall lyrical imagination be spoken of? A murmur of its ways and means traverses other writings which, down the centuries, have been devoted to the subject. I might offer two statements from unexpected quarters, in order to trace a provisional frame from groupings of ideas that are my underpinnings. Robert Byron, writing of the absence of any 'lyrical note' from the Russian architecture he had seen (in 1932), called that note an 'intimate perfection which reaches to the hidden places of the mind'.[1] Leonardo da Vinci observed: 'The man in the bird rests on an axis a little higher than his centre of gravity.'[2]

The essays are of different kinds and they were not written as a logical sequence. Tentative, hand-wringing, and often gauche, they range from discursive studies like the one on Hölderlin's 'Andenken', to the quite fragmentary 'Seventeen Hiccups'; from the remarks on translating Goethe (these might have had more rigour), to the slingshot prose of 'Louise Moillon's Apricots' and the finale, 'An Allegory of Erato.' In the last my pursuit of the kingfisher might well be thought to have imploded into a wild goose chase. References come at the end. Some can be perused separately, although most do footnote remarks in the text. My use of the words 'liminal' and 'liminality' in several essays needs to be explained. I was thinking along such lines when my attention was drawn to Victor Turner's writings in the field of anthropology.[3] He distinguishes between 'liminoid' and 'liminal', and I use 'liminal' where he would insist on 'liminoid', as a category for para-religious, para-spiritual events or documents. Turner reserves 'liminal' for the designation of institutionally religious happenings, such as rites of passage in Africa, or pilgrimages in Mexico and Europe. My avoidance of 'liminoid' need cause no confusion. I only substituted 'liminal' because the former term set my teeth on edge — it tastes of conferences. In this connection I would like to thank two friends, Barbara Babcock and Joel Sherzer, whose work and talk has been for some years always a delight and a lesson.

## 2

We live in terrible times. Much that has ringed and sustained human cultures for millennia is being extirpated. Investigation of such luminous substances can be stigmatized, easily enough, as stick-in-the-mud reaction, as connivance in the 'reactionary revolution' which for the present threatens to engulf West and East alike, mainly for the usual wrong reasons. I should hope that my curiosity and anxiety about lyrical imagination in the Western world might be understood contrariwise as pained concern about the future of that kind of imagination. I keep going back, but only because I want to suggest a *span*. Timeless or not, certain features of this Western lyrical imagination may be on the verge of leaving the world, or else we are on the verge of leaving them so far behind that they, like the godly presences in Cavafy's poem, seem to vanish into thin air. What human thing known as imagination can to the contrary be carried by us into the future? What is this marvel on which we might take hold before it abandons us, whose disappearance we must resist?

How to describe, let alone define, the fleeting combustible volatile gyroscopic *élan* of the nervous system in its creative condition which is called 'lyric'? Yet precisely that *élan* could be the climate, if not the cause, of the mobility of imagination in its other and heavier aesthetic forms — its invention also of the historic flesh through which societies protect, interpret, or doom themselves. One might conceive of lyrical imagination as a hearth of cultures, if only hearth were to be understood as a portable fire, rather than a fixed, geometric locus.

By this lyrical quality of imagination I do not mean escape, irresponsible *Erhebung*, or the 'sense of a universe' which sweeps across the heart-strings but atrophies conscience. One is covering 'dangerous ground': human beings, as creatures of language, are cruelly self-deceptive. If this self-deception is sterile, they block or distort the movements of a craving in them, so that the craving shocks them, with its liberating caprices — as if the spirit that craves cringed in horror at its own entombment in circumstance. How are intelligible symbols of lyrical imagination to be constructed? If they are constructed, what does that sort of utterance by the voice signify beyond itself? What role does nothingness, luminous or deadly, play in such signification? Against what modalities of nothingness does a lyrical imagination level its dialectical projections? With what creatures does it populate the void? These are some of the concerns I have tried to write about. If my gist comes to be dissipated by the pressure of impatience upon anxiety, suffice it to say that my oblivion was brooding upon scriptures as heterogeneous as Pound's *Cantos*, a host of German and French texts, and in crowded moments Ungaretti's four-word 'Alba' — 'M'illumino d'immenso'.

There is no formula, no conclusion. Yet lyrical imagination comes to be perceptible as a wild/free particle in the unsteady system of literature, enjoying 'the rare freedom of the particle to do what most particles never do'.[4]

Lyrical imagination lends itself accordingly to metaphors of air and flight. Yet the term '*Erhebung*' applied to acts of writing or reading does not suit what I had in mind. Besides, '*Erhebung*' is a German term describing uplift (psychic rather than moral), uplift of which heavy categorical Germans are frequently in need. It does not embrace the paradox and antagonisms of a poetry of volatility pursuing its own reverse: to come down to earth, to poise upon the laral domain of things, to nestle among everyday experiences. The Coptic tradition describes the poem as a composite of clay and gold. Clay jars were discovered inside walls during restoration work at St Sophia in Veliki Novgorod; originally they had been placed there to enhance the resonance of the chanting.

So the writer may feel, justifiably or not, that he is creating a world out of the contraries that crack like flowers the fortifications of his nature, irresolvable conflicts, the juice of his creations. But he can be deceiving himself. He is only adding his peculiar facet to the value structure of his time, his culture, and this peculiar facet is such that it breaks down, prismatically, the world into intelligible elements, coherent fields. To say as much, even then, is to put a good face on what is (more often) a singular despairing act of self-assertion against annihilating circumstances: he 'cries out before he is destroyed' (Baudelaire). Also this peculiar facet, this patch of real horizon which he can sight from his singular but erratic and largely unconscious point of purchase, might be a mere trick of the light, a gleam in the diabolic eye which elaborates the vision a writer believes he is himself projecting. Or else this facet — a batter, an inward leaning wall — may truly be a simple thrill which passes, pointless, through the socio-economic nexus of the writer's time, a mere shallow reflex of production relations.

One hopes not. The kind of lyrical imagination I try to speak of resists all the pious claptrap that, for want of something more sterile to do, reduces to economic dross the airy gold, the 'gold to airy thinness beat', of human souls giving voice to lyric frenzy with all the cool at their command.

### 3

I was flying across Texas with CM, the Polish poet; we sat in the front row of the cheaper seats, in 1969. In his hands he held a stout duodecimo volume of Polish poems. I looked across and down and saw the words on their no longer snowy pages. He had startling eyebrows, like feelers, wide sky-blue eyes, wrinkles of strain and laughter around them, a reception network. As we talked, he held the book affectionately between his hands. Of our talk I remember nothing.

### 4

Too weak a rebellion against prose decorum in the thinking of a poem tends to make its linguistic structure uniform, or tedious, hence to weaken its reflexion of unprompted, bizarre, aerial impulses at large in that thinking. What is to be looked for is a cross-coded music of signs, singularly arranged from horizon to foreground, a texture of allotropisms. That is the sort of texture which haunts memory and imagination; gradually, but in bursts, it reveals various 'meanings' when dwelt on — or caught up with — in mind. Actually the lyrical character is an ensemble, a gestalt: the clay around the gold, the vases which enhance the resonance. The wild particle needs to keep company with others, as early twentieth-century masters recognized (Pound, Eliot, Valéry). The breaking loose of the wild particle has a societal counterpart in the eruption of irrationality, however marked as expediency, rationale, or 'myth', in disintegrating communities (e.g., totalitarianism). Or so it has been alleged. A thinking person will be more apt to argue that institutionalized unreason, of whatever variety, is an absolute antithesis to the lyrical in art; and that the former is one poison we should by now have known what to do about (unhappily we do not). The pure ensemble of the poem can, however, slide the other way — into the somnolent, message-laden rationality, the moralistic sog, of cerebral or literary poetry *à l'anglaise*. There nothing intrinsically interesting, disturbing or disturbed, occurs in the waves of the poem's language. No subtly arresting successive alternations break the frame across distracted and contracted modalities of lyric frenzy, across calm and surge, coherence and fizz.

## 5

An open-eyed critique of power and its psychological bases may resemble, as Kafka's narrative critique still does, an all-dissolving nightmare of aphilia (lovelessness). Derrida's mode of metacriticism seems to be so fraught with the latter that its elevation toward the former — the critique of power — sets his hiccuping apostles, more often than not, on a slide backwards.

## 6

Once and for all, poetry, especially that of the lyrical imagination, should be treated as 'a secular art, free from the smears of mystery'.[5] That has been the drift, or the programme, since the Renaissance suspended the sacrality of home-made, human scripture. Yet there is a time-honoured view which holds that poetic speech does comprise — even in its vocal timbres — an esoteric dimension (gold, within the clay). The essays in this book liminalize an historic situation. The older view is not one that has been erased or invalidated by the evolution of consciousness in history, although anyone can tell the extent to which that older view has been taken in vain, smeared most piously, most abominably abused. As for the recuperation of 'sacred' poetry from archaic cultures, recently and still a 'going thing' in the USA, I have only doubts. Exquisite corpses, cerebral con-glomerations, may be read as pangs of a spiritual hunger which is devastating the profane world, but they do not solve the problem: the gnosis achieved is still voiced in the clamorous flat vocabulary of expensive 'research'. Mullahs and zaddiks cannot be impersonated.

**7**

The drummers have arrived. They pick up their sticks, and here goes. The writing that enacts imagination, specifically lyrical imagination, communicates infinitely more than a message conceived as a pack of words handed over for congruent redistribution. The range of a writer's perceptions (more strictly, apperceptions), as well as the depth or intensity of his powers of intellectual synthesis, are radiants of a star-stuff buried in the human mind, of the neural activity which is in the writer's trust, the writer as artist, uniquely. His horizons and interiorities do not necessarily blend into an exact equilibrium. The story of literature is the story of their ins and outs, gyrings, the separations, the touchings, the collusions of their cones, under the informing pressures of times and of circumstance. (The writer dwells in many times.) Once the writing is done, critical discourse and judgment can trace what it is that was done. Critical discourse may even serve to map, demystifyingly, as in the best pages of Coleridge or Barthes, the mental procedures by which the work came to be done, so and not otherwise. But how that which was done came to be done, so and not otherwise, is elusive. With wondrous alacrity it eludes the finer divining rods of those critics who dizzy us by phraseological shifts between doctrine, scepticism, and prattle-power. This HOW, was it play or plan, luck or cunning, gift or conquest? The reason intrinsic to lyrical imagination's projects has for its features manifold recessive declivities or acclivities sweeping out toward shrouded mountains, like great terraced valley slopes in Tibet; or else that reason is like the tiered mounds and hollows of sand clawed up or out by the sea on a beach pounded by a storm.

This HOW, even then, is the colour which detaches the work of imagination from the world of isolable messages. It is a filament which conducts a truth, through mazes of unknowns. Without an inkling of that truth we mischievous, self-deceiving, narrow-witted humans might forfeit all larger contact with our own beings, with one another across social realities, with the physical universe in which we share.

# On Translating Poems by Goethe

*O que será que será*
*Que andam suspirando pelas alcovas*
*Que andam sussurrando em versos e trovas*
*Que andam combinando no breu das tocas*
Chico Buarque

For two centuries Goethe has been the major figure in the history of
German literature. During the past century (since the Age of
Bismarck), he has become a principal turbine in what is now called,
disparagingly, the German 'culture industry'. But what sort of a poet
is he? Is it anomalous that a man with such massive powers of
reflection should have been actually not an intellectual poet? Odd
questions — if he was as great as they say, if fortune so favoured his
magnitude, they might have been settled long ago. It is astonishing
how many and various they were, the works of this single
imagination, works that were in one breath pioneering and
exemplary, whether they reconstituted a genre or broke away, like
*Faust*, into the transgeneric. But did his art shape the language and
temper of German writing after him beneficially? That question too
should have been settled. The critical literature is profuse, also
semioticians can now accurately fathom, we suppose, the workings
and effects of creative genius in language. When and why did Goethe
become an overwhelming 'classic'? Do people still read him for
pleasure, as Gottfried Keller in the 1840s did, responding wholly to
the warming golden light with which Goethe's writings, or so it is
said, wash reality? Has he been a beacon for hearts and minds far
afield in the civilized world, as other classics have been, or is he only a
name that awakens vague prejudice, does his spectre only provoke
conformingly, to quicken neither judgment nor desire? What a fatal
joke the Germans played on themselves when they adopted this
driven (but princely) immoralist as their Confucius, their Great
Educator! Worse, what features of Goethe's writings did his devotee
Nietzsche overlook that so enraged, in the year of confusion among
Surrealists and collapse in the Weimar Republic, 1932, a critic as

perceptive as the radical Carl Einstein?[1] Einstein bitterly denounced Goethe as a complacent windbag who never considered the gulfs of disorder between words and facts, a glib juggler employing 'eclectically a host of incoherent platitudes', and he lambasted him as the pernicious egotistical idolater of 'a conflictless, lazy unity, a roseate bat in an evolution belfry'.

Especially if fascination with Goethe deflects attention from a host of less comfortable older and younger writers of his time, Einstein's rage can still be shared by many. For others, Goethe has survived the petrifactions of adulation and exact scholarship alike. For sympathetic readers, his early ferocities are not empty, his middle 'classicism' is not leaden, the later wisdom is neither forbidding nor vaporous. It is possible to see Goethe at the opposite end of a tortuously long time-tunnel, as long as you can wriggle back through it, as a stark human being and as a poet whose best work is gravel in the machinery of the culture industry. At each stage in the growth of his labyrinthine individuality he was perhaps too fiercely hounded by vast imaginings to be found less than demonic. The famous later Master of Taxonomies, the tippling Privy Councillor in post-Napoleonic Weimar, in his utterances alternately Lear, Prospero, and Polonius, living finally surrounded by catalogued bibelots, lists and maps, collections of scientific and numismatic specimens, himself an imaginary museum (and easily outliving his only son, the alcoholic August), Goethe himself eludes all classification, he matches no literary or mythic archetype — unless it be the protean Magus. The questions begin with his being paradigmatic only of himself. So I shall only touch on the evergreen questions and address in this essay chiefly matters that are central to my theme: How does Goethe respond to English translation? What can a translator discover in the dark folds of his verse-textures? The views that follow are based solely on my own efforts to translate certain poems of his.

Translating a poem is not quite the inaugurative act of writing one. All the same, the synthesis of possibilities for which a translator settles is derived from his judgment as a feature of his linguistic imagination. He tries to weigh each value singly against all the others, grading also each to each as functions of a whole consortium, much as Kurt Schwitters required of the Merz artist. In Goethe's poems, rhyme belongs somehow with linearity, and linearity somehow belongs with a fluid resolution of stark-edged form. Rhyme belongs also with an air of improvisation, in so far as the lyrical speech-act flows, to all appearances, straight from a perception of circumstance (or an 'occasion'). At the same time, his poems always have a high finish. They are anything but stammered, although one or two might give the illusion of wandering (e.g., 'A Winter Journey in the Harz'). He was sensitive to the distances that can separate random from pure language. 'Language', he said in an undated poem called 'Etymologie', is 'ein reiner Himmelshauch', a pure breath of heaven, but conventions clog the channels, a great makeshifting occurs: and 'That which a people has stammeringly put together/Must be Eternal Law for heart and soul.' He was also sensitive to the veiling by illusion that makes absurdity and paradox in art mobilize the peculiar, intense image of experience which is a work of art. Not that his poems go off into the blue, on the contrary they are almost always addressed to some recipient or other, things, persons, or figments, or the spirits. But even lyrical apostrophe is a kind of absurdity — winged words addressed to a grape, a mountain, or to one's own eyes, even to unreceptive stars. Goethe made some apposite remarks to Eckermann on a landscape by Rubens in which the light comes from two opposed quarters, to throw impossible shadows: 'A picture as beautiful as this has never been seen in nature. . . . We would search reality in vain for it. . . . The artist wants to speak to the world by means of the All, and he does not find this All in nature: it is the fruit of his own genius, or, if you like, of the breath of a divine and fecundating spirit' (1827). So I would understand rhyme, linearity, the air of improvisation and other formal traits in his poems as means, among others by which he invites the pure to take over from the random, in radicalizing language, to 'shape an image' (as he says in 'Amor as Landscape Painter').

First, then, the question of end-rhyme. Obviously the mimetic translations I have attempted would miss the mark if they lacked rhyme entirely. But how can one invent in rhyme a 'believable modern English idiom'?[2] How, for translators or poets today, can a sense of the old *harmonia mundi* be restored, if only for a little time? A tacit faith in a cosmic harmony might seem to underlie the ability of older poets — think of Keats, of Byron — to rhyme with great zest and no effort. Rhyme was closure, proof of the veracity of the lyrical disclosure. It was also secretly linked with the onward thrusting of (apparent) extempore, with the crisp definition and suavity proper to any style, as the Latin classics had taught. At least, from Keats's letter of April 1819 to George and Georgiana we learn by the correction in his 'extempore'[3] canto xii, that rhyme always urged his imagination ahead of the act of writing, one line ahead or so, in a flow that crests in rhyme after rhyme. The same might be said of the interplay of rhyme and undulance in many of Goethe's poems.

Rhyme in translation, however, is likely to coarsen the effect, smell of the lamp. There is, then, a general problem: How to make rhyme sound as unprompted and as interesting as possible. This can be done, if coupled or alternate lines have sufficient flow and consonance in other phases, not over the line-breaks only, but in larger syntactical units, and in variant kinds of sound-patterning, such as assonance, whether final or inside the lines. Even then, assonance can dilute everything. For the feminine rhymes, in which English is poor and German rich, one can also substitute hidden tactful assonances with feminine endings — 'bedroom'/'zestful', 'kisses'/'shivers' in 'Wedding Night'. I also found that a phonetic shift (from feminine to masculine rhymes) might secure the tonal consistency of a translation, if the masculine ending had an open final vowel, not closing the word with a stop consonant, either. The point is, of course, to rhyme not because the original does, but because rhyming is proper to this English tonal m·⁻ ⸴is of the original poem's *decorum*. The mimesis crumbles, if there is no rhyme or if the assonance is inept, or inconspicuous, or random. The other point is to use no hackneyed rhymes, or, *nolens volens*, to rhyme interestingly on different parts of speech (something at which Alexander Pope was so deft). Verse-design is also a linguistic event in which rhyme relates closely to metric and its rhythmical fluctuations. It was necessary, for instance, in 'One and All', to lengthen the line by one measure from four to five beats, in order to make room for grammatical negotiations that would accommodate rhymes. This meant that the two poems 'One and All' and 'Testament' came to be translated into different metres, although the originals match, the latter picking up and modifying the theme of the former poem. Translations otherwise do observe the original metres, and only 'Pain, Dumb' breaks experimentally away.

Inevitably, the substitution of masculine for feminine rhyme, as in 'Universal Soul', modifies the tonal shape of the original. For that change to be made positive (mimesis being anything but replication) the translation ought to have its own tonal coherence and be, as regards rhyme, consistent. In 'Universal Soul' there is an inconsistency — one set of feminine rhymes (assonances) intrudes. Another translation with traces of the desirable intrinsic tonal coherence was the 'Night Song' of 1804. The original is a glossolalian rondeau with feminine endings. The translation with masculine endings sounds more clipped. But the insistent low pitches of the

English rhymes are meant to capture the original's dreamy murmur. To an attempt at translating acoustically the tiny arch-lyric 'Über allen Gipfeln' I was eventually taunted by Haroldo de Campos' Portuguese version (of 1966):

> Sobre os picos
> Paz.
> Nos cimos
> Quase
> Nenhum sopro.
> Calam aves nos ramos.
> Logo — vamos —
> Virá o repouso.
> (*From ms.*)

Goethe's poems do comprise, and not just sporadically, figures of sound (rather than 'figures of speech'). In 'Über allen Gipfeln', for instance, between the *u* of 'du' (line 3) and the next sound, the *k* of 'kaum', a tiny voiceless breath has to be breathed (and the poem is also saying 'hardly a breath'). The poem is not only *about* the 'Hauch', or about its mood or subject: it enacts mood pneumatically. In 'Wiederfinden' another such moment occurs, at the end of strophe 2: here the cosmogonic Alpha is kept in translation, but spliced with an apocalyptic Omega absent from the original:

> As he spoke the word 'Become!'
> An anguished 'Ah!' rang out, the All
> Exploded with a motion vast
> Into being actual.

Here the eschatological note may pass unheard; but to Goethe, versed as he was in the esoteric, the splicing would have signalled, aptly, Judgment Day, *apokatastasis*, the Restitution, in the End, of the Beginning.

Always end-rhyme is a cresting of sound-waves that move through other phases of the lines. If a rhyme scheme was changed, as in 'Primal Words. Orphic', or in 'Mignon', I still did what I could to get the right melodic clarity in the word-attunements interior to the lines, so as to recreate patterns of vocal quality (cf. the early 'Autumn Feeling'). Sometimes I had in mind Jean-Paul Richter's description of Goethe's voice in 1796: 'His reading is like deep-toned thunder, blended with soft, whispering raindrops.'[4] Charming, but not unhelpful. Goethe certainly liked words to roll. Homer was an open book to him, once he had read him in earshot of the sea near Naples. But he does also singularize sounds. Ezra Pound, in his 'A Few Don'ts' of 1913, when he tells 'the candidate' to 'dissect the lyrics of Goethe coldly into their component sound values'[5], was actually inviting him to notice the graduations of the shine on what Jean-Paul, as ear-witness, called 'raindrops'. Goethe is also the poet with a hundred voices, each with inflections of its own, and several are feminine ('The Spinner', 'Mignon', 'In Court', 'Nearness of the Beloved', and of course Gretchen.) This polyphony was instrumental in his becoming such a popular poet in some ways. Like the fifteenth-century Florentine artists under Lorenzo de' Medici, he so revised relations between popular (and oral) literature and humanistic culture, as to break down some of the barriers that separated them. People in his time also liked rhyme and they expected it, not as jingle, not as décor, but as a voicing of the *harmonia mundi*, of which poets were supposed to be the singing messengers.

Linearity is another feature of Goethe's poems which some readers might now find old-fangled. The verse-line is felt and delivered as a unit. This is not so noticeable in the quasi-Pindaric or proto-Expressionist poems of 1773–4, where a phrasing in clusters, or bursts, replaced linear design to some extent. But even in the earlier Sesenheim lyrics, and throughout the middle and later periods, the line is the backbone of the verse-design, even in such a strange song as 'Mignon'. This line-by-line, step-by-step progression of the poem is counterpointed, even in the hexameters and elegiac distichs, by Goethe's characteristic vocal undulation, which flows from the poem's imaginative matrix and 'organizes' everything. Now the original semantic of lines in sequence had to be kept. Transposition of words into different lines might be feasible, I thought, if it facilitated navigation of the straits of rhyme, or so long as it would make the undulation of the poetic logic more distinct. In practice, I found that any displacement of a word from its original line led to a slide, if not in the logic, then in the verse-texture itself. At the same time, adherence to the original linear sequence could lead, if one trod carelessly, to a loss of animation: the translation lacked the original's buoyancy. What I aimed at, then, was a balance between linearity and undulance — in Walt Whitman's sense of the poetic:

human thought, poetry or melody, must leave dim escapes and outlets — must possess a certain fluid, aerial character, akin to space itself, obscure to those of little or no imagination, but indispensable to the highest purposes. Poetic style, when addressed to the Soul, is less definite form, outline, sculpture, and becomes vista, music, half-tints, and even less than half-tints.'[6]

At the same time I had to observe the line's closure, when that was distinctively marked. Linearity is what makes gnomic phrasing possible; it provides the definition and clang of a 'truth', even if it may also open the door on cliché (and Goethe lent himself to quotation for all of life's occasions and ages, his gnomic lines have been embroidered into millions of samplers and mounted in bronze on many buildings). So if a rhyme scheme was changed (as the *ottava rima* was in 'Dedication'), this could mean the loss of just that rhyme in the original which marked closure, furnished the gnomic rondure. Such loss might be made up, I hoped, by some alliteration:

> Warum sucht ich den Weg so sehnsuchtsvoll,
> Wenn ich ihn nicht den Brüdern zeigen soll?

> Why did I seek the way with such a passion,
> If not to show my fellows what I found?

Eventually I was finding my way toward the nodal point at which linearity in rhyme is a dialectic of closure and disclosure. A line begins, opens up, closes (with or without rhyme); but no sooner has it closed than it is opening into the next line, in a fugitive instant, pure transition. This shutterflutter occurs even when the syntax entails complex subordination — those relative clauses, for instance, which in German promise a downward float into closure. What Goethe does is keep the shutterfluttering continuum in motion. There is an urgent forward motion, sometimes large like the roll of attacking momentum in Beethoven, sometimes microscopic, as in Goethe's handling of the word 'und' ('and'). To be sure, his 'und' can be a mere link between lines; but more often it is a sling from which an ensuant phrase or line is catapulted forward. In 'On the Lake', in an outrageous way at the time, he had an 'und' set off the poem's first burst. That particular 'und' signals an eruptiveness for which Goethe's early writings were duly notorious.

Constantly it was a question of gauging the specific energy in a line as one event in a nexus of lines, and of capturing that energy in its proper formal diffusion. This might require a transformation of grammatical types. For instance, the first line in 'Mignon': the original has a relative clause ('wo die Zitronen blühen'), but I substituted a straight English genitive with present participle ('of flowering lemon trees'). In other translations too a present participial clause replaces the original relative, without loss, I think, of the dynamic of the relative. These are small points, but a translator has to work like a pointillist. Goethe's celebrated dynamism (absent from so many translations, including French ones) can only be preserved by being punctiliously re-enacted. That re-enaction requires transformations which fly apart unless they are carefully controlled by respect for the channels, straight or twisting, through which the original line-energy came to be generated.

My next point, enhancement, also entailed a showing of respect. Translation into a believable modern English idiom, without the usual archaisms, requires a certain amount of judicious enhancement. One goes to work as a salvage archaeologist, or as a restorer of old paintings. Nothing may be distorted, but the treasure has to be raised in the nick of time. Thus it may be an enhancement, in 'Ganymede', when I make an appropriately mimetic triple rhyme undulate across the two lines

> Withal the nightingale lovingly
> Calls from the misty vale to me

— for which there is no phonetic match in the original. Again, in 'The Bride of Corinth', where I was adapting the Aytoun-Martin Victorian version, the original strophe 16 does not speak of 'muscle from the thrill of love'. It says 'youthful strength of love'. Here I felt that the change was due, the tissue of the line had to be fortified, and the 'muscle' phrase seemed to bring out, chastely enough, what the original implies, with the young man so amorous and 'durchmannt'. In 'Primal Words. Orphic', finding it impossible to recreate the original daisy-chain of feminine rhymes, I chose to toughen the phrasing here and there, in order to achieve a denser consistency on the semantic level. In strophe 2, line 4, the original says, literally: 'Likely you'll act as any other does'; 'other' is weak here, so I enhanced with 'manjack', which is a touch more robust (though little known in America). In strophe 3, line 8, the original says: 'The noblest, yet, themselves to one devote'; here again I wanted to avoid the colourless 'themselves', so I wrote, finally: '. . . their all to one devote', which is more clinching, yet fully consonant with the urbane wit which organizes the architecture of these monumental strophes. Seldom did I consciously intensify effects or meanings in ways that could be thought excessive. In 'Legend' I added a joke ('Or open it? For kicks?'), and in 'Shopping' I sharpened and modernized the anger. But that is all, or almost.

By and large my 'transcreations'[7] (the term Haroldo de Campos applied to those he has seen) are context-controlled. For instance, in 'Twilight Down From Heaven' the oscillating stress on 'unsteady' in line 14 brings out the shimmering by enacting it rhythmically, although the original shimmering is on the semantic level. In the same translation, 'a silver glow' is not quite 'Mondenglanz und – glut', accenting semantically as it does the colour, silver. The silver is proper, all the same, to the phanopoeia of these lines, and it is consistent with Goethe's feeling for that kind of light-effect elsewhere: in *Faust I*, Faust speaks of 'the silver figures of the ancestral world', and in *Faust II* there are the miraculous lines 'And in rolling waves of silver,/Seed to harvest urges on'.

Another aspect of this area is *antiquing*. Generally, I resisted it, as something adverse to enhancement, if not downright dilution. The last thing a translator must do is mistake turns of speech that became archaic after (or because of) his author's practices for any archaism or poeticism which might be embedded in the original. Yet that is the mistake made even by quite recent translators of Goethe. It is a curious situation: there was no English poetic idiom comparable to Goethe's in his own time, yet he has been translated till now in ways that simulate a 'period' style trashy in any age. Certainly his work became a mine for cliché-mongers, and he is not averse to mongering a little on the side himself. In principle all the translations I was making had to be free from outright archaism; but, inevitably, even those that have some flourish in phrasing and sentiment shrink the force of their originals by containing it in a confoundedly unmodern idiom.

In only a few poems did I risk a 'tis' or a 'thou', when such wording seemed both apt and inescapable. (It must be recalled that the German 'thou' is not archaic, but simply familiar.) 'On the Lake' was typical of another such difficulty. How to make outdated sentiment credible and strip archaism away? Who would now speak, as Goethe does here, and so anxiously, to his own eyes? Some readers will find a distinct change in 'Mignon' rather steep, perhaps. Her 'Dahin!' became 'Aiee!' Yet this (non-semantic, surface-phonetic) transposition into Flamenco Romany was carefully weighed against alternatives. One cannot ask Mignon to exclaim 'Thither!' 'Aiee!' suits her zither, and it is her cry, her sigh, her primal sorrow fully voiced in what they call, I believe, a 'phatic morpheme'.

Contextual control in the act of transcreation is what I was striving for. This was not only a question of rightness in texture, consistency, shape, or energy to be regenerated. It was also a question of honesty toward the quality, mass, and measure (*tempi*) of the perceptual experience which lines and rhymes and syntax unmistakably voice. 'Mignon', again, is an instance. I modified the rhyme scheme, true, but the English scheme does not blur the deep, symmetrical, intuitive design in the perceptual and imaginative scene which the poem tracks, line by line. There are three layers, or stages, of ubiquitous perception in this scene, in the three strophes: nature, culture, and myth (Goethe was at one time most receptive to Rousseau). With uncanny nonchalance Goethe may implant such deep designs in the lightest of his poems. The designs appear to have arisen out of his exceptionally clear and steady eidetic imagination. Another triangulation figures cryptically in the great 'floating buzzard' poem 'A Winter Journey in the Harz' and it is traceable in 'Über allen Gipfeln' ('Another Night Song'). When the nonchalance drifts toward cliché, the translator must be doubly careful to salvage the original dynamic from the cosmetic décor. He can do this by attending to the vocal values of the poems. Even in a single poem, those values may be versatile: naive, sly, jocose, pontifical, ironic notes conspire, but do not become bloated or slack. Did Goethe privilege a grand-bourgeois outlook and combine it with an art which cosmetically screens the wrinkles out of reality? Was there to be nothing nasty in the poetry of everyday? Yet he also knew of imagination as a 'violence within that protects us from a violence without . . . pressing back against the pressure of reality'.[8] In his time, the lyric poet, by definition, spoke to sublimate such violences; ugliness was outside his art's domain, even if he loathed or liked it as a human being.

Open and sensuous as Goethe's poems usually are, too, he seems to have quietly suspected that a poetic gnosis discloses a truth that is *sui generis*. Poetry in the last analysis was as different from other modes of speech or writing as the visual knowledge presented in a painting differs from linguistic or mathematical kinds of cognition. For Goethe, poetry and its gnosis arise from a clear apprehension of formal relationships between moves in the dance of his imagination among objects of sense — with those objects as partners in the dance. He glorifies the palpable. Yet discursive components of speech are not burned away in the process. When such components become 'poeticism', they inhibit the process, of course. But even an apparent cliché can be saturated with the formal-aesthetic patterning dynamism that informs the text as it unfolds. The cosmetic can condense the dew of cogitation and turn it into a nutrient for the inexcogitable inner thing. That thing is the patterning which is first and last in the process.

For all the ultimacy to be found in his work, Goethe is little known as a poet today. There are hardly any good translations into European languages. The English record is forlorn, but not unique. A false tone was set early on, by flummery translations from the great gossips Walter Scott and Thomas Carlyle. (In adopting some older translations,[9] I revised them, for the most part.) So the rebuffal of Goethe has been due, perhaps, to failure in translation. It might also be due to the fact that his *Lebensphilosophie* was too transcendental to interest ordinary people who have no patience with the vagaries, and with the lumberings, of the *mens teutonica* (as Balzac called it).[10] Besides, Goethe wrote so many other things. From every phase in his continuous work as a lyric poet came plays, narratives, memoirs, reflections, not to mention studies in natural science (from about the early 1790s). The rebuffal from the English-language side might have been due to something else also. Generally, readers have responded favourably, if slowly, to non-English European poets whose work has a dense and subtle intellectual foreground: Dante, Leopardi, recently Mandelstam. Rilke is somewhat of an anomaly. Even then, his Sonnets and Elegies have spellbound readers (of inadequate translations) with their uniquely sensuous intelligence, their intellectually pregnant metaphors. Likewise the Hölderlin to whom readers now defer is the later one, whose 'intellectualism' has a rigorous dialectical character, even when it is rhapsodic. Goethe seems to have missed the boat, on the other hand, because he is not critically argumentative, even though he may be dialectical, or prosy, in other ways. He is a sensuous, demonstrative, exploratory, divinatory poet. Hardly a poem of his presents an arguing poetic intellect in immediate action (as in Dante, Donne, Marvell, Browning). It is as if his poems, of whatever genre, unfold in some pre- or post-cognitive region of the mind. They deliver, enshrine, and codify ideas; but they do not enact ideas in the moment of collision with other ideas. This great transformer, this monarch, of German *Gedankenlyrik* (poetry of ideas) may have set his mark on its idiom so powerfully that it has remained to this day more apt for doctrinal than for witty critical thinking. Even Brecht hardly broke the pattern.

So much presence of mind, such a powerful emotional dynamic, such decorum, melodic rondure, wholeness, consonance, even such wisdom: yet he is nothing remotely like other 'classics', least of all like Góngora — because he never ceases to be an accessible poet, even a folk-minded one. His poems established, I venture to say, an uncommon linguistic ground, which may no longer be home ground, even for honest-to-goodness German loyalists. This ground oscillates at various frequencies, between directness and remoteness, immediacy and sublimity, folk-mode and highmindedness; but, for all the intimacy that he carved out room for in German poetry, he is never savage or vulgar in his wordliness. And he writes his poem, it would seem, after the fecundating conflicts have been adjudicated by his steady imagination, but without ever becoming a mere 'fair-weather' poet. In some later doctrinal poems, 'Urworte. Orphisch', for instance, just when we might expect a poet to interrogate his vision, he indulges a fatalism that might seem trite, were it not so grim, and still seems to beg the questions of free will, justice, and choice which Aquinas and Dante[11] addressed with such realism and acumen. The one poem in which an argumentative foreground might be discerned, densely composed (at a first shot) in *terza rima*, is the late one about contemplating Schiller's skull. Here he might come close to the old Yeats, but that would be because Yeats had learned how to cry in the teeth of philosophy, coming full circle from 'abstract dark' to a vision of the world as a symbolic construct of man's 'bitter soul'. Even in this late poem of Goethe's there are traces of an immediate circumstance in which the utterance occurs, and there is the characteristic address to the *object* in question. The 'occasion' as such is perhaps not so distinct as in many poems, but there is still the contour of the given, an aerial contour. Translating Goethe showed me, even then, something seldom noticed. This contour of the given is delicate and mobile, because it frames the fundamental experience voiced in most of his more celebrated poems: the experience of moving back and forth across limits, a transition of thresholds. It is the real stuff of rituals: the liminal experience. Whether its dimensions are miniature or cosmic, light or dark, deadly or redemptive, that is perhaps the core of lyric experience, and not in Goethe's work alone.

Here, too, is the mobile point amid known bounds and clear

proportions from which Goethe fills his world far or near with metaphors, ideas, feelings, analogies, to create a living texture of meaning. He was one of the last poets of the old projective imagination. Poetic creation here is one leap away from the kind which Mallarmé later came to view as the unique poetic world: a world of purest 'conjecture'. Soon after Goethe, all such totalizations were to become suspect. He lived in apocalyptic times. Forty when the French Revolution began, he eyed the upheavals of the next quarter-century with curiosity, much doubt, some dismay, and (later) considerable disdain. In history as such he watched for signs of an infinite but not inscrutable plan: and he saw symbolic events, polarized confluences of minds human and divine, rather than moves in a finite dialectic. (Not untypically of his tough outlook in this area, he is to be found rambling through the great Valmy bombardment, of 20 September 1792, studying the effects of shockwaves on eyesight, of light on dust.) For it was also a time of splendid systems: classical harmony in music, the Critical Philosophy, Hegel's Phenomenology, and the promise of a synthesis between art and the cognitive disciplines — all systems that were not totalitarian, unlike Napoleon's ubiquitous secret police. Not without anguish and rage, not in all confidence, Goethe fashioned in the recalcitrant German language a living texture which might have served, if all things had ever been equal, to defend human beings against their own worst aptitudes, their Gorgons, and against the voids that fill with demons when the positive projections are withdrawn. Small wonder if the attempt to capture in translation some fragments of that enterprise might seem like an absurd signal, sent into the past, but saying that the enterprise continues, here and there, in other ways.

By way of conclusion, some remarks on a vignette of Goethe by the old Rococo poet J. W. Gleim.[12] Gleim describes a reading that took place in 1777, in the apartments of the Duchess Anna Amalia of Saxe-Weimar. He has brought the latest issue of a wellknown poetry journal, the *Göttinger Musenalmanach*, and a 'young man' has just come in, booted and spurred, wearing an unbuttoned green hunting coat. This 'huntsman' sits opposite Gleim and listens carefully, although 'apart from his gleaming dark Italian eyes I hardly noticed anything about him'. During a short pause, he borrows the journal from Gleim, very politely, and asks if he might read too. Gleim condescends — even though the stranger is only a huntsman. The stranger reads some poems that are typical of the time, by Voss, Stollberg and Bürger. Then something happens:

Suddenly it was as if Satan had the reader by the short hairs, and I thought I was seeing with my own eyes the Devil's Huntsman. He was reading poems that were not in the journal at all, he was modulating into all possible vocal sounds and melodies, in hexameters, iambic lines, doggerel, anything and everything, all mixed up, as if he was shaking it out of his sleeves. . . . With what humour he brought all his fantasies together that evening! Sometimes such splendid thoughts came out of him, however fugitive, in fragments, that the authors to whom he ascribed them should have thanked God on their knees, if ever those thoughts had come to them at their desks. And for every person present he had something to offer . . .

Goethe's virtuosity depicted here has a history in Renaissance beliefs about the ordering and creative power of the word, a power that 'bespeaks a great confidence in the mind's authority over nature'.[13] Romantic and post-Romantic poetry, on the other hand, reflects a momentous shift away from that confidence. Poets perceive varieties of agonizing separation between mind and nature, words and things: a gulf has to be bridged, or closed. Goethe's poems span the epochs and are remarkable for the ways in which the conduct of poetic language and the spectacle of the world coalesce effortlessly in them. He was a master of that kind of supreme fiction by which the poem becomes 'part of the *res* itself, and not about it' (Wallace Stevens).

Yet this is the crux, at which contemporary readers of his poems, at least, might find his sanguine temperament too beaming, his confidence too easy, his reality too unresistant. Unlike Auden's 'governess', who gives the universe nought for behaviour, Goethe offends us by giving it a sort of placating A. Not that his language overwhelms the real; rather, it can seem to be remote from those realities which we experience without mediation, without help from any ordering forms or formalities. Hence the decorum of his poems is strange to us. We may be averse to his rhetoric, as 'old hat'. Inside the rhetoric, however, and not so far inside it either, there is a body of vital lyric experience which a reader can feel on his own skin, once he has made the imaginative effort, the effort that translation may or may not provoke. That experience is coherent and intact. It is partly the experience of an undulatory relationship, mediated by countless sensory and linguistic correspondences, metaphoric or not, between the act of speech and the whole scope of finite existence, from luminous spirits to deadly darkness, from psychic liberation to confinement in a body of fate. To that extent, Goethe's fictions of concord, born of this undulatory experience, should not so much tax our patience as train it. The supposed 'power' of speech to order real experience is here not a violence. Rather it is a kind of ductile vigilance in tune with an unshaken sense of the interrelatedness of things, with humanity as 'part of the natural continuum, and all nature indivisibly divine'.[14]

One of the themes which Goethe modulates, largely or in miniature, is thus the integration of opposites, the consorting of Yin and Yang. Another is the momentum of flowering (in the very motion of the poem), the unfolding of being, in and out of mind, which is generated by such instants of integration. The pneumatic power of the word gives access to the Law, it is the 'Gate' to the Law, in so far as the word is the Now, fully articulated. It is this Now about which Kafka's country simpleton asks, in the famous parable, even though the simpleton is not really conscious of what he is asking about. To this Now he can gain no access, stupefied as he is by the answers of the Gate-Keeper. Because of the latter's Authority, the simpleton cannot even risk a glimpse into the interior of the literal.

For us, too, Goethe is strange because he fathered something we simply take for granted: the interiority of modern German lyric language. He also made intimacy over to the public world — for every person, as Gleim said, he had something to offer. There were notable antecedents, to be sure, but Goethe enriched and subtilized the emotional, tonal, and semantic range of German poetry in ways that were unheard-of. (A century later, Debussy was to conjure likewise an otherworld of tonalities from the piano.) How then is one to perceive the enduring *Gestalt* of his poetry? — not forgetting that the *Gestalt* concept of today was shaped by his manner of thinking. Nineteenth-century positivist critics invited readers to interpret the poems as confessional works. Goethe had prompted this, calling his poems 'fragments of a great confession'; and he was a godsend for both positivist scholars and readers pursuing vicarious experience in lieu of none at all. Every poem sprang from a vital occasion, it was thought, and so he was celebrated as the founder of *Erlebnislyrik*, the poetry of experience. We now insist that a poem is a distinct linguistic event, a transformation of whatever elements may have ignited it. We care far less for biographical ingredients than for the semiotic process of the poem itself. I would simply hope that a reader will come to intuit the

*Gestalt* by enjoying some poems as a feast: if the feast is translated, still it is not just leftovers or the menu-card.

I say 'feast' with specific emphasis. Inherent in language there is a pneumatic and festive power, or a joy, which, like Aristotle's Infinite, initiates variety, as it orders development, and which links the dissimilar logics of civil liberty and art. The play of Goethe's verse-textures testifies to the latencies and activities of that power, whether or not it is 'god-given' (as Goethe's Tasso claimed). Currently there is much talk about language as a 'ritual event' having effects that are 'repressive' or occlusive. Such talk can be salutory, if it disposes of the brouhaha, and if it reflects a strict philosophical delight in the integrity of the translinguistic, if it makes recognizable the pristine values of beings and things neither tainted nor falsified by our linguistic ways of rendering them to ourselves. The talk is otiose if it only parrots fashionable theories, of course; it is thoughtless if it ignores the existential (historic) experience upon which those theories are predicated. For there are two historic moments. First, the majesty and joy of the creative word engages human communities in the awesome task of civilization. Second, a disenchantment occurs, oddly shared at the start of this century by Alfred Jarry's King Ubu and Hugo von Hofmannsthal's Lord Chandos: the pneumatic and festive power of the word has withdrawn, it withdrew long ago, from our not-so-civilized midst, we are immobilized, and only *now* do we know it.

What is the festive power of the first moment? It enables its vehicles to return to a virgin condition, to be renewed, and it dwells in words, just as it dwells in aquifers, so long as the words and the water are left to themselves for long enough. To dismiss language *in toto* as an oppressive ritual is to deny that feasts of refreshment are there for the eating, and for the cooking. It is to puncture with a sort of puritanic acid — let us call it the Savonarola Solution — the very eyes upon which the rainbow of being depends. It is to *ob-literate* the 'Event', which in authentic feasts like those of the Pueblo or of the Kannapuram spirit-dancers in South Asia configures commonplace life with what is variously called The Time of Beginning, The Dawn of Becoming, the Originative Now. More topically, it is to recommend that we become like the Americanized Poles in *The Deerhunter*, a film that so tellingly diagnosed the last years: slaves of the inarticulate, delivered up to existence as a gamble complete and militarized, a game of Russian roulette. The bullet waiting in the chamber of that pistol is rather different from the one that was waiting for Goethe's Werther.

Five Poems by Goethe

## Herbstgefühl

Fetter grüne, du Laub,
Am Rebengeländer
Hier mein Fenster herauf!
Gedrängter quellet,
Zwillingsbeeren, und reifet
Schneller und glänzend voller!
Euch brütet der Mutter Sonne
Scheideblick, euch umsäuselt
Des holden Himmels
Fruchtende Fülle;
Euch kühlet des Mondes
Freundlicher Zauberhauch,
Und euch betauen, ach!
Aus diesen Augen
Der ewig belebenden Liebe
Vollschwellende Tränen.

## Amor als Landschaftsmaler

Saß ich früh auf einer Felsenspitze,
Sah mit starren Augen in den Nebel;
Wie ein grau grundiertes Tuch gespannet,
Deckt' er alles in die Breit und Höhe.

Stellt' ein Knabe sich mir an die Seite,
Sagte: Lieber Freund, wie magst du starrend
Auf das leere Tuch gelassen schauen?
Hast du denn zum Malen und zum Bilden
Alle Lust auf ewig wohl verloren?

Sah ich an das Kind, und dachte heimlich:
Will das Bübchen doch den Meister machen!

*Autumn Feeling (1775)*

More fatly greening climb
The trellis, you, vine leaf
Up to my window!
Gush, denser, berries
Twin, and ripen
Shining fuller, faster!
Last gaze of sun
Broods you, maternal;
Of tender sky the fruiting
Fullness wafts around you;
Cooled you are, by the moon
Magic, a friendly breath,
And from these eyes,
Of ever quickening Love, ah,
Upon you falls a dew, the tumid
Brimming tears.

*Amor as Landscape Painter (1787)*

Sat upon a rocky peak at daybreak,
Staring fix-eyed through the mist before me;
Stretched like canvas primed with gray it mantled
Everything on either side and upward.

A little boy now came and stood beside me:
Friend, he said, I wonder what you're up to,
Peering, supine, at that empty canvas.
Might you have lost for now, if not for ever,
Pleasure in painting, shaping out an image?

Glancing at the child, I thought in secret:
Perhaps the boy thinks he can act the master.

Willst du immer trüb and müßig bleiben,
Sprach der Knabe, kann nichts Kluges werden;
Sieh, ich will dir gleich ein Bildchen malen,
Dich ein hübsches Bildchen malen lehren.

Und er richtete den Zeigefinger,
Der so rötlich war wie eine Rose,
Nach dem weiten ausgespannten Teppich,
Fing mit seinem Finger an zu zeichnen.

Oben malt' er eine schöne Sonne,
Die mir in die Augen mächtig glänzte,
Und den Saum der Wolken macht' er golden,
Ließ die Strahlen durch die Wolken dringen;
Malte dann die zarten leichten Wipfel
Frisch erquickter Bäume, zog die Hügel,
Einen nach dem andern, frei dahinter;
Unten ließ ers nicht an Wasser fehlen,
Zeichnete den Fluß so ganz natürlich,
Daß er schien im Sonnenstrahl zu glitzern,
Daß er schien am hohen Rand zu rauschen.

Ach, da standen Blumen an dem Flusse,
Und da waren Farben auf der Wiese,
Gold und Schmelz und Purpur und ein Grünes,
Alles wie Smaragd und wie Karfunkel!
Hell und rein lasiert' er drauf den Himmel
Und die blauen Berge fern und ferner,
Daß ich, ganz entzückt und neugeboren,
Bald den Maler, bald das Bild beschaute.

Hab ich doch, so sagt' er, dir bewiesen,
Daß ich dieses Handwerk gut verstehe;
Doch es ist das Schwerste noch zurücke.

Zeichnete darnach mit spitzem Finger
Und mit großer Sorgfalt an dem Wäldchen,
Grad ans Ende, wo die Sonne kräftig
Von dem hellen Boden widerglänzte,
Zeichnete das allerliebste Mädchen,
Wohlegebildet, zierlich angekleidet,

If you sit there, sullen, doing nothing,
Said the boy, no good will be the outcome.
Watch, I'll paint a smidgeon of a picture
Now, for you, a pretty one to learn from.

Then he lifted up his index finger,
Which was quite as rosy as a rose is;
Pointing to the fabric stretched before him,
Now the boy began to trace a picture.

At the top a beauteous sun he painted,
I was almost blinded by the dazzle;
Borders of the clouds, he made them golden,
Rays of sun to perforate the cloud mass;
Painted then the delicate and tender
Tops of freshly quickened trees, with hillocks
Touched into place and freely grouped behind them;
Lower down — water he put, and plenty,
Drew the river, as it is in nature,
So much so, it seemed to glint with sunlight
And murmur as it rose against its edges.

Ah, beside the river flowers had sprouted,
And the meadow was a blaze of colour,
Gold, enamel sheen, a green, and crimson,
All aglow like emerald and carbuncle.
Bright and clear, above, he glazed the sky in,
Mountains, blue, receding in the distance,
So that born anew I looked, ecstatic,
Now upon the painter, now the picture.

You'll admit, says he, I've demonstrated
This is a handiwork I have some skill in;
The hardest part is still to come, however.

Then, with pointing fingertip and very
Solicitously, by the little forest,
Right on the brink of it, where sunlight gathered
To be reflected off the shining humus,
He traced the loveliest girl you could set eyes on,
Pretty figure, and a graceful garment,

Frische Wangen unter braunen Haaren,
Und die Wangen waren von der Farbe
Wie das Fingerchen, das sie gebildet.

O du Knabe! rief ich, welch ein Meister
Hat in seine Schule dich genommen,
Daß du so geschwind und so natürlich
Alles klug beginnst und gut vollendest?

Da ich noch so rede, sieh, da rühret
Sich ein Windchen und bewegt die Gipfel,
Kräuselt alle Wellen auf dem Flusse,
Füllt den Schleier des vollkommnen Mädchens
Und, was mich Erstaunten mehr erstaunte,
Fängt das Mädchen an den Fuß zu rühren,
Geht zu kommen, nähert sich dem Orte,
Wo ich mit dem losen Lehrer sitze.

Da nun alles, alles sich bewegte,
Bäume, Fluß and Blumen und der Schleier
Und der zarte Fuß der Allerschönsten,
Glaubt ihr wohl, ich sei auf meinem Felsen
Wie ein Felsen still und fest geblieben?


*Nachtgesang*

O gib, vom weichen Pfühle,
Träumend, ein halb Gehör!
Bei meinem Saitenspiele
Schlafe! was willst du mehr?

Bei meinem Saitenspiele
Segnet der Sterne Heer
Die ewigen Gefühle;
Schlafe! was willst du mehr?

Die ewigen Gefühle
Heben mich, hoch und hehr,
Aus irdischem Gewühle;
Schlafe! was willst du mehr?

Cheeks a fresh complexion, all around them
Tawny hair, and more, the cheeks were tinted
Like the tiny finger that had shaped them.

Little boy, I now exclaimed, what master
Can it be who took you as his pupil,
That your designs should be swift, so clever,
And finished, as by nature, to perfection?

Even as I'm speaking, look, a zephyr
Gently stirs, it agitates the treetops,
Ruffles all the river into wavelets,
Fills the filmy robe that she is wearing,
The perfect girl, amazed I am, and more so
When she starts to set her feet in motion,
And she moves, she walks, she's coming this way
To where I sit beside my wicked teacher.

Now everything, but everything was moving,
Trees, the flowers, filmy robe, the river,
Delicate feet of the girl in all her beauty —
Do you think I sat so calm and steadfast
Rocklike on my rock a moment longer?


*Night Song (1804)*

Pillowed so soft, dream on,
Half listen, I implore,
To this my zithersong,
Sleep, could you wish for more?

To this my zithersong
Is heart's eternal core
Blessed by the starry throng;
Sleep, could you wish for more?

Blessed by the starry throng,
Out of this world I soar
Endless desires among;
Sleep, could you wish for more?

Vom irdischen Gewühle
Trennst du mich nur zu sehr,
Bannst mich in diese Kühle;
Schlafe! was willst du mehr?

Bannst mich in diese Kühle,
Gibst nur im Traum Gehör.
Ach, auf dem weichen Pfühle
Schlafe! was willst du mehr?

*Urworte. Orphisch*

## ΔΑΙΜΩΝ, Dämon

Wie an dem Tag, der dich der Welt verliehen,
Die Sonne stand zum Gruße der Planeten,
Bist alsobald und fort und fort gediehen
Nach dem Gesetz, wonach du angetreten.
So mußt du sein, dir kannst du nicht entfliehen,
So sagten schon Sibyllen, so Propheten;
Und keine Zeit und keine Macht zerstückelt
Geprägte Form, die lebend sich entwickelt.

## ΤΥΧΗ, das Zufällige

Die strenge Grenze doch umgeht gefällig
Ein Wandelndes, das mit und um uns wandelt;
Nicht einsam bleibst du, bildest dich gesellig,
Und handelst wohl so, wie ein andrer handelt:
Im Leben ists bald hin-, bald widerfällig,
Es ist ein Tand und wird so durchgetandelt.
Schon hat sich still der Jahre Kreis geründet,
Die Lampe harrt der Flamme, die entzündet.

## ΕΡΩΣ, Liebe

Die bleibt nicht aus! — Er stürzt vom Himmel nieder,
Wohin er sich aus alter Öde schwang,
Er schwebt heran auf luftigem Gefieder
Um Stirn und Brust den Frühlingstag entlang,

Endless desires among –
Yet you have shut your door,
Cool is the night and long;
Sleep, could you wish for more?

Cool, ah, the night and long,
Only in dreams, on your
Pillow, you hear my song,
Sleep, could you wish for more?

*Primal Words. Orphic (1817–18)*

## ΔΑΙΜΩΝ, Daemon

As stood the sun to the salute of planets
Upon the day that gave you to the earth,
You grew forthwith, and prospered, in your growing
Heeded the law presiding at your birth.
Sibyls and prophets told it: You must be
None but yourself, from self you cannot flee.
No time there is, no power, can decompose
The minted form that lives and living grows.

## ΤΥΧΗ, Chance

Strict the limit, yet a drifting, pleasant,
Moves around it, with us, circling us;
You are not long alone, you learn decorum,
And likely act as any manjack does:
It comes and goes, in life, you lose or win,
It is a trinket, toyed with, wearing thin.
Full circle come the years, the end is sighted,
The lamp awaits the flame, to be ignited.

## ΕΡΩΣ, Love

Love is not absent! Down from heaven swooping,
Whither from ancient emptiness he flew,
This way he flutters, borne by airy feathers,
Round heart and head the day of Springtime through,

Scheint jetzt zu fliehn, vom Fliehen kehrt er wieder:
Da wird ein Wohl im Weh, so süß und bang.
Gar manches Herz verschwebt im Allgemeinen,
Doch widmet sich das edelste dem Einen.

## ΑΝΑΓΚΗ, Nötigung

Da ists denn wieder, wie die Sterne wollten:
Bedingung und Gesetz; und aller Wille
Ist nur ein Wollen, weil wir eben sollten,
Und vor dem Willen schweigt die Willkür stille;
Das Liebste wird vom Herzen weggescholten,
Dem harten Muß bequemt sich Will und Grille.
So sind wir scheinfrei denn nach manchen Jahren
Nur enger dran, als wir am Anfang waren.

## ΕΛΠΙΣ, Hoffnung

Doch solcher Grenze, solcher ehrnen Mauer
Höchst widerwärtge Pforte wird entriegelt,
Sie stehe nur mit alter Felsendauer!
Ein Wesen regt sich leicht und ungezügelt:
Aus Wolkendecke, Nebel, Regenschauer
Erhebt sie uns, mit ihr, durch sie beflügelt,
Ihr kennt sie wohl, sie schwärmt durch alle Zonen —
Ein Flügelschlag — und hinter uns Äonen!

## *Dämmerung senkte sich von oben*

Dämmerung senkte sich von oben,
Schon ist alle Nähe fern;
Doch zuerst emporgehoben
Holden Lichts der Abendstern!
Alles schwankt ins Ungewisse
Nebel schleichen in die Höh;
Schwarzvertiefte Finsternisse
Widerspiegelnd ruht der See.

Apparently escapes, returns anon,
So sweet and nervous, pain to pleasure gone.
Some hearts away in general loving float,
The noblest, yet, their all to one devote.

## ΑΝΑΓΚΗ, Necessity

Then back it comes, what in the stars was written:
Law and circumstance; each will is tried,
All willing simply forced, by obligation:
In face of it, the free will's tongue is tied.
Man's heart forswears what most was loved by him,
To iron 'Must' comply both will and whim.
It only seems we're free, years hem us in,
Constraining more than at our origin.

## ΕΛΠΙΣ, Hope

Yet the repulsive gate can be unbolted
Within such bounds, their adamantine wall,
Though it may stand, that gate, like rock for ever;
One being moves, unchecked, ethereal:
From heavy cloud, from fog, from squall of rain
She lifts us to herself, we're winged again,
You know her well, to nowhere she's confined —
A wingbeat — aeons vanish far behind.

## Twilight Down From Heaven (1827)

Twilight down from heaven wafted,
What was near, now it is far;
Gentle, though, and firstly lofted
Lustre of the evening star.
Off all things the contours shiver,
Sliding mist, way up it goes;
Mirrored deeps more black than ever
Darken the lake in its repose.

Nun am östlichen Bereiche
Ahn ich Mondenglanz und-glut,
Schlanker Weiden Haargezweige
Scherzen auf der nächsten Flut.
Durch bewegter Schatten Spiele
Zittert Lunas Zauberschein,
Und durchs Auge schleicht die Kühle
Sänftigend ins Herz hinein.

Now a hint of moon, I wonder,
From the east, a silver glow,
Boughs of hair the willow slender
Dandles in the flood below.
Through the sport of shadows gliding
Luna's unsteady auras dart,
Through the eye the coolness sliding
Touches with a calm the heart.

# For Márton, Erwin, and Miklos

I ask myself first what kind of statement about poetry I might make, in a certain situation. Invited statements often have an air of blank formality about them; and so I envisage a situation, in which my three Hungarian friends, a poet, a composer, and a novelist, ask me to talk. I have to tell them what I think about poetry. I no longer know whether we are in my house among the hills in Texas, or in the room where Miklos lived in Berlin. The reader must know that the fragmentary conjectures which follow are not programmatic but a part of a possible conversation.

To begin: I feel uncertain and ignorant about poetry, especially when there are scholars around. Remember this if I seem to become assertive. I can read poetry in three European languages, and from one of them I have made translations. In translation, too, I have read many poems from non-European cultures. My own poems have been written amid constant feelings of uncertainty and ignorance. This world is not such a place as to allow one to declare, blithely, that poetry is play, or a luxury, that it happens in the exceedingly fragile and uncomfortable substance of language, and that it voices the interdependence of what is essential and what is actual, of the oneiric and the ordinary domains of human attention. Why, too, are poems so often misinterpreted? Why, again, is so much of it, poetry I mean, pompous blather?

I ask myself this: is poetry, an art with a long, variegated, and difficult history, fundamental now to human life on this planet? Have we any evidence of a profound biological impulse at the roots of poetic imagination? Perhaps it matters, or perhaps not. Most people, if you told them that a poem can pump fresh air through certain vents in the walls of sense which imprison the human brain, would say you are making a stupid category mistake.

Then someone might ask: Do you mean that certain kinds of word-tissue present an active pattern of mental energy, which can reveal to me my own capacity for ordering my mental energies in an economical and productive way, feeling along the lifelines between biosphere and noosphere . . . ? After a doubtful silence, someone else says: Show me, then, a poem, which is a model of ordered and articulate mental energy, a model which integrates interior and exterior worlds. For once I would like to see the spectrum of my passions as a rainbow. So you do show him, or better, recite to him Baudelaire's 'Invitation', then a certain poem by Wang Wei, also Rilke's 'Archaischer Torso Apollos' plus, for good measure, Rimbaud's 'Mémoire' and Pound's Canto XVII. Too much. Dismal demonstrations. Soon he's pulling from his pocket the text of Tzara's 'Maison Flake' and asking: Can this be called order, this incredible flying zigzag, this pure movement of delight?

Aha, says he, somewhat later, so it is the dialectic of outward appearances as they interlock with your unfathomable imaginative projections; the great biological motors of chance and design breathe in the rhythms which compose these particles of language; we catch, red-handed, the spirit of paradox, beauty as a form of tension, is that it? Yes, or something like that, you might reply, if you could be sure that he was joking.

Still you are wondering. Was it the poems that made you wonder? Is wonder the word we assign to the event of a mind's suddenly admitting and expelling this magical breath, which is the information poetry brings about life and death? Sometimes, to be sure, you are reading a poem and are assailed by awareness of a fresh kind and of a quality which makes your whole being glow in the presence of a structure peculiar to consciousness and yet, somehow, other than it. Quoted with approval by Montaigne, St Augustine said: 'The mean (*modus*) is clearly wonderful, whereby spirits cleave to our bodies, nor can it be comprehended by man, and that is very man (*et hoc ipse homo est*)'.

## 2

Having said as much, I have to remind myself that much of the writing called poetry is as dead as a doornail. Certainly much of it is not a conquest or critique of the *dismal* — once a Franco-English noun meaning 'a bad day'; nor is it a 'victory of existence' such as that which Francis Ponge attributed in 1948 to a pebble: 'individual, concrete: the victory of coming into my sight and coming to life with the word' (*Méthodes*).[1]

Another statement by Ponge, a rather grand one, concerns the receptive side of any such 'conquest', the boundless receptivity of poetic intelligence and its being transferred to the reader: 'the function of poetry is to nourish the spirit of man by giving him the cosmos to suckle. We have only to lower our standard of dominating nature and to raise our standard of participating in it in order to make the reconciliation take place.'

Zen thought and Owen Barfield's book, *Saving the Appearances*, took life from considerations like these. You could cautiously substitute, for Ponge's word 'nature', the words 'the unknown' or 'the unconscious' — strange relations begin to establish themselves between the plight of our ecosystem and certain 'bad days' in the history of poetry, as a reflector of emergent mind. Hence certain doubts. You cannot wonder about the universals which persist in the language of poetry without feeling horror and perplexity at the conditions which threaten life on this planet.

### 3

Next I want to say something about description in poetry and its neural basis. If you read a taxonomic description by a botanist, you are struck by its almost hallucinatory precision, which seems to interact with the presence of unknown words (technical words). Poetry, too, can have that kind of precision, without unknown words coming into the picture, although unusual words give special interest to the texture.

However, a poetic description animates what it presents and it does so by distortion — something a botanist avoids. This distorting animation in poetry is what liberates the reader's imagination from a supposed 'real' scene, and binds it to the composition of the linguistic signs themselves. The signs and their composition have intrinsic interest. In some epochs, descriptive poetry flourishes; in others, due to shifts and changes in linguistic usage, which reflect psychic and social changes, for better or worse, descriptive poetry becomes flat, inanimate, devoid of intrinsic interest. (Two old descriptive poems which still have intense charm for me are Cowper's 'Yardley Oak' and Goldsmith's 'The Deserted Village'.)

More often than not, when such poetry becomes inanimate, when its language becomes schematic or perfunctory, its descriptive features will be found to have displaced something else, or to have cut loose from something else. This 'something else', which always has virtue in a poem, is, I believe, the neural base of the mimetic impulse.

Even in poetry which invokes unknown presences and so is not descriptive, the activity of that base, of that deep impulse, can be detected in strength.

This 'something else' occurs when a phrase (or larger unit) has the breathtaking balance of a great dancer's motions; when an elegant orphic line scintillates in its context, like Keats' 'To bend with apples the moss'd cottage trees'; and when syntax enacts what it says (Robert Duncan's 'Infant snails, pearl pure of the first moisture and light, rise from their cradles of lettuce'). These and like events are signs that the quality of the perceptions voiced in a text (or in the air) make all the difference between a singular poem and a speechless one. They are signs of what I am going to call 'body-consciousness' (even though it sounds like jargon).

Example: the end of George Seferis' poem (1937) 'Mathias Paskalis Among the Roses',[2] where the speaker is walking down steps in a garden, thinking:

And then I read of her death in old newspapers
of Antigone's marriage and the marriage of Antigone's daughter
without the steps coming to an end or my tobacco
which leaves on my lips the taste of a haunted ship
with a mermaid crucified to the wheel while she was still beautiful.

It is not just that the lines have a continuous sensory track. Certain motor-muscular ingredients of experience are active there: and such ingredients are radical to poetry, however abstruse, lofty, or 'pure' its intellectual ingredients may be. If the motor-muscular ingredients are absent even from ordinary speech, it is a sign that speakers are under pressure to allow their language to become desiccated and their minds programmed by external agents — which is what seems to be happening in the USA. Poetic pleasure and muscular pleasure, their kinship springs perhaps from contact between the antagonistic impulses which are voiced, historically, in poetry's time-honoured themes of love and death.

The kind of pleasure I'm talking about transmits signals to other sensory-motor centres and in a moment, as if embraced, the body itself becomes attentive to the 'volume' of words, their 'colour' and their 'musical' value. The matter has been much discussed. Yet it is not an obvious matter or easily determined, nor have its psychic implications been pondered much. I'd rather not harp on it, but mention a book nobody seems to have read: André Spire's *Plaisir poétique et plaisir musculaire* (New York: S.F. Vanni, 1949).

The poetic functions at which I'm hinting cannot just be due to poetry's happening in the mouth or in the mind. The respiratory and cardiac systems are pleasingly affected by the presentation to consciousness of what is normally hidden, suppressed, or not perceived. The solar plexus 'does' something; the lunar plexus too, no doubt. It is in and through the breath-rhythms that a kind of transfiguration of body-mind comes about.

Precisely this body-consciousness has been lacking in much of the descriptive and demonstrative poetry which dominates the English scene. When it does appear, can it still be recognized? Or has everyone become so bookish, set in their ways, and one-dimensional (or indifferent) that they wouldn't notice? My own poems do contain some traces of it, in conjunction with my compulsive themes of being and not-being, here and there, this and 'the other'. But English reviewers have castigated my poems for being 'cold' and 'impersonal', also for being disjointed, obscure, and 'skinny'. As if my product were a poor relation of Dr Frankenstein's. The question of personality (whose voice is this?) does arise; readers expect in my poems to meet an open and concordant individual who joins the conversation — they find, instead, a scatty hermit feeling out formal relations between cobwebs and starlight. But relations like those are the stuff of life for the body-consciousness. And I would point out that Montaigne was an intent observer of its operations, its wave-structure of inconstant impulses, its outlines and impressions. Nietzsche discovered it during his 'psychologist' phase; later it forms the infrastructure of Kafka's nightmares.

**4**

I shall put it this way: Poetry has the power to make transparent and self-aware the mysterious, undulant body-consciousness which features grammatically in poems as the 'I'. Poetry makes audible the voice of imagination as it projects itself upon the unstable aggregate of impulse and impression I have been calling body-consciousness.

'If a sparrow come before my window I take part in its existence and pick about the gravel', said Keats. So, on the one hand, body-consciousness circumscribes to the limit our 'apprehension, our judgment, and our soul's faculties in general' (Montaigne). On the other hand, in poetry it is the base upon which a model of reality may be constructed, a model with its own distinct linguistic physiognomy, the poem as a 'world' which, although it is objective, other, even alien, has been penetrated and radically transformed by imagination. Hence the violent, but coherent, changes in attitude undergone by the poet in imagining, and, if communication is made, by the reader in responding.

Another statement by Ponge comes to mind: 'Hope therefore lies in a poetry through which the world so invades the spirit of man that he becomes speechless, and later reinvents a language.' Insofar as poetry is about itself, it is about this revision of attitudes. The revision occurs as the poem subverts (often by remodelling) the clichés, when it overturns stereotypes, when it *infuriates* the world into showing its hand. Poetry can thus function as a catalyst to precipitate what therapists of the Gregory Bateson persuasion, like Watzlawick, call secondary changes — your whole frame of reference is changed. In the language of shamanology this is called 'breaking the plane', or 'deconditioning' (disinhibition in the language of neurologists). Here is an illustration, showing that poetry is one of those things that makes you attentive to originality and other enigmas as they penetrate your world at any point. In the summer of 1846 the poet Eduard Mörike went out for a walk; after a time he sat down beneath a tree, became pensive, and then, suddenly, he saw with amazement before him a presence hitherto unseen, unrecognized: his own two feet. Before that moment, in terms of projective imagination, his feet had never even existed.

Mörike's feet and Ponge's pebble figure importantly in my scale of poetic values. So does Cézanne's outburst: 'The day is coming when a single original carrot shall be pregnant with revolution.' So I go about cultivating microscopism and trying to write in such a way as to undercut the 'foolish-boldness of speech'.

## 5

Once there was the vision, shared by poets and sages (in spite of Plato), of the world as a great pattern of interlocking depths and surfaces, a continuous physiognomy or semiotic system, from which could be read, with a little luck, much study, and a measure of belief, the features of a divine mind. Poetry was a minute exegesis of creation, scrupulously composed by one who could believe that he participated in creation's formative processes. And this is what Baudelaire still meant, with his poetics of 'reciprocal analogy', where metaphor is the linguistic agent which divines links between microcosm and macrocosm, between individual body-consciousness and the life of the universe.

Poetry could still, theoretically, function as a bridge between the opaque and the luminous, the unstable body-world and the spiritual-electric aura of supreme fictions. Since then the aura has been lost (Walter Benjamin) and poetry's ground has shifted. The bridge, or the backbone, has been smashed. A poem is now, more or less, a contest with the opaque, conducted in silence, until the human combatant screams out in agony before being crushed ('and later reinvents a language'). My language here is too melodramatic. But I mean to distinguish between suave poetry which has been pushed to the margins, and exigent poetry, hard-bitten poetry, which goes to the limits of the conceivable and thus relocates the centre.

This exigent poetry tends to have archipelagic structures. Its movement tends to be a dance, not a walk. It is a poetry balanced over gulfs of silence, a poetry of surprises, of enigmas, scrutiny followed by vertiginous distance, a poetry of broken uncertain surfaces, of foregrounded hinterlands. Prototypes early in the century were some of the 1911–13 poems by Apollinaire ('Le musicien de Saint-Merry'), some poems by Tzara (later his *L'homme approximatif*), Eliot's *The Waste Land*, Pound's *Sextus Propertius*. I cannot rightly say what has become of this particular sensibility in the versions of it appearing in poems by several New York poets. John Ashbery certainly has roots in it. The American zigzag has an optics determined by American urbanity (including the soul-shredding experience of big-city life). If I prefer the archipelagic zigzag to the sturdy continuous 'prose tradition' of English, it is because the latter has been made, somehow, inaccessible to me by experiences of my own, which are not American experiences. I have battled, often tongue-tied, with my own ambivalences and uncertainties. The multiple 'ego' can easily become a mass of variables which jam the lines of perception. Then again, suddenly, comes an insight, just a modicum, a microscopic 'triumph' of order, in existence, as this or that set of words. Then the laughter is shaken out of the apple tree, as Tzara said: poetry becomes exploration beyond the frontiers of the ego. To poets reduced to anecdotage and confession by their monomania, I submit these words — from a prison in Africa: 'One begins to see all one's efforts and entire life in clear terms of action. How idle we have been, mesmerized by our own ringing voices and bad verse. The true poetry lies in a vast and incalculable suffering, and the will to resist and endure.'

**6**

That said, dear Hungarians, you won't mind if I tell a kind of anecdote about my first meeting with substance in poetry. I was about sixteen at the time. And I was convalescing at an old country house used as a school sanatorium, far out in the western hills of England. I am sitting in the grass beside a stream and looking at a Greek poem, by Alcman, the four lines invoking halcyons. My Greek is feeble. Suddenly I am spellbound by the Greek vowels, how their pitches differ, sound like colours, a web of colours, fragile but indelible, I hear them float and see the colours. In those days one did not know how protected one was; yet one did feel the pressure of a fear, by which the protectors tried to control eveything.

Two years before I had begun to study cuneiform and hieroglyphics, inspired by Dmitri Merejkovsky's novel about Leonardo da Vinci. Those studies, like Greek, were never continued. It seems I am a persistent inventor of zigzags, some of them false tracks. Later what I liked about Dada, when studying it during the 1960s, was its energetic and volatile zigzag anti-poetics. I liked the long nose Dada made at everything *chic* and *poncif*, everything portentous that sat upon a mess of 'normal' iniquity. In sum: I am still in pursuit of the halcyons, the sea kingfishers.

That pursuit does not allow me to write as much or as regularly as some people do. They say: yours is not a serious approach to the task of constructing a work. I question the topos of 'approach', on the grounds that you have to be already in the middle of a poem (knowing it or not) before you can assemble all its flying particles. I question too the topos of 'the work'.

Cézanne, Ferdinand Cheval, Jean-Henri Fabre — workers of such heroic stature as these men are exemplary because they lifted the curse from the nineteenth century work-ethic which propelled them. They never indulged in production for production's sake (ugly sister of art for art's sake); hard put as they were, they took and gave pleasure in creation.

One certainly does 'work'. But poetic work reverses the modern work scheme: it reverses reification, insofar as it projects into the opaque world of objects signs of intense mental life (sometimes just this side of madness). Poetic work declares: Here, at least, is a limit to manipulation at the hands of human beings who have been turned into functions of the economic system, here is a limit to enslavement. A poetic text, even then, may be subject to manipulation, if it is not *reflektiert*, as the Germans say, to the point of structural transparency.

Mind you, poetry is a curse, altogether *sui generis*. Not the curse of work but the curse of indeterminacy lies upon it, a curse from which its semantic value does not escape. A poem reflects, after all, its human source, in throwing open to experience quite singular planes and volumes of consciousness. For all its integratedness, a good text explodes with difference. It may not change life, but it gives an indication of how life might be differently perceived. No, it is naive to suppose that poetry can change life, change the ways in which people construe life. Yet it does subvert norms with which people mystify and atrophy themselves. It can enable imaginations to see through general ideas (the terrible simplifications) to the naked living universe. By anatomizing idols, a good text overthrows them. Perhaps it is as inhospitable as that universe. Perhaps indeterminacy here is a precise sign of that forbidding and immense presence, of the mystery we experience when we wonder about that universe and how we are placed in it.

So you go in pursuit of the kingfisher and are fortunate if you so much as glimpse a sparrow. You cannot really fly, at least not always. You don't even mean to catch the kingfisher. You only want to know from the inside how it creates its own bones, the bones which display the colours and sustain the flight.

# Pai Ch'iu's Arm Chair

For obvious reasons, any account of a poem in translation will be hazardous. Even then, a translation can manifest a structure — give or take a little — which validates itself so nicely that one could hope its conception matched that of the original. There may be some details, in the wording of the translation, that are somewhat 'off', but the substance asks to be taken on faith. In return, one asks for the translation's credentials. It happens that this translation of Pai Chi'iu's 'Arm Chair' has good ones. Precisely its articulate structure, rising clear of presumably unique original features, bridges the distance between modern Chinese and English.

> My two hands are open as usual;
> In the cavernous room, made conspicuous by
> The slanting sunbeams, right in front of me,
> It seems that, amid the darkness, something
> Comes leaping.
>
> That squat form, taut
> As a catcher awaiting the ball in a glimmering ball park at twilight;
> Like a determination, nakedly
> Awaiting the explosive collision of planets.
>
> Life is silent with solitude; upon the broad earth,
> A still body without sound or breath —
> With its own image, transforms solidity
> Into a glittering phrase
> Quietly standing there.

At a first reading, one might be inclined to infer that the speaker, with his indicative grammar, is sitting in a room and looking across to the arm chair situated in a dark part of the room. He invents, provoked by this arm chair, the two powerful metaphors of the second paragraph. The grammar of these metaphors is not indicative, but deiktic, or 'gestic', in Brecht's sense 'That squat form . . .' and no verb to go with it. This is perhaps a kind of low-key apostrophe, but the grammar is pugnacious, rather than lofty or vaporous.

The metaphors are not developed in the concluding paragraph, where the grammar is again indicative. Yet this sequel is a fresh opening of sense, a movement forwards, into the first phrases — life-solitude-earth — and on into the quiet transformation, as the chair becomes 'a glittering phrase'. Then one might falter for a moment. 'With its own image, transforms solidity . . .' — what about this? Isn't this 'image' not one of the chair's own, but something laid upon it by the speaker, a last tremble, as it were, from his metaphors of the catcher and the determination? Metaphors can be made, true enough, out of the body-images which a poet's mind entertains; or one has the Platonic option, e.g., an artifact latent in its eventual maker's mind. Here one needs the original Chinese: perhaps it says 'With an image of itself . . .'

A second reading could revise the first one slightly, or more than slightly. Is it not the poet at all, but the chair itself, which is speaking? Is the 'something that comes leaping' the poet himself, and is he also the 'squat form'? Whose are the 'two hands' which are 'open as usual'? The poet's? Couldn't they be the 'hands' in which the chair's arms terminate? Is this 'still body without sound or breath' in the concluding paragraph the poet's, or is it the chair itself? The poet's body could be still, without sound or breath, if he were 'quietly standing', breathless, seeing that he and the chair are, in that instant of lyric insight, as one. Far-fetched as this reverse reading might seem to be, it makes sense of the phrase 'with its own image', for that image would be the one with which the poet has transformed this chair into a 'glittering phrase' of his own making — the poem.

There could be, at least, a dialectic of contrasts here, reinforced by several details in the wording. Paragraph 1 — cavernous . . . darkness/conspicuous . . . sunbeams. Paragraph 2 — squat form . . . catcher/ball . . . twilight (where twilight suggests a massive spaciousness antithetic to 'squat' and to 'ball'). Paragraph 3 — silent/phrase; broad earth/still body (again a switch across perspectives, from macro- to microperspective); solidity/glittering phrase. One could think of these contrasts as the crossing-points of threads in a woven fabric, or else as the pressure points in knots. Either way, contrasts, splicings, and oppositions generate a tensed and economical structure, which still fluctuates elastically in its scope of reference, from local and interior to cosmic and exterior context.

A third reading might make more of the reverse aspect and figure the text as a rebus. It is the poet, having his 'two hands open as usual', who becomes the 'catcher' (baseball is alive and well in Taiwan); but at the same time it is the chair which is the 'squat form' crouching as a catcher crouches waiting for the ball. Who leaps? Has the poet rushed into the room? Or are his perceptions, as he enters the room at a normal speed, so accelerated as to conceive of the chair leaping at him out of the darkness? Has there also been, in the last lines, a similar union of speaker and subject, so that, within the terms of the poem's logic, it can legitimately be said that the chair's *own* image transforms (its) solidity into a glittering phrase which is (*now*) quietly standing there (as the poem itself has come to do)?

Inevitably one recalls the riddle about Chuang tzu: Did he dream the butterfly, or is the butterfly dreaming him?

The 'explosive collision of planets', which the 'determination' is waiting for, 'nakedly', metaphorizes with absurd brilliance the chair waiting for the impact of the body that will settle into it, as the poet's receptive imagination, simultaneously, waits for the collision between chair and the language concerning it, which he is still in the act of penning. The 'glittering phrase' would then be the flare that follows the planetary 'collision' — the whole poem an incandescent kinetic impulse of imagination wrought as a crisscrossing of language-particles in the space of the page.

If one is still not confident about the rebus, one might settle for a reading which regards the circling of the planets before collision as a metaphor, however cryptic in its vastness, of the circling of poet and chair, in the 'cavernous' room of the universe, 'made conspicuous by/ The slanting sunbeams'(which in turn, eventually, cohabit in the text with 'glittering phrase'). The consistency of the text is wrought, I think, whether or not the translation attenuates the original, by traces of what Mandelstam called 'polynomial comparison', in his 'Conversation about Dante'.[1]

It is conceivable, too, that no such readings of the text would have occurred without certain quite inconspicuous sound-patternings for which the translator must be thanked: generally deep vowel-tones slowly ascending through the poem to the higher pitches of the last two lines. It is this not indistinct sonority which magics the structure across the cultural and linguistic distance. And it also enables a reader to respond to the fine threads which give the poem, immediately, accessible texture — threads along which the straight or paradoxical speech-thrusts move. There is something wholly consonant with traditional Chinese lyric feeling in this cross-hatching of the straight and the paradoxical. One thinks of ancient woven silk; one thinks of a fence, a gate, or a roof, made from crossed bamboo poles, or of a bamboo window lattice.

# The Pursuit of the Kingfisher:
# Writing as Expression

> A quoi bon ces grands enthousiasmes fragiles,
> ces sauts de joie déséchés. Nous ne savons plus
> rien que les astres morts; nous regardons les
> visages; et nous soupirons de plaisir. Notre
> bouche est plus sèche que les pages perdues;
> nos yeux tournent sans but, sans espoir.
>
> André Breton and Philippe Soupault
> *Les champs magnétiques*, 1920

I have precious little hard knowledge about expression, but mean here to coordinate some thoughts about it. Since my reading in the works of semiologists has been scant, the risk is that I may contribute only parochial follies to their global debate.

## 1

In the realm of nature, display is spontaneous and pragmatic. Certain signs, like coloured petals and plumage, the emission of scents and seeds, songs and pollen, the formations of geese when they migrate, can be read as a message that an identity is being articulated. Invocation and, at the same time, warning. The mocking-bird is at once highly territorial in its conduct and highly inventive in its song. Aggressively (attacking cats and human beings alike) and vocally it declares where it is and what it is. The male painted bunting, on the other hand, twitters briefly and with modesty; his only longer song in summer is addressed with rapture to the setting sun, from high on a treetop, to catch the sun's last rays. But his plumage displays his presence with triple emphasis: the breast crimson, head electric blue, iridescent greenish gold flashing down his back. Both he and his much less flamboyant female are also intrepid birds, yielding not a flit to the pugnacious red cardinal when they feed together. Display, self-assurance, pride in identity, the gift of being distinct but not rigid, not falsifying the fluid surprise of life — attractive human females consolidate these traits.

So, if you put a human construction on it, the message, identity, may comprise several moments, distinct but simultaneous. In announcing myself I invoke my kin and ask them to recognize, in what I announce, both our common grounds and my difference. Here at least the sign is warm. But the sign given has another moment, colder: it fends off whatever might threaten the group, and whatever might threaten 'me' from within the group. It is a challenge to whatever is 'other', if hostile, as the possible eraser of my differences or of the group which feels that those differences are life-signs. Rilke's lines at the end of Duino Elegy 7, about the hand beckoning to the angel and keeping him also at bay, do imitate nature in her mode of operation.

Human dreams are also groups of signs in display. The nervous system selects elements from experience and converts them, somehow, into the images with which we entertain ourselves in dreams. Perhaps the nervous system, as a transforming agent of extreme complexity, has a particular message to deliver through the image. Possibly the system itself is the message. Most theories of dream decompose the image, in order to read the message it 'contains'. The signified is thought of as something that lurks behind the sign or beyond it.

Goethe had much to say about this. It is still a perplexing matter. The phenomenon, as image, is fraught with the beholder's sensory and emotional responses to it. But a trained, vital response does not convert the phenomenon into a mere toy to be manipulated by human projections. For Goethe, the phenomenon, or the image, is 'real' and not illusory. It embodies 'das Geistige', and 'das Geistige' is a spiritual substratum which implants (encodes) throughout appearances, external or internal, a legible order, an order which is indelible, though perhaps only faintly perceivable. That was the old theory. For all its insistence on order, it allowed plenty of luminous free space to mediate between the substratum and the sense datum.

The erosion of the old theory (Goethe defended its anthropomorphism against Newton's physics) occurred along with the slow demise of capacity for belief in a transcendent *logos*. People now had to operate within different parameters. We say that in poetic expression, as in most imaginative approaches to truth, language functions as a kind of switchboard. By means of the switchboard, the nervous system and its object-world exchange messages of a special kind, a quite special kind, so that to speak of spiritual interference (or support) is to look where you can't see — behind language. It is also understood that any given nervous system as such speaks no known language. Sometimes its behaviour is intelligible, then elusive, now barbarous, then elegant, then again a jumble of absurdities. Time-skeins and space-skeins in the perceptual world of the individual are always apt to become tangled. This is particularly true in old age when individuals lose much of the ego-stability they had earlier; and it is true of the imaginative behaviour of individuals in ageing societies. Also it is understood that the object-world, although it may recede (without loss of presence) into vistas ruled by pure silence, is linguistically structured and always drenched in historical flux. No escape. Moreover, the individual has been apt at all times to compose his image of things in such a way as to deflect his attention from the things in their manifold overwhelming concreteness (in vain the individual struggles to achieve a wisdom conceivable only to the group, and in the group unthinkable, hence invariably tacit). That kind of image, also in the dream, lacks ultimacy; it may be positively feeble, if not false. This is Kafka's theme, he explores it even in 'The Great Wall of China', a fiction which is much more 'warm' and seemingly carefree than, say, 'The Judgement' or 'In the Penal Colony'.

So in one way or another the language of a poem is generated during attempts to decipher the code in which the nervous system expresses itself while communing with the world. The potency of the resulting image is an index of the skill exercised by a mind straining against horizons which the image imposes. Such attempts are the outcome of a profound receptiveness. They are loving, deliberate, desperate, impulsive, and they proceed by the steady elimination of inessentials. Anyone who does not know his stuff should not engage in such attempts. Even the purest phrase may give only a weak signal, or a deceptive one, if it is left in a surround of 'raw' language (confessional anecdotage — distractive texts of the type widely appreciated now in the USA).

Any attempt meets or invents obstructions. By this I do not mean the provision of resistance like those of rhyme or metre. I mean that open-textured elements in your language (even in language you have made all your own) easily slide into fixity and so falsify the nervous system's code itself, a code which is recognizable, as in dreams, by the mobility of its signs, by the polyvalence of the significations. There are no replicas for that code. A poem as spellbinding and subtle as a dream must be an invented dream, a modulation of oneiric tonalities, composed in a different medium according to the rules of a different game. In that game precisest thought is provoked, life itself is at stake. In society, on the other hand, as in a world apart, it is the fixed elements, the clichés, which provide an illusion of coherence, even when deadly games are being played (as in diplomacy).

For the poet, as for birds, what is expressed has validity and interest only insofar as it initiates, elaborates, and projects a distinct structure. An appropriate structure. In the distinct structuring it is the relatedness of the systemic elements (images in dreams, words in the poem) which delivers from bondage the inchoate dark thing that insists on being said. That is one side of a many-sided process. Out of that relatedness as from a bath words rise up in all the freshness and singularity, all the livingness, of which they are capable. Someone said: 'I would like to be able to see things just as they were before they showed themselves to me.' The real poem presents words in that unbeheld state.

Wordsworth and Mandelstam were both mumblers. They mumbled to themselves (not communicating with someone else) until a distinct structure began to inch into the open, becoming symphonic. This was not confession. It was the art of producing out of the maze of speech an essential code with which to illuminate, if only in flashes, entire landscapes of possible human expression, from the most abyssal glossolalia to the most glittering awesome peaks of insight. The genesis of a structure may depend on phonic values fathering semantic values.

## 2

Confession and self-analysis were twin by-products of the discovery of 'subjective depth'. They marked a directional change, of great significance, in the evolution of mind in the Western world. What do we mean by this metaphor of depth? Among other things we should mean that subjectivity has found that it is an essential factor in language, and is thus essential for the self-revelation of life itself. It also means that *logos* and language begin to go their separate ways; 'otherness' enters into everything. Subjectivity: a transforming agent, which enables life immediate or remote to take a long and deep look at itself. St Augustine, supposedly one of the first men to be interested in himself as a container of 'depth', was also the man who said, concerning the fabulous hippogriff: 'What matters is not whether or not it exists, but what it signifies.' He was, you might say, putting the more difficult question: the question as to the inspirational value to be assigned to that which, as an entity, is neither here nor there. Or: what does something signify which is made only of words? Kafka is pointing to treacherous areas in the depths when he has K say of the messenger Barnabas, during the early stages of his talk with Olga (in *The Castle*): 'I have set hopes upon him and suffered disappointments through him, both based simply on his words, that is to say, with almost no basis.'[1] If unconscious trust is converted without residue into doubtful fear, you are living in the present world and taking it for granted.

The word that you liberate from the dense mass of latent language (*langue*), the word that shimmers with the subjective life, must provide, if it is to be a lyrical word in truth, the semblance of having a basis. In some cases a semblance is provided by the word's being set in a peculiar relation to other words. The latter may have a less lyrical shimmer in themselves, but by virtue of the peculiar relation they are touched by the surprise, by the magic, of the original word, and they vibrate along with it. Or there may be no magical words at all. There may be, instead, fine grammatical or syntactical structures which furnish the energy-context, the variety, tension, elegance, and so forth, in the basis (Brecht's Svendborg poems, for example). I also have in mind structures which admit extreme discrepancy. The subjective experiences from which they arise are not to be framed by 'fictions of concord' (the term Frank Kermode gave to certain parameters of English modernism, although he disregarded modernisms elsewhere).

Emile Benveniste's linguistic analysis of subjectivity confirms Peter Schilder's psychoanalytic and neurological argument about the 'body image' in brain-functions. Schilder said (1935): 'There is no sense in "ego" where there is no "thou",' and again — here in J. Z. Young's approving paraphrase: 'The individual bases all his actions on an anticipatory plan, which is based on the (body) image.'[2] Young's paraphrase also says: 'The "I" of the internal sensations is related to the "thou" of the outside world.'

Benveniste says this: 'language is possible only because each speaker sets himself up as a subject by referring to himself as *I* in his discourse.'[3] He continues as follows: 'Because of this, *I* posits another person, the one who, being, as he is, completely exterior to "me", becomes my echo to whom I can say *you* and who says *you* to me. This polarity of persons is the fundamental condition of language . . . neither of the terms can be conceived of without the other . . . and at the same time, they are reversible. . . . It is in a dialectic reality that will incorporate the two terms and define them by mutual relationship that the linguistic basis of subjectivity is discovered.'

Here Benveniste is addressing himself not only to communicative language, not only to public language. He is saying that language as we know it could not even exist without the 'inner dimension'. It is quite remarkable how poets revise public language – which tends always to cancel the concrete subject — in ways which conform it to the intimate patterns of their own nervous systems. I am reminded (reading René Char, for instance) of the Hopi Indians. Dorothy Eggan established that certain Hopis modify the myths of the group by re-dreaming those myths and communicating the results.[4] I can imagine how the faces of their interpreters scowl or smile, depending on the value of the recycled product, its value for the 'basis'.


### 3

There are writers who invent images which do not communicate as subject-predicate sentences do. Such images are extracted from abundant subjective depths. My writings, said Kafka to Gustav Janouch, are images, only images. (By this he did not mean that they were 'symbols' in any Goethean sense, far from it.) Paul Celan said to someone, too, that his poems were meant to be accepted as 'concrete imagery, not as codes needing deciphering'.[5] Michel Deguy might say the same of his splendid 'Chant Royale', even though that poem is also, if non-discursively, an *ars poetica*.

The point here is that some modes of writing are, as it were, not reproducible. Their codes cannot be cracked. It now seems that Kafka invented such a mode. His polyvalent imagery and his grammar of 'sliding paradox'·(G. Neumann) resist interpretation in admirable ways. The imagery forbids semantic interpretation of the reductive type, the type that aims to 'fix' a meaning. Hence countless critics have read Kafka at cross-purposes. The sliding paradox surpasses straight paradox, and it does not rest at merely apparent contradiction. It represents, as a means of registering delicately convoluted tremors of subjective life, a subversion of public language no less momentous than St Augustine's revisions of Latin. Kafka's shorter prose functions in several ways that are desirable for poetry, and it does so by transposing lyrical intelligence, not excluding it but reworking it from the roots up.


**4**

Hermetic and subversive: two terms often used to distinguish those lyrical structures that became thinkable once Rimbaud had tied his knot in the psychological linearity of poetic grammar, by asserting 'I is another'.

Whatever Rimbaud may have meant at that moment, the pursuit of the other, the pursuit of translogical elements dwelling in language or in the unconscious, soon developed its curious circularity. Also its own negative/positive productivity. The world and the *you* became vanishing points. Soon enough, even as tacit presences, the world and the *you* came to be seen as constructs of language. Europe meanwhile was sinking into a marshy waste of words. Sinyavsky quotes a fellow prisoner as saying: 'What is Western culture? It's carrying snot around in your pocket: you blow it into a handkerchief and carry it about with you.'[6] Disrespectful, but to the point.

Yet the poem, as uniquely possible, occasional ecstasy, can still burst clear of the circle in which the poet, in pursuit of his kingfisher, confuses himslf, torments himself, tracks his own echo. The poem which bursts clear of the snot is a fabulous linguistic projectile launched toward the *logos*.

Or I contemplate the figure of the poem as a labyrinthine nest in which the kingfisher might want to settle. The poem is a lure for an elusive and speechless spirit which we can think of as the real basis of the lyrical impulse. Then suddenly I remember that I built a nest for a bird once, in my childhood. Of course, no bird ever so much as looked at it. Absence and contradiction: the structures of discrepancy are likely to be singular ones that voice radical doubt as to the efficacy of the poetic word, doubt of its power to knit into a reciprocal relation the 'inner' and 'outer' spheres. The poem is the place where I and thou fall apart. Or at best they gaze past one another, mouth to mouth, fingertip to fingertip. The prints of the fingertips may be traced, even with our pens, which we dream are shaped like birds. And at the slightest shift of context, the pen may become a deadly instrument. Torn away from its ancient roots in the body and the voice, the lyrical impulse, though capable of many metamorphoses, may be deadened by the mere act of writing.

5

A certain healthy impurity in the lyrical strain goes back to Archilochus, the first known subjective poet. But there have been epochs in which a lyrical substance was at large in the pure state. The strain has been crossed and recrossed with many other strains, not necessarily adverse ones. And since the original animated word is so elusive, we are inclined to think that it cannot even manifest itself unless it is coupled with other strains, other and contrary ones. Hölderlin discovered this, and went on to develop an ontological poetics of total paradox, a positively Bach-like metric of paradox. The splicing and grafting and cross-pollinating have continued: Eliot, Brecht, Khlebnikov, Valéry, Seferis, and Cavafy still at a slight angle to the universe.

Now in the English canon a poem is fraught with messages which it *communicates*, with distinctive and authentic emotion, thought, imagination, and so on. The density of the poem is such that communication occurs at every point along all the lines across which the poem advances toward the reader. Poems are admired if they are 'beautifully controlled', like athletes in motion, notably long-distance runners. The communication and the control may admit impulse and hazard, but concord is the rule. Any clowning, any inattention, onstage or in the back rows, is generally frowned upon. Discrepancy may be admitted (humour!), but only as long as it eventually melts away into an overall *style* of congruity. Its piquancy is, at length, washed away by a draught of port. (The culinary analogy haunts much poetry-reviewing.) This has been made canonical as a set of stylistic options, all of which put *suavitas* before magnitude and *sanitas* before the grand old madness. So you have a poetry which is programmed, if not to taste of port, then to leave you psychologically prepared for the next tea party.

Behind this orthodoxy stands a noble and hard-tested tradition, in which the poem embodies an equilibrium. The equilibrium of impulse and control, emotion and intellect, imagination and a fine sense of fact, has to be legible in the text. Equilibrium is fundamental to the civilizing values which the tradition spells out in each important text, from Chaucer to the present. Respect for equilibrium sustains the life-stream of English poetry. Hence the immense appeal of William Blake to counterculture poets, although Blake was the master of exceptions, not their slave.

It is possible that the main tradition has reached a stage at which entropy sets in. Even with its extraordinary breadth of perspective, that tradition, you might say, was only a bundle of perspectives. Patriarchally self-perpetuating, it may now be fostering wanton self-deception. Is English poetry now merely blinking, paralytic because deprived of any vision, of any radical lyric thrust? Has the lyric sensibility been crushed by an overlay of ancillary strains, strains which originally sprang from the impulse toward lyric expression? Has Orc been silenced by Urizen?

I don't know. But it does occur to me that few English poets or critics have an antenna for poems like Tzara's *L'homme approximatif* or even Lawrence Durrell's 'Elegy on the Closing of the French Brothels'. I think that these poems provide models of high-spirited, rebellious, and completely lucid language, as poems of genuine lyric inspiration.

Well and good, if the lyrical impulse has been excluded on the grounds that it brought a wet and wistful sweetness into poetry, that it had degenerated into a factory for bagatelles and formulas, or that it fed on self-deception, nurturing false consciousness. But the exclusion also seems to have arisen in part of its own accord, in the general English perplexity. English social and intellectual life is marked by a genius for trivializing. Embarrassed by any impulse issuing from real depths of experience, people seek in trivialization a moment's relief from muddle. It is a mechanism which enables the mass of the population to survive. But with it belongs a short-sightedness, which, in the longer biological run, can bring havoc (the general snigger gives place to a grinding of residual teeth). No true homeostasis can be sustained if a body or mass of bodies fails to accommodate the other which is its nourishment. Exclude that other, and you have the diabolic situation. *Diabolos* is not only the one who injects himself into everything (the everlasting busybody). He is also the one who 'casts himself through himself'. He is the parochial monomaniac, not the volatile and sensitive island spirit. He is the protoplasmic bore.

## 6

What I have to say next is, by and large, a personal and speculative reply to the popular question, 'Why write?' There are the urbane answers, such as: I write so that my readers will be helped to achieve and maintain an independent, balanced, and critical stance in their historical worlds. Or (no less demonstratively): I write to alert people to a version of reality which puts pleasure in the forefront, but pleasure so clear and so intense that no power on earth will be able to regiment them: I decipher the dreams of the victims who had no chance to speak. Equally valid, albeit venomous, is the reply: I write from hatred of this painful world, from self-hatred, from passionate fear for my fellow-beings, I have to shed this hatred or I would go crazy. Striding before and limping behind such answers is the least revealing one: I write to live.

How is it that a writer entrusts to his words that intricate entanglement of moods, sensations, thoughts, dreams which make up the signature of his supposed identity? How can a writer still believe that his words might sink in, have some solid significance in this unfathomable world-mass of improvisations? Our mass-mediated, techno-economically programmed contexts cramp our sense of a tradition, or they obliterate it. We may believe that a lifeline of intelligence passing from one social structure to another in global historic time is within reach. Yet we might be smiling faces already down full fathom five, some smiling to have exotericized the implacable old mysteries, others to have ignored them.

In Loren Eiseley's book *The Unexpected Universe*, there is one answer to which even Kafka might have assented: 'Each man deciphers from the ancient alphabets of nature only those secrets that his own deeps possess the power to endow with meaning.'[7] A formidable answer. So a voice speaks to the writer and he replies with all his energetic curiosity. Then a dialogue begins. Out of his 'nature' he draws historically inflected structures of consciousness. The latter are his 'expression'; finely wrought, resistant, yet also sensitive to every tug of his own vital currents. The grip of adventitious matter is weakened; a writer's 'metaphoric' version of reality can be a continuation of something that began in the unthinkable back of beyond, when the first sparks of mind were ignited. It is not mere continuation, either, for he transforms what went before, what preceded the 'creative act', the primary *données* of his private context or of his tradition. By means of fictions he resists the confusion with which existence sprays his consciousness. Or those fictions are islands, each an island in an archipelago, on which he can take a critical stand. So he watches the sea while exploring the interior of the island which he invents as he invents himself.

Generalizations. I say 'while' exploring the interior. But did I mean 'then'? Can observation and insight be simultaneous events voicing themselves, in chorus, as one writes; or is there an interval, through which all sorts of variables and lies crowd into the text, fingering the inventions? And I say 'interior', but what if this is not another metaphor? It all sounds, too, a bit bland, visions of Aegean islands, occasional earthquakes, true, but the windmills are not deterred, the writer goes on writing, fighting against greyness, against suppressors, against protectors. Uncertainty surrounds what the subject and the object actually do when they are communing, rapt in the relationship that gives birth to a spirited word.

## 7

When the will diabolically splits away from emotion it stagnates in self-possession, while fantasies swell and flit from thing to thing, person to person, in a way which bloats the writer's ego and makes his work a flimsy narcissistic husk. What value can it possibly have, the work of a writer whose self-dissections are a benign substitute for suicide? Plenty, the disciples of Artaud would say. But that is not me, no, for while writing I am under the reverse impression, namely, that I am pulling my particles together. Contraction, coupled or alternating with a widening of all the apertures. Something in imagination challenges the law of identity upon which our vocabularies are founded.

True enough, to be in touch with your own body is what matters, the sensation of multiple identity, many-limbed, radiating from a tacit centre. The word as display shelters the body of which it is a tacit sign. A coincidence: while I was writing, not long ago, about body-consciousness in poetry, I bought a copy of Andrei Sinyavsky's prison book, *A Voice from the Chorus*. It was lying at my elbow for several days, then I began to read it and found Sinyavsky saying this — about his feelings on being released after six years in a labour camp: 'The main thing is not some kind of special inner "self-awareness", nor the intellect or the will. But, I would say, the sensation of your own limbs. The consciousness that you have a body, that you are you.' Here there is something akin to the archaic idea of incarnation. Grossly secular as our world is, there are writers whose art, on good days, keeps vital a very old and uncomfortable mystery. Mandelstam can be quoted here, because he was such an artist, whose instinct told him that life was not meaningless but a drama with changing styles, changing textures, changing depths:

> The word is a psyche. The living word does not signify an object, but freely chooses, as though for a dwelling place, this or that

objective significance, materiality, some beloved body. And around the thing the word hovers freely, like a soul around a body that has been abandoned but not forgotten.[8]

A dot in the eye, that statement, for doctrinaire ideologues, one-dimensionalists, nominalists, and idolaters generally; and it is amply borne out by Mandelstam's poem 'The Horseshoe Finder'. It is a statement that is soaked in knowledge of the most dangerous and the most innocent games the writer plays. (If the statement does have ideological colours, a 'pure' Heraclitan light shines through all their tints.)

## 8

When the need for adventure seizes me, or when I am anxious to write, I am searching for signs of this single truth about the body in the word, the word in the body. The flesh-detail: it is nothing necessarily profound, it is the colours of the kingfisher, the splendour or the darkness of and in human faces, human limbs, human sayings.

Icons, Sinyavsky says, are illuminated faces. The ancient image in stone was no portrait but a soul's dwelling. The face — a window out of which the soul gazes, like one of those great Berlin ladies leaning over her cushion of an evening. Sinyavsky's model for observation of the living human face was the icon. In the art of the icon he found the most concentrated awareness of what the transfigured human face is and means: the distance out of which it comes, a mystery, but legible, a fluid set of signs, a conquest of the opaque. The transfigured flesh is not the flesh up point-blank for display, or for deceit, but the flesh in its ancient and present hieratic action.

Even then, most of the time, inhabiting history, one is deceived. Does my pursuit of the kingfisher also turn out to be a deceived and self-deceiving escapist's form of domination? Does the sporadic writer, in this case, become a continuous deserter, a fugitive? And is this my impulse, when I write, to dominate the fugitive flesh so harshly, or so tenderly, it hardly matters which, that in despair at my self-deception it transfigures itself into something unspeakably humdrum, and so escapes from me? This 'I' which has only its moments can hardly see history whole. History appears as a constellation of epiphanies, grandly patterned, yes, but outside of them time grinds away mechanically, pulverizing the flesh. Or: I have no horizon, only a keyhole. Past this keyhole, occasionally, on the other side of the enormous Byzantine door, the kingfisher flashes. The thrill of life passes through me but, it would seem, at its last gasp, always at its last gasp. Then if I grant that time is the purest, most intangible part of creation, however horribly human enterprise and greed encrust it with historic systems, I am seized with vertigo, for it seems that my stance is upside down.

I cannot yet establish, but want to assert, a connection between my kind of vehemence, this passion for the abstruse, the esoteric, the magical (even for ornithology), and a profound grief which gnaws at the roots of my consciousness. I call it grief, but it is oddly unspecific. Consciousness admits it in various ways: directly as a blankness, in negative shapings of reality, weaknesses, blindness in human relationships, a compulsion to gainsay everything. It is death, of course. It suppresses love, if love is a capacity to break through one's own limits: the 'one' goes out and is with the 'other', in the true radiant imagination. Short of that, even compassion projects nothingness. This is, I suppose, what Nietzsche diagnosed as unconscious nihilism. My curiosity about certain writers, Eliot and Kafka, Mandelstam and Seferis, is due not least to their having known it, suffered it, and made something out of it.

## 9

All this time I am chewing something, as in a dream; it is not cake, but fat. I sit down at a table, opposite me another man is sitting, ordinary, without features. I start to spit out lumps of fat, turning politely aside. Nauseous, the feel of them in my mouth, soft and cold, but some pieces won't come out. I spit four times or five, and still a last piece sticks in or behind my teeth. I am ashamed, disgusted, the grief is seizing me now, I say something to the man opposite, he turns away with a shrug, not a word, but he (who is I) cannot help me. Then I stop spitting, I put my hands to my head, lower my head to the table and say, only for myself, weeping now, slowly: 'The terrible suffering.'

What desperate compulsions dwell in the brain and in the guts, compulsions that make us 'chew the fat' and never let go of the notion of expression? With or without forethought, we drum the messages through certain transformations. Doing this we engage mysterious receptive passions that possess our bodies. As we rock, back and forth, between waking and dream, our horizons expand and contract. The dew-sparkling nerves filter information about the world through their spiderweb, the sensorium, but what alternative signals do our powers of reflection and our voices eliminate? Knowledge that the image is an image, the sign a sign, wakens us to the world of difference, but also to the negations: not this, not that.

# Ideas about Voice in Poetry

Expert studies of sound in poetry tend to take for granted the phenomenon of voice. My purpose here is to set up some thoughts about voice and its imprints in poetry. The physiological side of the matter is not what I have in mind, and rhythmic profilings of voice-sound are so all-important as to require separate treatment. I shall record, without much elaboration, as brief notes, some of the ideas, interrogatory ideas, that have occurred to me while reading poems and listening to voices in them.

## 1

The imprints of voice in poetry, pervasive and elusive, are fundamental to the whole range of lyric expression. The question is: What is meant by 'voice', and how does a reader or listener read or listen to it? The field is one in which variables matter, and they may matter significantly even within settled types of sound-patterning. We might discriminate, somewhat as follows: Textuality attracts, directs, and structures the literary intelligence of a reader, and sometimes it may transform his whole predisposition. His training, susceptibilities, detective skills, dialectical powers, all come into play when he gathers, in the act of reading, the manifold shimmering entity that is an imaginative text in its context. Vocality, on the other hand, is, in a sense, the very authority, or source of the shimmer, in a lyrical text. When a poem lacks vocality, as it may do with good reason, or otherwise, because the bird is dead, then this lack too merits attention.

I do not think that vocality is a subform of textuality. I do not think, either, that lyric vocality is exhaustible semantically in terms of suppressed 'differential structures', terms being used — and widely abused — today in studies of the nature of textuality. Even outside the lyric field, vocality may be paramount, as the voice of a narrator,[1] the voices of his characters. There are poems, it is true, that race ahead of the consciousness of their epochs; but poetry also tends to carry into its present some rooty old features of pre-literate speech. It erupts — even when the text has been assembled over typographical and syntactical lacunae — erupts into its present, streaming with the ichor of the archaic.

Some voices are irretrievably lost, of course. It might just be possible for phonologists to reconstruct some of those that lie dismantled in the Chinese *Book of Songs*. The dynastic Chinese voices, too, even when originally bound to given tunes, had characteristics which are still to be identified (e.g., the tender swinging voice of Li Ch'ing-chao, of the Sung Dynasty).

## 2

The world consists of manifold signals which any individual, any animal or plant likewise, picks up and interprets sensorily. The sound signals in that manifold, or in segments of it, are not less crucial for being frequently and massively nonlinguistic. If I hear footsteps crossing the roof of my house, I do not go and fry an egg, but wonder who or what is up there. A solitary fisherman, offshore from Halicarnassus in 604 BC, had he attended to the splash and ripple of waves against the hull of his boat, might have thought that some other being was around him, at large, but within earshot, even if that other being authorized his element, water, to speak through a different phonetic system from that of the fisherman's Carian.

The manifold voices of the ancient cosmos, subhuman or superhuman voices, might also have engendered in the fisherman's inquiring mind the tremendous thought: 'They alone speak truly who, having learned and understood them, utter the voices of the cosmos.' Instead of accommodating that thought, and as they became Western and aggressive in their ways, peoples of the north-eastern Mediterranean entrusted their fate to another thought: 'They alone shall possess the earth who live from the powers of the cosmos.'

## 3

Even then, that latter thought — if it can be taken as a 'one-legged' epitome of the mind of antiquity, as Walter Benjamin suggested[2] — blazed a trail from archaic polytheism to the hermetic Magian teachings of the West, out of which 'modern science' was deviantly to develop. That trail, it is evident, was signposted with linguistic (or pictorial) markers, some of which retained the imprint of the other thought, the one that might have been.

From what essential and regulative power acting through the human vocal apparatus does poetry draw that authority with which it seems to subjugate, if only for its fatal moment, the demons of earth? What is this voice that makes the earth, not as territory but as planet, a freely valued possession of whole historic societies, treasured especially by their nonconforming members? If subjugation and possession are vitiated terms here, we might think, instead, in terms of placative wooing and tenancy, as North American Indians did, and as some still do, at least on ceremonial occasions (the Hopi, the Pueblo).

### 4

Braiding of narrative and lyrical codes: a patterning of sounds woven so subtly — even inconspicuously — that one might think the passage in question is a 'narratized' and lexicalized phonic poem. It is as purely phonic, inside its lexical clothing, as anything by the pre-audio-laboratory innovators Kurt Schwitters (1920s) and Ernst Jandl (1960s). Certainly, even then, its tonal tincture is more *cantabile* than theirs ever tended to be:

> She weeps alone for pleasures not to be;
>     Sorely she wept until the night came on,
> And then, instead of love, O misery!
>     She brooded o'er the luxury alone:
> His image in the dusk she seem'd to see,
>     And to the silence made a gentle moan,
> Spreading her perfect arms upon the air,
> And on her couch low murmuring 'Where? O where?'
>                     (John Keats, 'Isabella, or The Pot of Basil')

Line after line (except for the fourth) there is an oscillation here, a blending back and forth between *o* and *e*, into which 'perfect' blends as a soft resolution of the sharp antecedent 'seem'd to see'. There are also several of the strong vocalic contrasts (lines 5 and 6), which Keats eased out of the pitch resources of English, and which raised the hackles of some of his contemporaries, who found such bold contrast, it can be presumed, to be eruptive, not suave enough for 'poetry'.

The aptness of 'perfect' is due not only to sound. Somehow the sounds of the whole line, with its light alliteration — *spreading/perfect*, *arms/air* — enact an *opening*. 'Perfect' can be read as alluding to the shapeliness of the arms, or, with a pained irony, on a more cryptic level, to their being now *done for* — having no lover to embrace. An opening is somehow enacted prosodically: the gesture portrayed certainly lends itself to visualization. But any image thrown before the mind's eye here, even a glimpse, not unthinkable, nor so shadowy, of Isabella moaning as she bends back and forth to the *o/e* oscillation, is floated by phonic means, and so the reader's response is a manifold one. 'Inner eye' and 'inner ear' are invited to interact. These features stand out, being mounted on the delicate braiding of end-rhymes in the *ottava rima* — by this time, at stanza XXX, a reader will be taking the verse-form in his stride.

Yet whose voice is this? It was that of John Keats. Now it is an imaginary voice, a voice that was launched by his, but one that has a life of its own in the contemporary air, while it retains his un-mistakable, distinct imprint. That imaginary and unmistakable voice is a kind of *endophone*. I propose this designation as one that distinguishes this kind of voice, with its time-traversing potency, from the exophones or voices with which we speak and to which we listen under ordinary conditions.

## 5

The term *endophone* might conceivably be of some use to readers who are attentive to sound-patterns imprinted in poetry. How is the endophone likely to behave? How is it detected?

(a)   The point about vocality in poetry is that sounds are picked up and assembled in timed stretches by an 'inner ear', and they issue from an 'inner voice', this endophone. (Probably we need to rescue the idea of an 'inner voice' from the coils of religious parlance — which indicates only that religious parlance is habitually in a bad state.) Performance can raise such sound-sequences into profile. Actual vocalizing, unless it is vitiated by histrionics, can nourish the inner ear's competence to pick up and assemble sequences. Yet the inner ear is capable of an auditory complexity which exceeds almost any audible vocalizing: the latter tends to be reductive, if not falsifying, also it may straighten out shocks and distortions which, to the inner ear, are part of the real thing that is the voice in the text and the delight of the text.

In performance, which should be the best instance, there occurs the falling away of mental entity from linguistic entity, or vice versa. The rift appears, gunfire and screams.

(b)    It could be argued that it is the act of silent, or at most murmured, reading — that act alone — which can realize the vocal qualities of a text, the sequences of sounds, the timbres, the tonal colourings. That kind of act, reading from a page or recital from memory, can also *dwell* on patterns of sound, as they exfoliate and intertwine, so as to arrive at a fullbodied perception of the relations (phonic, semantic, syntagmatic) which are being voiced here and now in the text. Thus the silent or murmuring reader construes the text as a symbolic analogue of the planes upon and through which the poet's endophone did once move.

The subtle differential harmonies of the text as voice, are these picked up by the ear alone? Possibly not. The reader's eyes do part of the listening, do their part in identifying and selecting sound-patterns, in the presence or audition of which a delight is experienced and 'soul takes wing'. (It can take wing, too, in the subtly ordered air given off by grammatical balance in the prosiest poems of Brecht, or of Lawrence.)

This collaboration between ear and eye may also be reinforced by the other senses, if not subliminally regulated by those senses. The spreading of the perfect arms has a tactile aspect, for instance. More, as the patternings of sound in the lines are blent into a narrative sequence which, itself, tells of the sounds being uttered by Isabella, a phonetic-semantic chord is struck which vibrates — or it is diffused like an arpeggio — through a reader's imagination. The reader imaginatively somatizes the vocality of the text, for it has aroused in him various other sense-traces, which may be hard to fix. Is it a temperature, a scent, a response of the flesh to the enfolding dusk, through which Isabella spreads her perfect arms?

# 6

A hypothesis: the activities, even along a brief continuum, of the inner ear depend on a profound and stable rapport between the central nervous system (psyche) and externals, whether the latter are actual, or, via a text, virtual. In one of his most cryptic sayings, Mandelstam indicated how far the poetic word can go against the whole grain of the Saussurian view of language as a system of conventional signs: 'The word is a psyche. The living word does not signify an object, but freely chooses, as though for a dwelling place, this or that objective significance, materiality, some beloved body. And around the thing the word hovers, freely, like the soul around a body that has been abandoned but not forgotten.'[3]

The indistinctness of voice, the absence of this *pneumatic* word, in much poetry being written today, written and attended to, is the mark of a poisoned relationship between psyche and externals. In the old listenings of poets, the psyche (again, central nervous system) could in its own good time enter into communication with particulars no less concrete and critical than the sound of a dog lapping water from a gutter, the flit of an eyelid, rustlings of rag or taffeta, an owl's heartbeat. The furore of street traffic (spatial displacement) and the uncertainty (time-desiccation) of living (only partly and anxiously living) have shut inner ears, thresholds to the psyche and its manifold perceptions, shut them off from secret and unbidden resonances of the present here and now likewise.

As far as the inner ear is concerned, the world has been silenced; and the sound-values of single words or word-groups have been largely marginalized. This silencing is concurrent with a kind of suspicious hyper-reflexivity affecting prose: witness the types of erudite discourse which put one in mind of jottings, complete with the usual flourishes and groundlessness, in the dossiers of an intellectual secret police. If dead souls can be said to have speech, that speech is so mouthed as to have little or no interior auditory value. It is noise, like the noise of American or German voices to be noticed among tougher, soft-spoken people like the Turks, who nurse their fires in secret: glib and piercing voices, they chop the foreign air and do not signify.

Signifying in poetry, to the contrary, occurs as a phonic event. That event may occur, however, on an ultravocal level, and its experiential density, subtlety, and volatility may call upon a reader to exercise a kind of clair-audience.


## 7

With such terms as *endophone* and *ultravocal* I seem to be reaching out toward a revised conception of 'classic restraint'. What was the ancient magic power, the aura, of the sacred word, in pre-and proto-literate societies, if not its rarity and volatility? The power brims, but does not overflow. The reticence commended in classical poetics was, perhaps, an attempt to recuperate that power, which secularism was eroding. Longinus, if he may be invoked in this rough-hewn context of mine, argued that the 'sublime' occurs when all the soul's powers are brought to a harmonious head in the play of lyric utterance. Hölderlin rephrased this finely in his last version of 'Griechenland':

> But he sets
> A limit to the stride unchecked
> By measure, then
> The soul's powers and
> Affinities draw in tight,
> As golden blossoms do, together,
> So that beauty may dwell on earth
> More fondly, and a spirit of some kind
> Makes commoner cause with men.[4]

What a pity that sublime utterance ended up as orotundity and as what plain folks call hogwash.

Reticence matters, in crime as in theology: like God, the arch-criminal wisely refrains from obtruding singly, in overt action, or directly in the public view — otherwise he forfeits power. The prattle of much everyday speech spilling over into poetry has a similar effect. The loosening of restraint, in expressions that are linguistic but voiceless, vocal but without artistic discretion, numbs or kills the nerve of lyric vocality.

— Decomposing fruits of the inescapable 'Fall of language-mind' — to quote Benjamin again: there's no gainsaying that Fall, by which (in Benjamin's phraseology) 'mental' and 'linguistic' entities come apart; does not their being wholly coalescent, as some suppose, rest on an illusion which is also laid upon us by that Fall?

## 8

The tract I am living on goes with access rights to a small wooden dock five minutes' walk away, built by bricoleurs thirty years ago, and from this dock you can swim in this neck of Lake Austin. At this point it is an old river course. On the far side there is a great limestone cliff stretching in either direction as far as you can see, densely overgrown with oak, elm, and towering water-cypress. You can dispose yourself on the planks of the dock and contemplate the water, the cliff, and the vegetation. Quite soon, if not prepossessed by self-interest, you come to sense an affinity between your body and the landscape. The landscape is hardly landscape any more: it is a space, as closely knit, variable, integral, necessary, muscular, and functional, as your own body is. The water is liminal: there could be something about the motion and weight of the water that qualifies it to act as mediator between body-space and this segment of world-space. Aeons ago, the water carved out that cliff, which, on days when the water hasn't a ripple, looms across at you, mirrored without fault. Your body consists also, in some part, of water. It goes sideways, this water; the cliff goes up as well as sideways, trees too. Your body does similar things. Its concerns are posited by its occupying, in simultaneity, a vertical and a horizontal axis. I'm not saying that oaks have elbows or thoughts, or that rocks are subject to sunburn. The inter-metaphoricity of body and space has limits, upon which you alone can decide. Sound-patterns in poems likewise: when Roman Jakobson microanalyses sounds in lines by Blake, or Khlebnikov, he is leaving common sense to others who may have some use for it.[5] When the great French archaeologist Capitan was trying to read palaeolithic glyphs out of weathering marks on a rock surface, he was suffering from senile lithomania. No: the intermetaphoricity of body and space, mediated by water, has a real weight, to which measured fantastic play may contribute much, but which eludes perfect measurement, because of the Fall of language-mind away from body, on its unpredictable evolutionary track athwart consciousness or with it.

Yet this manifold which may be intuited, whatever the ego is doing to interfere, alerts imagination to its task, a ludic task. As endophone rather than reductive exophone, voice can perform this task. It is, if I may risk saying so, and by saying so not be taken to mean anything nostalgic or otiose, the task of moving minds, by weaving tissues of linguistic sound, toward a restitution of the lost flesh of God, at least toward a re-membering of his forgotten flesh.

In that now lost, forgotten, or abandoned flesh, the old thinkers — being disinclined, unlike their successors, to drain the colours out of everything — felt the multiplicity of the One. Was it ever palpable? Were they right? Does presence, after all, not not-exist in a world of total inter-reflexivity, but have being, as this or that phenomenon, once the perceiver has been granted the transparency from which reflection has been flushed? Cannot then imagination, which is a power of wondering, activate the whole body of consciousness to play, like an orchestra, as One? In the course of history, any guarantee of such actual presence, actual perfection, was scrapped. Where *ananke* is sovereign, there are no guarantees. Yet there are poems, which paradigmatically bite on the flesh, lost, forgotten, or our own. For one, Valéry's 'Le cimetière marin'. At the end, vast abstractions epitomizing the dramatic thrusts of Ionian thought, with all the consequences, come to rest concretely in the sound-radicles of the last lines — 'Ce toit tranquille où picoraient les focs'. Hardly any actual *focs* forage in the green lake I am poising over, but my dove-sailed reflections pick about its 'roof', and now if I swim I am foraging for an order, for a sense of Change, a way to kick the world awake, as it passes by, snoring in the unthrottled motors, trapped in the pointless revolutions of propellers.

## 9

The timbre of the voice launched by Alexander Pope can be at times as viscerally thrilling as that of Josephine Baker, in her songs of the thirties. Her flips from coyness to headstrong and dizzying femininity are a match, any time, for Pope's turns of architectonic wit. The one has a wicked intelligence, the other a spellbinding presence: both had the edge over most performers, for they practised a wizardry that shatters the very folderol such visceral voicings are prone to generate:

*a voice-net*

*shrivels us*
*in its       chimeras*[6]

## 10

Oral tradition and the pneumatic word:
(a)   George Borrow's *The Romany Rye* has been as good as forgotten. Yet it is a narrative museum of all the varieties of English spoken in those areas where Borrow travelled in the 1820s. The sounds of those varieties are articulated as cadence and as syntax, quite apart from vocabulary. What an ear he must have had. The imprints of voices in their speech-cadences and syntax are as audible, as indelible, as any pneumatic phrasing, or polyphonic designing, in poems by unforgotten poets. What a memory, what powers of endophonic mimicry Borrow must have had, at the tip of tongue and pen, to write everything down, just as if he had *invented* it.
(b)   The endophone, as it voices the internality peculiar to lyric speech, is likely to generate 'deep' sound-structures. These may be immediately detectible, or they may lurk so far below the 'surface' as to be audible only in a theoretical way. (A sage in music will detect

scarce-performable instrumental values in a score.) Keats's 'Ode on a Grecian Urn' might be read as a five-part orchestration of the vowels of English, accenting each in the following sequence, while breathing patterns of others around them: i/e/u/o/a (corresponding to the five strophes).

This hypothesis will be meaningless to many, unprovable to the rest. It is a hunch, however, which can have some heuristic value, clarifying the celebrated crux of the last few lines.[7] What I perceive as a vowel-orchestration alerts me to the hidden foundation of the whole Ode, perhaps the foundation running under all the Odes that Keats wrote in 1819. That foundation could be described as an *état d'âme* of perceptive wonder at the profound fluidity of experience, and about the liminal character of objects in experience, their suspension across life and death being one limit to such a psychic perception.

The arresting of vowel-flow by means of orchestral thickenings — or groupings — corresponds as a phonic event to the dialectical interplay of then and now, there and here, action and portrayal, pursuit and capture, which is the vibrant fabric of the Ode's language as an aesthetics of eternity. Keats sublimated this aesthetic from the roots of the English sounds, or he radicalized it, down into those roots, as if it had always been there, latent in those roots, waiting for this voice to raise it up. The riddle posed by the end — Who speaks? The poet or the urn? — might be answered with 'Both; but constraints of grammar and punctuation required the duet to sound like a solo.'

This answer is a legitimate guess, prompted by reading the putative deep phonic structure as an analogue to Keats's vision of a great undulance traversing all things, here momentarily crystallized in an image of presence, an inexhaustible image of fleeting presence.

This coherent vision of liminality is the Ode's orchestral voicing of a wonder, in a breath of time, that subject and object, reader and text, object and portrayal, such a richly figured 'thing' and such a profoundly responsive imagination, can blend into one another and still be, through all similarity, separable. In that separability dwells the distancing and paradoxical movement of a freedom. The wonder, with this freedom, here, as its authority, is a primal mode of lyric imagination, lyric sensibility. It is the mode through which, mediated by the endophone, the essential and regulative 'power', mentioned earlier, arrives in the world as a formative agent, benign, fructifying — as language.

Without the elasticity of that freedom, which actualizes self for engagement in the historical world, for the contest with *ananke*, for the struggle against indistinctness in that world, wonder is prone to play havoc with everything. It will play havoc until something turns it back on itself; lacking any freedom to apply itself otherwise, it is turned back on itself, to meet its own awful interior medusa — voiceless void.

# Reflections on a Viking Prow

## 1

To recapture poetic reality in a tottering world, we may have to revise, once more, the idea of a poem as an expression of the 'contents' of a subjectivity. Some poems, at least, and some types of poetic language, constitute structures of a singularly radiant kind, where 'self-expression' has undergone a profound change of function. We experience these structures, if not as revelations of being, then as apertures upon being. We experience them as we experience nothing else.

Yet we say that a poetic text is not this or that thing out there. We say that such a virtual thing as a text is not an actual thing, that it is not even thinglike at all. Or we say that this or that text occupies an interface between things and persons, but has its ontological status only c/o the addressee, who is itinerant and anonymous. Look at the problem this way: Might it be that we are forgetting what a thing as artifact firstly is and secondly signifies? We might be forgetting, in particular, about the intrinsic virtues of pre-industrial artifacts, not only ones that had explicitly sacred value.

Lace, icons, handblown glass, handstruck Greek coins, bone implements, masks, figurines, old books, paintings, carts, and bedspreads and ploughs — such handmade things are real, did become real, because they were brought to life by currents of formalized energy, desire crystallizing as it passed from imagination to skilled hands, through to treasured materials, and back again in a circuit never broken. Some artifacts were charged with a 'spirit' which, as in Kwakiutl masks, formalized itself while the skill of the artificer conducted it, like lightning, and crystallized it into socially significant objects illuminating the whole time/space context of the artificer and his tribe. Such an artificer is not confessing, not foregrounding his own subjective compulsions, not cataloguing impressions, not hanging an edict from an anecdote. There is nothing random which is not absorbed into the structure of the artifact. The artificer fashions a group wisdom in the thing which speaks for itself.

That is, at least, one way of viewing, now, certain objects and practices older than ours and other than ours. We may dismiss such practices as fetishism. Seldom do we recognize the watery fetishism, or idolatry, that we ourselves bring to bear on cars, washing-machines, cigarette lighters, a glittering host of technoid commodities. The older practices were informed by vigorous, even fierce animistic feeling about the materials at hand, the wood, the jade, the bronze, to which people could relate as once to animals and to the gods in animals. The animism may not always have been lucid. At least it resourcefully furnished knowledge through the conduit of the material, as we can still see in old cathedrals. Our practices are evidently less animate. We fetishize commodities on the basis of yawning indifference — or tight-lipped hostility — toward a world of objects that confuse perception and multiply signs of our alienation. Yet, worse, faced with this forbidding world, bothered by it, we finally cease to care. The profit motive, blunted by high taxation, sees to it that we seldom take joy in putting body and soul into things we make for sale or even for our own consumption. A tiny fraction of the mass world, west or east, can still find gratification in handmaking perfect things in leisure time stolen from money time. Artisanal work is coming back, yes, and in the USA, of all places, a little good cooking. But the mainline production mechanisms keep these changes peripheral, for an élite. For the rest: plastics and apathy, sinister twins. Plastix and Apathy: twin *croque-morts* stuffing the corpse of Western civilization.

The old animistic practices, the old view of *things*, had a great range of vital significance: from witchcraft to Rilke, from soothsaying to apparel, from Viking ships to the most delicate French and German portrait miniatures of the later eighteenth century. The artifact as icon: if you lived in that world, an icon actually contained for you the soul-substance of the person portrayed. Portrayal was not descriptive or derived. It was presentation, immediate and precise, of the being resonantly invoked by the image and stored in the image. There was more to this than idolatry. By the image the viewer was freed from some snags in the circuitry of response to the world, snags which for us stop growth in two general ways. One is the opacity, compounded of dread and habit, which bottles subjectivity up. The other is the NOHOW feeling which liquefies subjectivity. No wonder that throughout the 1840s hundreds of thousands of North American people rushed into the daguerreotype studios, hoping to achieve structure, identity, in the form of a perfect and detailed image.

I must edge away from this frame of reference to approach another question. It may be impossible to reconstruct exactly an older world's quasi-magical reality, the texture of its beliefs. But we can do so conjecturally, in this case, by asking how artifacts behaved, or else were thought to reach out and touch the boundaries of space, physical and social space, which defined them. First I shall outline a conjecture, then trace correspondences between that touch relation (artifact/environment) and poems experienced as apertures upon specific spaces, or places.

Artifact and environment: a dramatic example is the prow of the Oseberg Viking ship. The photo I'm looking at as I write shows a curved piece of wood, elaborately carved, sweeping up out of the rocks and mud which buried the ship for eleven centuries. Placed in receding layers behind the carved wooden curve, secured by the wooden plugs, are eight boards, quite slender, the front of the hull, their own curve following the axe-edge upward curve of the prow. Then comes another carved board, as if to reinforce the significance of the prow board. The leading edge of the prow board is about as wide as a kitchen matchbox. It is blank and is paralleled by another blank, the trailing edge. Inside this frame come the carved figures.

The figures are carved in low relief, curlings and weavings and interlacing, dragonlike designs. On what is left of the prow board you can count seven major areas, interlocking. The anterior reinforcing board, eight boards back, has a similar but not identical configuration of interlaced and interlocking squirls, tendrils, sticklike ligaments, and broader body-areas — again dragonlike. This figuration is not representational. It is something else, but what? The body-areas are cross-hatched all over, with striations less deep than the squirl outlines: little elevated rectangles, like those which are concave ('coffered') in a waffle — dragon scales, if dragons were intended at all. But nowhere does this intricate ornamentation obliterate the woody nature of the wood. You can see the grain. Nowhere, either, does the carving weaken the wood. You see what they mean, the etymologists who derive from the word 'cosmos' the word 'cosmetic'. Essential virtù explicit in accented palpable form.

People say that the dragons, whose claws invariably point outward to the sea, were meant to protect the oarsmen from evil spirits. I would go further. The dragons are sea foam formalized into (mythic) animal shapes. They are animal formalizations of the sea foam that crashes against the prow or lies briefly on the ocean surface. At the same time, the dragons in no way deform the wood. They are realized directly out of the wood and its grain. The carver carved the protoforms of sea substance into the wood, because then, he thought, even if portrayed as dragons, these protoforms, at home in the wood, know also how to deal with the sea, they being made of the sea, while sharing too the life of the wood.

The ship was protected and guided by marine protoforms carved — into symbols — out of the wood whose axe-edge shape cut through the salty matter of the sea. The symbols worked a magical substitution. The substitute, as symbol, participates communicatively in the brute life, sea, from which it is extracted. Because of that communicative participation, because it knows its double origin, the dragon wood knows how to grip the sea, cope with it, deflect its onslaughts, and how not to be smashed. That was how the carver of wood served his fellow beings, with capable hands. Enormous muscles on the backs and arms of the oarsmen would otherwise have been helpless. They needed these delicate and incisive woodcarver's hands, needed this information, and they needed the dragons as helpers, to anticipate and disperse the horrors of the sea.

The carving which induces the magical substitution has not only a sheltering (or passive, apotropaic) role to play. Its role is transitive too. The carving acts in and upon the sea, cuts into the sea the shape of the human journey. Finally, the carving is a model of order, good energy in good order. It signified — even if it did not always achieve — a conquest of randomness. By its transitive action this model made sense of the hazardous sea. To the oarsmen's muscles it signalled orientation among the whirling cross-currents, the heaving labyrinthine web of high tensions between order and chaos, ship and ocean.

Thinking about artifice of this kind — the prow system is not isolated, nor need we lose sight of social implications for ourselves — one comes to have doubts about poems which conform to the scripts of subjective expression; doubts also about anecdotal or confessional poems, poems that catalogue impressions additively, and so forth. I say doubts, but the key to value in any text is the character (quality) of the writing; so perhaps I have simply crept a long way around in order to concede an obvious distinction. This would be a distinction between two kinds of text, the configural and the confessional. Either may appeal to sound aesthetic judgement. If my doubts apply at all, it would be because the (broadly) confessional mode is more apt to encourage limp, self-indulgent, and haphazard writing, also because it makes room for what is fake.

The scripts for self-expression are not all formulae, not by any means. The liberating force of poetry as we know it today derives much from volcanic expressions of the recent past. From Whitman to Artaud — crises in the guts, psyche and voice, oceanic feeling, democracy, elaborate invention of human interiors, not excluding the anguish of Artaud's anus. The great confessional crowing, at its most intense, can show what reckless and savage stuff a creative individual is made of. But the artificer poets, who contend with their seas on other levels, at disparate angles, have different ways of making that stuff luminous. Many of the artificer poets, unlike the unwinders of intestines or excavators of the void, are connected with historic places. At the very roots and altogether transparently they are connected with specific places, solid scenes. I wonder if their sense of dwelling along a particular time/space axis implies an imagination akin to that of the prow-carver.

Propertius, Musil, Lorca, Kafka, Baudelaire, Mandelstam, Balzac, Fontane, Joyce, Mörike, Proust, Leopardi, Pindar, and Ladislas Nowak in Trebic today, or Fritzi Mayröcker in her Zentagasse room — they are anything but milieu writers. They all wrestle, respectfully, with arbitrariness. Their cities, landscapes, and rooms are not photographically literal. Never frontal reportage about apparent localities, their writings are formal creations which enshrine and radiate poetic space. A particular time/space axis, as 'world of appearance', may be recognized, certainly, in the words and the imagination words embody. But that embodiment includes a crucial moment of change. Nothing is neutral any more, all is transvalued and animated by the rhythms of a unique formal vision grounded in an original sensibility. (There are many women among such writers; their keen and rich sense of space, oddly, is less mixed with artifice.)

Mörike's Swabia, Propertius' Rome, René Char's Vaucluse, all are structures — or I should say structurings — which relate transitively to the extraneous world whose form they gaily enshrine. Hence we experience these places as *world*, as *cosmos*, once we have experienced them in these forms of words. The inaugual word-forms are distinct from expression in the usual sense; they are vocal, but not thought/feeling arbitrarily vociferated. Almost they put us in perceptual contact with being; almost we perceive, in their organization, being as most subtle and integral form. It does not matter much whether the point of contact is a gutter or a fountain, a 'ship under sail' or 'a hog in a high wind', as Byron said. Perhaps the actual place, in all its dense psychic variety, was in the last analysis a focus for the creation of a vision: a vision of being as an enigmatic and deep structuring, a structuring full of conflict, but pervasive.

At which point I hear my academic hat whistling through the air, aiming to clamp itself back on my head. Yet, if I emphasize structure as a radical linguistic happening, if I consider that some structurings imply magic, I do not advocate making structure conspicuous or exclusive. No neo-Parnassian frigidity. Any doctrinaire purism repels me, even that of Gerhard Rühm. I do admire some French poets who are working intelligently to deregulate the sentence-mechanism, who have a fine sense of fragmentariness, and who rid a text of random feeling. But keep at arm's length, I tell myself, the attractive idea of a non-discursive, trans-reflexive poetry which, as it presents complex lyrical experience, is said to be a disclosure of being. At arm's length — partly because this idea lends itself to academic wordspinning, partly because conscious effort so to write results in an esotericism both vacant and prim.

All I have tried to do in these notes is propose, as one possible model for the poem, the significant and useful ancient artifact. In doing so, I stand by figurative speech, as a time-tested access to truth in finite existence, and more, as speech which tells of the impact of the world upon the body. Figures offer an access — to truth and to death — which might be called physiognomical, because it does not sheer away feeling and randomness, but admits them, whatever the pain, in a purged and dynamic condition. Purged and dynamic: it is the evolving structure which, as you write your artifact into life, tests and tempers this or that feeling, this or that random particle. The testing and tempering is what eventually makes a text radiant, polysemous, and redeems it from the flat modes of confessional anecdotage or impression-cataloguing.

It is understandable that in the Bundesrepublik younger poets should place imagination, the source of figures, under suspicion (or arrest?), because of its erratic tonal flights and its deceptiveness. Understandable too, but less so for me, that in England not only younger poets seem to regard imagination much as their forebears regarded sex, as a release not often permitted, and then only if it helps you to feel better. Imagination, precisely because it is deceptive and demonic, needs artifice, needs the pressure of craft, the pleasure of artistry, for a dialectical counterpart. As another set of controls one can practise the critique of imagination suggested by Wen I, the Chinese Ch'an (Zen) master of the 10th century: 'All appearances lack in essence and all names arise from that which is nowhere.'

So the world is tottering and still you do what you can to make the prow that shall make sense of the sea, with all the times of your life and of your fellowbeings to propel the ship it guides and shields. Let subjectivity rip, in a poetry of panic and egomaniacal delirium — and the volatile, animated word, the figural form, as an aperture upon being, will very likely be splintered.

## 2

(See References for a list of exhibits and texts which illustrated the lecture on which this part of the essay was based: prehistorical figurines and tools, Arabic, Kufic, and Greek calligraphy, pictures by Kandinsky, Klee, Malevitch, Hartung, and Carlfriedrich Claus, typography by Iliazd, concrete poems, a Rilke manuscript, and inscriptions on walls in Facteur Cheval's 'Palais Idéal'.)

These exhibits and texts are not aired in order to exemplify anything. I wanted simply to show two sets of signs with which an imagination might play, after it had been taken by the thought that between text and artifact a theoretical relation might exist, and that this relation might not interfere with tedious old distinctions between the fine, the verbal, and the useful arts. If you study Rimbaud's poem, 'Marine', you notice that an invention in words can come close to realizing an artifact model. In this case the model would be the process of braiding. Braiding goes into hair, furniture, metalwork, bread, clothing, and so on. Rimbaud was braiding images of sea and land, prow and plough, forest and jetty.

But then a model is not devised for realization; it is a theoretical construct. In the froth of phenomena models keep disappearing. Another matter to be remembered is this: As we attend to texts, things, artifacts, making and writing, we are like refugees frightened and baffled by real dangers. We look at the exhibits and see all around these limpid inventions the opaque times we are living in. Our time is the second or third phase in the age of reproducibility of works of art and of the mass replication, for commercial ends, of what George Kubler called prime objects.[1] Years ago, Walter Benjamin mapped the new situation — 'loss of aura'.[2] What troubles us now is the likelihood that some sort of vacuum, having eroded the presences of original things, artifacts and handiworks, is eating away the awesome reality of individual human lives. Adjoining Benjamin's map of the developing terrain there are terrible regions like that around the filing cabinet in chapter 1 of György Konrad's novel, *The Case Worker*. Around that cabinet there are stupefying regions crammed with futile objects that constitute no clear cut world at all, only a 'hieroglyphic pattern of . . . murderous devices'.[3] The totally politicized world, with its economic imperatives, grievances, greeds, is punctured all over by ideological syringes that suck and pump singularity out of everything, and flood, with embalming fluids, every vein of difference, every muscle of human oddity.

A nightmare of designification is running its course. This understood, we should consider, not without pangs and qualms, how down the centuries since somebody told how the shield of Achilles was made, poets have learned from significant things about the naming of such things and significations. They learned how essential the right words are, particularizing or flighted, words like shingle, lip, spandril, dovetail, tuft, byssus, garboard strake, topsail, stitch, clerestory, burdock, or the beautiful Greek *sphrinx*. By observing things and contemplating them steadily, they came to see things in the making, and to know how craftsmen go to work on things. They understood things as messages telling how things are made, the thing telling of its own generative process, not just a dead end-product. Some poets, like Gérard de Nerval, madly or not, also recognized in a set of material objects the play of id-forces, a universal dreamwork, their own inmost soul-drama crystallizing, puzzling itself out, in the thing or in the fluid webs of things. The regard resting on the object is thus, as sometimes in Kurosawa's films,[4] the key to self-affirmation: a self reclaims itself from nonentity and, as the object reveals itself in a certain light, that self can gaze into its own depths as an agent of interiority, no longer a mere blob to be pushed around in a flat world. Between 'I am' and 'This is' there can be strange ligatures — a magico-grammatical tissue links first and third persons singular.

In Gerard Manley Hopkins' journals[5] (1860s) there are prose studies of the distinctive forms of things (inscapes), in which the prose itself is a signature of the designing force that Hopkins called instress. Studying the way an oak tree evolves, as a unified design, he instresses into the grain of his prose the oak's gnarled and rooty gestalt. (His study of a bluebell is a brilliant exegesis of the flower's gestalt — but then Hopkins could read the flower as a sacred text.) A surprise in this area — Kipling's travel letters.[6] Kipling is invariably specific, at times a bit careless, but always curiously mixing metaphor and fact, actualizing, together with the design of the thing he presents, the delicacy and force of his perception of it. His prose goes all the way around the thing. The thing is shown as a decisive event in consciousness, as language.

All the same, a text is not in itself a thing. In some ways it is the reverse of a thing. It may be about a thing, embrace a thing and make intimate to thought a thing's hidden vital sense. But I'm trying now to look past the fascination of poems about things,[7] poems in which, as in Mörike, Rilke, and Williams, verbal design mimes an extrinsic concrete thing or kinetic grouping of things, but mimes in such a way as to melt reference into wording of high intrinsic interest. The miming would not be thinkable, let alone interesting, were it not for the fact that, even when type-face and lay-out are enlisted, as in cummings, text is non-identical with thing. This non-identity is perfectly obvious, but it matters a good deal to the distinction that also has to be made between text and artifact.

An intelligible inscription on an artifact, a painting or a bowl, contributes to the artifact's thinginess, but is not itself a thing. In cases where a phrase or letter has been shredded and attached as graphic element to a material surface, as in Franz Mon's 'Abstraktion', we might think of the whole outcome as a thing, or, more specifically, as an artifact. But we cannot fail to recognize that the verbal-graphic element is contributive only, not self-sufficient, in the ensemble of that artifact. For millennia, inscriptions have been adjuncts to the presences of things. In this century, and before it, alphabets and syllabaries have been plundered by artists for graphic and calligraphic ends and put into pictures or upon objects that we can think of as being things. Yet we do not think of language as a thing. After all, language is not made by the hands, and it has a weird way of moving around in the body-mind, not occupying a fixed position outside it.

We also call a book a thing, but the texts which compose the book are not thought of as things (except in some such special sense as that of Francis Ponge). The book has its three dimensions, like a cup or a tombstone, you can handle it, but does a text 'have' anything at all? A Chinese scroll, Tutankhamun's lotiform chalice, or Ian Hamilton Finlay's glass sheet with words sandblasted into it — these are things. But the moment those words, ideograms, or hieroglyphs, are detached from their tangible vehicle and appear as themselves alone, they re-enter the open field of non-things, non-artifacts.

A verbal design so well wrought, or so spontaneous, that it enables a reader to feel the 'very feel' of a thing, is still not itself a thing, we say. The extrinsic thing out there, or the feeling for it, is actually reinvented in the instrumentation of language called a poem. Besides, the 'very feel' comes about only through this or that unique instrumentation, which mediates the arousal of the poet in the presence, memory, or imagination, of his thing, even when the pull of the thing is reversed by the poem. All this is representation, and the textual design holds up a representation as an unbinding of the spell of idolatry. The text is an image, if you like, even when it may strain to be transparent. From the extrinsic thing the text that unbinds the spell and measures the depth of the writer's arousal is lifted by an interpreting touch. I do say lifted by an interpreting touch, because the intervention need be by no means as vast and divinatory as, say, Rilke's gaze on the head of Amenophis IV in a Berlin museum. 'Feel', he wrote to Benvenuta, 'feel from this face what it means to confront the infinite world and in a surface thus confined, through the intensified ordering of a few features, to form a counterweight to the whole manifest universe'.[8]

Rilke had more to say (and this was before he met Benvenuta and started to address her extravagantly). He wrote: 'Could not one turn away from a night sky full of stars and find in this face the same law blossoming, the same magnitude, depth, inexhaustibility to thought? From things like this I learned to see.' Extreme as this sounds, surely the delight a reader can experience in textual design, a delight with roots going down deep into his creaturely fear and trembling, comes about as a dawn of insight across this distance between star and face, thing and text. It is a distance of non-identity, which sets intelligence free to intuit a common law between star and face. The delight liberates. A re-ordering of perceptual schemata releases intellectual energy. This energy has been wrung from the inchoate and it configures in the design of the text.

Every text is singular and so is each degree of delight in the experience of each singular reader. Singularity is the term that seems best to embrace a host of foreground and background features in the experience of delight in design. The experience is one that singularizes the agent of the experience, to start with. You are on your own. Momentarily, at least, you are set apart from engulfing things by which 'we' are *bedingt* (cf. Heidegger). Singularity here, what is more, does not mean just oddity. The word comes from the Latin root *sim-* , and the derivates of *sim-* denote self-sameness, identity, integrity, consonance of the whole person or thing, rather than similarity (to something else) in our sense. This kind of singularity of the person who responds consonantly to design, or this singularity of the text itself that embodies the design, is never actually final. Design configures the text and marks non-identity between text and thing. Design also displaces, for the singular reader, the flat confusions formerly programmed as reality. A new identity is coming into sight, uniquely the design as such, singular, also self-renewing, re-readable, because in each performance never quite the self-same. Here, I suppose, are some of the variables implied in the young Ezra Pound's *aperçu* that a 'sense of sudden growth' is what a reader feels as he responds to a complex poetic image. Hopkins, it is true, was put out when he felt that 'instress cannot come' on account of the presence of a companion; and yet, he wrote, 'I saw the inscape though freshly, as if my eye were still growing . . .' The truth we are after belongs, I think, in that very growing.

The braiding design in Rimbaud's poem can also be read this way. He was braiding images of sea and land. At the same time, he was dispersing, singularizing, and reinventing the world in which, habitually and referentially, sea is perceived as sea and land as land: the pedestrian world where inertia is king and metaphor the fool. The text communicating itself as immaterial reinvention of reality forcibly delivers imagination from the tyranny of things. The text as a cosmos of signs is a system with its own controls and balances — but it is not shut off or out, nor is its deliverance from things necessarily contrived by violence, a violence at once positive and distortive. No wonder it can be argued that a certain range of signs, artifacts or texts, has sacramental value.[9] In the Zuni world, for example (a basic example), what we might comfortably call reinvention was understood as a restitution of the first creation, the dawn of being, before the big fire brought the creator's wrath. The Zuni sculptor might put no more than a notch in a small stone shaped like a horned toad. For his people, that notch nevertheless was sign enough that the stone he had found could be identified, for sacramental use, as a horned toad left over from the primal creation.

Unlike a stone or a horned toad, the text has no weight. It has no volume and no pages. It is a memory trace of a complex and radiant kind. Even if it is discontinuous, even if it is a spectre come to drink at the pool of involuntary memory, you can summon it to bring otherwise inchoate feeling into focus. The text as a non-dimensional, mental event is also a sign that in non-identity a freedom is available.

Certainly your first delight is free to modulate, in quality, in its own way. Should you forget about the text, your delight is free to die. Dying, it may transform itself into a component of your general feeling. Severed from its first occasion, this delight can persist in your capacity for delight generally, in the delight you cathect into the world you are full of. It seasons your sensibility, and you can converse with it. Perhaps it opens, as an intelligible design, your mind to yourself. Formal closure of some kind might well be the mark of a text and of an artifact; at least a good sense of limit was the mark of societies neither madly classical nor madly self-destructive. Yet closure in the design of a text is not only what stimulates the sense of growth for a reader; it is also the measure of how, on some levels of signification, a text is branching out into the unknown, ramifying toward or out of the unsayable.

One step more, beyond the humanistic solecisms, then I mean to draw back and look around. Perhaps a text in all its singularity, as a dematerialization of thing into sign, as a structured but not rigid event in consciousness, with a design as fine as that of an artifact, but not identical with any artifact or thing, might show you a way toward an otherwise shuttered world of infinite delight that you carry around with you, gnash your teeth as you may. But I would not insist that the immateriality of any text points the way to a private door into 'divine nature', the private door which St. Augustine[10] said was intrinsic to each soul, and beyond which, for the soul, 'all things come to nought'. The reverse might be the case. Textual design in sedated self-destructive societies may often imply cushioning devices that absorb the shock of unholy terrors in the thing-bewitched world. That is the trouble.

Now to look around a little. How do these ideas relate to the idea of the artifact as model for a poetic text? I have proposed that you can talk back to a text which you have experienced with delight. You can also talk to a thing. Yet a thing is mute. So when you do talk to it, you are not talking back to it. You are talking to yourself through the circuitry of the thing. Or you might be talking vicariously to other people not present. (If language originated in the furious urge to communicate with oneself, not with other people, then other people too are originals.)

Does what Heidegger called 'the heavenly' talk to itself vicariously through us, or through our artifacts? A tall thought, and we are little informed about this. If things are mute to us, must our artifacts be mute to angels? Rilke did not think so, in the ninth Duino Elegy.

There he insisted: 'Show him (the angel of the Elegies) a thing', and 'Tell him things'.

Rilke's figurative hyperboles here cannot be transposed on to a practical level, in a designified world, without a dimming of their suggestive power. They might bring pangs of despair to people less eloquent than he, or less intimate with things than an old woman who makes rhythmic speeches to her dog and can talk to God about her knitting, as well as vice versa. Any 'angelic' illumination is made problematic, or is indefinitely postponed, by the existence of things in a world of subjectivity that is inexhaustibly self-reflexive. In Kafka nothing grows toward illumination. It is things, with their inscrutable penumbra, that spellbind the self-reflexive subject and eclipse illumination with anxiety. This human *Bedingtsein* is figured in a gigantic newspaper, a closet of whips, a cart in the corner of a nocturnal courtyard, or in Fraülein Bürstner's utterly ordinary pincushion. Thus *bedingt*, people wander around like zombies, not even knowing that is what they are, crowding history's corridors, erratic, obstructed, crushed. Kleist too seems to have thought of things as entangled fractions whirling in the vortex of erratic subjective actions. Seldom are his things stable reference points that might measure the deeper pulsations of a psyche, or might help the will to achieve some degree of orientation, retrieve the lost lucidity of instinct. St. Augustine, also Meister Eckhart, and indeed the main East-West metaphysical tradition, with its roots in the oldest strata of human self-consciousness, are intent on extricating the soul from the damnation of things, extricating it too from the gravitational force we put around things and call beauty.

So consistent is this, that one might almost think the artisanal traditions of the world were plain contrary from the start, that the metaphysicians were right, and that with materialism East or West, whoever owns the means of production, people have got what they deserved — rockets, egomania, TV dinners, and rotten operas for light relief. Even if this were not the case, puritanical fanaticism in the West has done its spiteful worst to replace things with nothing. Even the Platonic-Buddhist strain in Western poetic idioms tends to subvert the artisanal contrariness, with a few exceptions, Keats for one. (It is noticeable that in our time Williams and Ponge are distinctly anti-Platonic, Brecht too, who had a passion for old handtools, and knives and forks.) If Goethe and Wordsworth differ here, Goethe still cannot be seen as an undeviating critic of the metaphysical tradition. The old pagan is always on the lookout for archetypal 'bleibende Verhältnisse', transcendent paradigms. On 9 October, 1786, in Venice, he writes à propos shellfish: 'What a delightful, glorious thing a living entity is! How well adapted to its conditions, how true, how being!' Six months later, in Naples, à propos Rousseau, he writes: 'If I didn't have such sympathy with things of nature, or see that there are ways of sorting out and comparing hundreds of observations despite the apparent confusion — as a surveyor does when with a single straight line he checks many separate measurements — I should often think I was mad myself.'[11] Time and again Goethe's fantastic sympathy for things in nature compels him to sing them to sleep for a while, so that he can speculate about entelechies (in paintings he also looks for the story-line). We should note: Had he subtracted from the irreducible singular thing his feeling of partnership with it, or his abstractive gaze upon it, either way that thing in the immediate confusion of things could for him have been more like a knocker on the gate of a madhouse, than a latch on the soul's private door into 'divine nature'.

Now it is intriguing that we should except writings from our categories of things. Horrendously rugged proto-Germans may have had some such word as 'dinc'. By 'dinc' their successors meant 'assembly', possibly too the common concern, focusing event or crisis, which might occasion the elders of a group to reason together. The Latin 'res' had originally the same sense. In neither case was the word for thing applied in our narrower sense, to particular external objects. It almost looks as if an old semantic muddle, or else a fabulous psychological transformation, underlies our reluctance to think of a significant text as a 'thing' belonging in the orders of prophetic dreams, invasions, oracles, incest, or famine.

French 'chose', similarly, comes from Latin 'causa', again the word for a concern, and for a case (like German 'Sache'), but not, it seems, for cause in the sense of ground (German 'Ursache'). Heidegger plots these etymologies and prefers, for his priceless speculations on a jug, an ancient sense of thing as 'gathering'.[12] He also carried across into them the sense of Greek 'on', Latin 'ens', as 'that which is present . . . put here, put before us, presented'. He does not refer to Sanskrit levels of Indo-European.

Etymology gives us a glimpse behind current usage, but still we are in the dark as regards which word prehistoric speakers might have used, if ever they wanted to pronounce sounds in order to refer non-specifically to such things as 'stone', 'shaft', or later 'hoe', and 'pick'. Perhaps there was no non-specific word. If there was none, how should we think about events in the mind of a typical prehistoric speaker, who might never have been able to say: 'Look, northward, what is that thing out there?'

It is possible that such a person, for all his amazing skills and other powers of communication, linguistic powers included, lacked any organ to locate and identify natural objects or artifacts as 'entities' altogether *separate* from his own person. Discussion in our terms becomes doubly difficult if you think that he might have thought of his own person not as 'I' but as 'he'. Only, perhaps, with the accumulation of spare things, in a world that had marched away from subsistence economy, a world with power-centralization and property, a world that had shifted from right hemisphere to left hemisphere thinking, a world with a grammar that arose with the neural shift away from magical thinking toward cortical or subjective thinking, did a term as non-specific as 'thing' in our sense enter ancient man's vocabulary.

Only then, again perhaps, did a later variant of 'dinc' come into use as a term with which to designate a discrete, exterior, objective, manipulable entity, separate from consciousness, but serving it — a genuine *Gegenstand*. In this case, the notion 'thing', as object, comes to life along with individual self-consciousness, as contrasted to group-consciousness. It comes to life with the breakdown of some very ancient magical cohesion, in which mind had been a shared social coagulant, and not really subjective — here I'm leaning on Julian Jaynes's set of arguable hypotheses.[13] It comes to life with trade between magically coherent societies, if it was trade (besides vast geophysical catastrophes and difficult encounters between foreigners) that transformed, or shattered, the unconscious semantic bonds that kept those societies discrete and insulated. Far back, one might speculate, the concept 'thing' is already to be linked with diversification, economics, alienation, and finally reification.

Bleak thought: the word once still used to signify a common concern now signifies objects for which we compete, over which we squabble, with which we pretend to be on top and well off, commodities replicating themselves *ad infinitum*, jealously guarded acquisitions, cold comforters for our slowly powdering bones. Yet even in our sense certain things have retained some of their ancient energy. Out of things, and quite especially out of artifacts, we can still draw the fine fugitive tunes and harmonies of consciousness as language. Even if we no longer construct Gothic cathedrals, some things, even good cars, can still embody for us the intellectual and social configurations which linguistic interpretations of them convoke.

Other things do gather the rays of feeling with which we — in our indelibly animistic afterthoughts — pretend to penetrate them, and they reply to those rays with presence. Briefly, even when things retain their trans-linguistic purity in silence, they are essential to our social and private coherences; and our artifacts do encode those coherences in peculiarly transparent ciphers. To go back to the contrary old artisans: they were right. They did not contradict spirit really. They were designing spaces in which spirit, on its adventures, might call in, or rest awhile, after shaking hands with a few people. Or else they really did contradict spirit, and that contradiction was just what spirit was calling for, because spirit needed to be provoked — paradox was the condition of its appearing.

Artifacts are highly organized, distinct, and subtle things. Contemplate a Yurok basket, try to embrace its intricate formal weave as well as the skill and work that have 'gone into it'. The contemplator and the thing conspire to bring matter back into the spontaneous motives of thought, to retrieve matter into the rumorous life of reflection, deliver matter from separateness while not violating its difference. A text, as a mental event, as a common concern, is also an ensign that convokes us and even emboldens us in the fight for interior life. It is, to this extent, just as provocative as an artifact can be, even if its status, that of the text, is unstable, or liminal, itinerant between interiority and externals, the imaginable and the actual, the silence and the speaking.

What is this will to retrieval? Is it a real function of so-called intentionality in a text as work of art? Intentionality might be the fiat which sets certain elements loose in play; as that play becomes determinate as text, the elements configure into a design, and that design asserts, like an arrow shot from a bow in perfect tension, the central fact of language, which is relation. I think this may be so. But I can think of many texts that just do not do what I say they are meant to do. The fundamental notion here is that intentionality institutes play first, the determinations only later. A Yurok basketmaker, too, is quoted as saying: 'While basket-weaving sit with your back to the fire. Do not think of it as hard work or the basket will not be good.'[14]

Yet this fiat of intentionality, also this retrieval, are what a reader can feel when the text is before him, growing into his world as he grows into its world. This is what he feels when this text, as artifact, 'res', or 'dinc' or imagination, defies and dissolves the fossil codes, those determinate yet so slippery things out there, the fictions we institutionalize in our fear and with our all-entombing idolatry. Without demonstrating anything, a text can at least recall to us our gifts of being free, singular, and grateful. This in-stance of the text as a thing presented, though not a thing, as a thing recovered into thought and shining anew with the aureole of thought that gave birth to it, this very nearness of the text to its own origination restores to us the feel of distance, our own distance, for it is we who are performing that text and closing that distance.

The distance which is performed as a closing is recognized as the afterglow of a design, because an optimum response to a textual design is a going out from the person reading. I go out first as regards the text as an alien external. Then, as regards that text's intrinsic radiation, I go out toward the whole field of reference and connotation it projects — its 'thing'. The in-stance of the text and the distance to the thing are convoked by the authority of a linguistic design alone. In-stance and distance are dialectical co-ordinates that regulate a reader's responses as he reads, they are his fabulous or plain frame of interpretation. They continue to nourish his general responsiveness thereafter. The freedom of non-identity modulates into the freedom of self-discovery, and then into the freedom of this going out from person to the thing invoked by the text. In this transaction, it is not so much the person of the artificer that counts. What counts is the authority with which that person has invested the textual design, an authority behind which he stands. That authority in the design laughs at the comical set of contrivances called 'person'.

Finally, it would seem that this kind of design, which attunes and regulates the text, inconspicuous as it may be, also this experience for the reader, are peculiar to lyric utterance rather than any other. Conceivably they might help us to fathom some of the ways in which lyric utterance can, in one fell swoop, invoke a spirit and be radiant with bodiliness. Apostrophe, the invocation of a spirit, though now archaic, is still fundamental to the lyric in one form or another. Mörike modulated the old spirit-invoking apostrophe into the thou-address of his poem 'Auf eine Lampe'. Rilke, before he could modulate from his juvenile Ah and Oh of *Das Stundenbuch* to the questing celebrations and invocations of the Elegies and Sonnets, had to discipline his whole imagination toward 'sachliches Sagen' — concretely realizing utterance — which he found as exemplary pictorial presence in Cézanne. In both poets there is respect for the thing with its distance, respect for the design as in-stance, and respect for the perfection of the text that sustains caprice as a vital factor in design but delivers design from the flipflop of subjective randomness.

My theme of poem and artifact was provoked by a picture of a Viking prow, as the prow came out of the mud and before it was restored. Rimbaud's 'Marine' kept other thoughts in motion, thoughts about the poetic reinvention of reality. I am still haunted by a third sea image. Xenophon, in the *Anabasis,* describing the situation of the Greeks as they struggled out of Asia, along the Euxine coast, and across into Thrace, mentions a headland on which, after a shipwreck, a book might be washed ashore. The book would have been on its way eastward, to a Greek colonial city, perhaps into the possession of a Crimean barbarian learning Greek. But it was washed ashore, along with other artifacts in the cargo, wooden beds, oars, chests of oak or olive wood. The book's pages, of papyrus or goatskin parchment, would have been soaked, its wooden covers stained and warped by the sea. Once it reached land, the wind might have riffled the pages and dried them. The text, though blurred, was still not unclear — perhaps a play, or a dialogue, or a song. Suppose an illiterate beachcomber picked it up and took a look: what use or meaning could the book have had for him? Or else this book was not rescued. It fell apart, became débris, among seashells, the shit of gulls, pearly like their feathers, and other changeful artifacts of nature, epiphanies of chance. Three angles for a fix on cosmogenesis: a book disintegrating into the Bosphorus; a text, not lost, Xenophon, the only reminder of it; and ourselves in this moment, remembering the sound the book made as it fell through the air, when the beachcomber let it drop.

# Syntax and Signification in Hölderlin's 'Andenken'

## 1

'Andenken' is probably the best known of Hölderlin's later poems. Customarily dated 1802–3, it is supposed to have been written during the same winter months as 'Patmos' (first version), 'Der Ister', 'Der Einzige', and 'Mnemosyne'. All five poems are lustrous and enigmatic texts which explore vast, but infolded, visionary spaces. They are also texts in which Hölderlin's imagination — he was thirty-two in 1802 — begins to turn from idealizations of Greece to historic Germany. It was Hölderlin's project to celebrate the arrival in Germany of an etheric and fiery Spirit, whose metamorphoses are the successive historical cultures. The task of the poet is to compose, from the materials of his language, a gnosis telling of the Spirit's voyage and its intrinsic, recurrent structure.

'Andenken' must certainly have been written after Hölderlin's return from France to Swabia in 1802. In January he had crossed the Auvergne on foot, through ice and snow, a pistol under his pillow at night, to arrive at the house of the German consul in Bordeaux on 28 January. In the middle of May, for reasons not known, he left Bordeaux. Perhaps he found this fourth household tutorship as tiresome as the others had been. So he walked north, through the battle-torn Vendée, and late in May he reached Paris. It is alleged that he saw here the Greek sculptures in the Musée Napoleon. From Paris he continued, still on foot, or as best he could, to Strassburg. He crossed the border on 7 June, and by mid-June he was in Stuttgart, exhausted, bearded, in rags, and in a poor mental state, if not quite demented. His heroine Diotima (Susette Gontard) died in Frankfurt on 22 June, Hölderlin was told of her death on 30 June. He spent most of July and August in his mother's house in Nürtingen. Then, during the first half of October, he travelled with his friend Izaak Sinclair to Regensburg in Bavaria, for a political conference: Regensburg was the seat of a permanent council for the settlement of affairs, and of the ongoing hostilities, in post-Revolutionary Europe. Sinclair said that he had never seen Hölderlin more intellectually alive and psychologically sound. With the Landgrave of Hessen Hölderlin evidently discussed religious matters; the poem 'Patmos' was an outcome of these discussions, likewise 'Der Einzige'. Both poems exist in several versions, in which Hölderlin is agonizedly seeking to forge a 'true image' of Christ. The Christology of 'Der Einzige' is peculiarly problematic, because here he was working out a hazardous conception of affinities between Christ and his preferred Greek gods, especially Herakles, as a god of action. Home again by late October, Hölderlin spent the winter in Nürtingen. One might fondly imagine him recollecting the sunlit Bordeaux scenes on a gloomy Swabian afternoon, being fussed over by his mother, who places before him on a table a glass of red wine, which is also appropriated into the poem, together with thoughts about relationships between near and far, poetry and action, land and sea, presence and memory.

## 2

So much for the background. What I propose to do now is track the syntactical design of 'Andenken'. The peculiar consistency of the poem is evident, I believe, in its syntax. Certain obscurities, as well as poetic functions, become more clear once the pulse embedded in the syntax has been felt. Two points are at once to be noted. In studying a poem's syntax, one is studying an aspect of poiesis which is likely to be less 'conscious' than some other aspects. Hölderlin did not predetermine the syntax of 'Andenken'; it was no accident, but it 'happened'. That 'happening' is the moment of epiphany, in fact, as an old Eskimo poet has testified: 'When the words we need sprout up by themselves, we get a new song' (Orpingelik, of the Netsilik People). Orpingelik also said: 'Songs are thoughts that are sung out with breathing when people let themselves be moved by great force and no longer can be satisfied with ordinary speech.'[1] Second, I would align with Orpingelik's words those of Mallarmé, who considered syntax to be 'the mobility or principle' of words, 'being that part of discourse which is not spoken' ('Le mystère dans les lettres'). In studying syntax, one is studying perhaps the 'unspoken' but legible signs of the originative animation which brought these and only these words into these and no other sequences. Syntax is the breathing in the 'singing out'. Further, this breathing of syntax is the 'great force' that connects the diverse memory-traces which the poem recalls or recollects into a consonance. The syntax conducts one form through the many elements which it animates and harmonizes.

Even before the poem is read sentence by sentence it can be felt as a structure of speech waves having different lengths: some rolling, some abrupt. One certainly wonders, too, that the memories, or 'objects' of *an-denken* (thinking-of), are localized around Bordeaux, thus in a liminal situation, between land and sea: Hölderlin followed an older spelling, but *Bord d'eaux* means 'Waters' Edge'. Soon one is alerted to other aspects of this liminality: solid and liquid, permanence and flux — the sea/land nexus pervades the whole text. One thing not noticed at once is this: The poet is not so placeable as his recollections are. Where is he? In Swabia? It is odd — from the first words he is so close to what he is recollecting that one might forget that he is not actually in a faraway French place, to which the north-east wind from Swabia is blowing, and that finally he is not actually witnessing the confluence of the rivers as they flow into the sea. Presence and memory are coalescent, even if they do not quite coalesce. Yet the voice has only said: 'The northeaster blows,/Best loved of all the winds/To me, for it promises/Fiery spirit and a good voyage/For the mariners.' Then he tells the wind to 'go and greet the beautiful Garonne/And the gardens of Bordeaux', and he seems himself to have flown there with the message-bearing wind.

Now to the hazards of figuring the design of the sentences.

1 The first sentence provides a formal triadic matrix which subsequent sentences amplify and modulate:
(a) a declarative verb phrase (*Der Nordost wehet*)
(b) a qualifying phrase (*Der liebste unter den Winden/Mir*)
(c) another qualifying phrase, here with a two-tiered main component and a conjunction at the outset (*Weil er feurigen Geist/Und gute Fahrt verheißet den Schiffern*).

2 The second sentence amplifies typically the triadic matrix:
(a) a verb phrase, of a different type from the first. This one is two-tiered and imperative: *Geh aber nun und grüße*. The shift in verb mood is abrupt, there has been an ellipsis, also there is a temporary shift from third to second person singular, and from declarative to apostrophic grammar.
(b) a two-tiered qualifying (specifying) noun phrase (*Die schöne Garonne/Und die Gärten von Bourdeaux*)
(c) another qualifying phrase amplifies (b) and is introduced now by *dort, wo*. (In (1) the introducer of (c) was a conjunction; here the 'there,

where' represents a quite distinct gesture, the gesture caught in Johann Georg Schreiner's pencil sketch of Hölderlin, 1825–6, in which Hölderlin is pointing his famous finger.) The amplification in the dependent verb phrases follows; each phrase is two-tiered, bracketing another 'pointing' phrase, *darüber aber*:

> *Dort, wo am scharfen Ufer*
> *Hingehet der Steg und in den Strom*
> *Tief fällt der Bach, darüber aber*
> *Hinschauet ein edel Paar*
> *Von Eichen und Silberpappeln*;

The phrasing here is chiasmic: *dort, wo* is internally paralleled by *darüber aber*, while *Steg . . . Strom* is paralleled by *ein edel Paar*, *Hingehet* by *Hinschauet*. The syntax is the movement of an *ordering* of memories.

3  The third sentence is a further amplification. It is also continuous with the second sentence which ends with the semicolon: the sentence-continuum overruns the strophic division:
(a)  an introductory verb phrase (*Noch denket das mir wohl* = I still remember well)
(b)  an amplifier (*und wie* . . . etc.)
(c)  another amplifier (*Im Hofe aber* . . . etc.)

The two amplifiers allude to two sights recollected: the elm wood bending its treetops over the mill, the figtree in the courtyard.

4  Fourth sentence:
(a)  a verb phrase (extending through four lines)
(b)  an amplifier (conjunctional phrase, *wenn* . . .)
(c)  another amplifier (*und über* . . . )

There are contrasts in the mobile figures presented. (a) the brown women walk, (c) breezes move: one action is that of human bodies, the other that of invisible elemental forces (*Lüfte*), although the latter have a subtle visual and muscular trait, for these breezes are 'heavy with golden dreams', and that heaviness is felt in their being *einwiegende Lüfte* (cradling-lulling). The almost immaterial second subject, *Lüfte*, is left almost to the last in this structure (which is again chiasmic):

> *Die braunen Frauen daselbst*    (plural noun)
> *Auf seidnen Boden*            (preposition)

*Über langsamen Stegen*    (preposition)
*Einwiegende Lüfte*    (plural noun)

The *wenn* phrase in the middle is zeugmatic: The brown women walk
. . . when night and day are equal/When night and day are equal . . .
breezes move. In the midst of this delicate veining there comes a
cryptic association: there are the women, and there are the cradling-
lulling winds (*Wiege* (n.) = cradle). Yet here the breezes lull and oddly
the paths, not people on them, are slow, *langsam*. This inconspicuous
distortion prepares the shift toward sleepy interiority in strophe 3.
But the chiasm noted above does something else. It fixes, in a perfect
grammatical balance across the liminal *wenn* phrase, an instant at
which an image still *contains* its idea, before the idea has become
explicit or broken loose into independent discourse. In this instant of
the intact image, all the potential development of the text is infolded.
The image is a little pocket, wrought by recollection, in reverie, of
specific sights which connote silken softness, lulling, dreams,
communion (of night and day), dreaming and waking states of mind.
It is the syntax that stitches that pocket.

5 Strophe 3, fifth sentence, beginning *Es reiche aber . . . mir einer den
duftenden Becher*. Here there seems to be a fairly abrupt shift, the
phrasing is choppier than before, the word order 'anomalous' insofar
as the norm would be *Es reiche mir aber einer den duftenden Becher voll
dunklen Lichts*. The shift is somewhat cryptic, but it is arising from a
sudden recognition, *enacted in the syntax*, of a metonymic association:
'*lulling* breezes . . . that I may *sleep*.' The verb mood shifts, at the same
time, from indicative to subjunctive, via an imperative — *Es reiche*.
Graduations of such delicacy, inconspicuous as they may be, make
the syntactical symmetries in the triadic movement vitally vocal. This
crypticism is not that of a voice entombed.

(a) The sentence begins with an imperative verb phrase
(b) an adjectival qualifier amplifies, preceding the noun phrase (*des
dunklen Lichtes voll*/*Den duftenden Becher*)
(c) further amplification comes in the dependent phrase *damit ich
ruhen möge*, and that phrase is in turn amplified by the *denn* phrase and
the second subjunctive (*süß wär . . . der Schlummer*).
This triad is structurally similar to the earlier ones, but it is
contracted, as the associations distributed across strophes 2 and 3
('lulling breezes . . . that I may sleep') are rapid as well as cryptic.
The contraction precedes a most abrupt shift to the deeply cryptic

declarative phrases which begin the sixth sentence. Not suavity now, but 'hard linking' (*harte Fügung* Hölderlin called this) is at work in the composing of recollections.

6 and 7   The sense: 'It is not good to lose one's soul in mortal thoughts. But it is good to converse, say heart's opinion, hear much, of days of love, and of deeds done.' The (a), (b), (c) arrangement for each sentence seems hardly to work here. What has happened? The developing *harte Fügung* and contraction of phrasing incline the reader to skip the period before *Doch* (But) as the sense continues across it into sentence 7 (*Doch gut ist ein Gespräch* . . .). So the period after *zu sein* is no more conclusive than was the strophic division between strophes 1 and 2. Sentence 6 amplifies itself into sentence 7. What we have here can best be called a disseminatory structure, which hereafter moves with the triads. We might say that, at this point, it goes like this (to the end of Strophe 3):

(a)   the verb phrase *Nicht ist es gut . . . zu sein*
(b)   the qualifying amplifier *Doch gut ist ein Gespräch*
(c)   further amplification with (1) *zu sagen* and (2) *zu hören*.

In this frame there are, as before, two-tiered phrases:

> *Ist ein Gespräch und zu sagen*
> *Zu hören viel/ Von Tagen . . . und Taten*

There are also tempo changes in strophe 3: it begins lento, the choppier middle section is rubato, the end a brisk allegro. These changes mark a perspectival change. In strophes 3 and 4 we find a dwelling in reflection on what has been recollected in the images of strophes 1 and 2; we find that an interpretation of those reflections is unfolding, also. We enter the sphere of what Hölderlin called the *ideal* ('reflective', as contrasted with *naiv*) tone, as one may read in his sketches of 1799. The *ideal* tone is now given *heroisch* characteristics: for the mariners of strophe 1, line 4, are being reflected upon.

What we have in strophe 4 is, in fact, a sudden flaring of the signifiers *Quelle* and *Meer* (source and sea) which appear in lines 3 and 5 of the strophe. Sparks were implicit in the opening lines of the poem, with their emphatic placing of *Mir* and *den Schiffern*. But now comes a flaring, in lines 2–12 of the strophe: a dramatic vision of the voyage away from the familiar world of the first two strophes, and thus developing the poet's own voyage away, or more deeply into that world, in strophe 3. Poetry and action: nowhere does Hölderlin abandon his idea of their essential interdependence, even though, in 'Andenken', communication is strained (and refined) to a limit.

Before figuring syntax in strophe 4, I should attend to the word *Quelle* (source). It might mean the source of the river whose delta the mariners might find on reaching the far shore on their voyage westward. That shore Hölderlin conceived as being 'Indian', that is to say, ultimately 'eastern', even if, like another of his later heroes, Columbus, his mariners were sailing to the west. (A draft of 'Andenken' has the phrase *Nach Indien* — to India.) Yet there might be a hitherto unsuspected liminality in his mental geography here. It is curious that he introduced *brown women* in strophe 2, and that in strophe 4 he introduced *natives* dancing. Might it be that the *Quelle* is not on the far side of the Atlantic, but in Europe, and that everything else, too, is the other way round? In his letter of 4 December, 1801, to Boehlendorff, after announcing his Bordeaux plan, Hölderlin did mention Tahiti: ' . . . to leave my country, perhaps for ever. I shall remain a German, even if my heart's distress and my need to make a living should drive me to Tahiti.' Is there a drift toward double vision at this point in the reverie? The Bordeaux women are presented as being brown, from a viewpoint far to the north-east of Bordeaux — brown as the 'Indians' even farther west of Bordeaux. *Eingeborene* in strophe 4 means distinctly natives, not European country people. Those people might not be ones the mariners left behind in Europe, but people they are soon to find, or soon to leave behind, in the Americas, or the 'Indies'. The options fade in and out of one another. 'Brown' women would anyway have scandalized German readers in 1802, who tended to suppose that women should be white and swooning. One need not invoke double vision here, to justify the epithet 'brown' — the exposure of southern French people to the elements was something Hölderlin observed in his November 1802 letter to Boehlendorff. But in reverie, writing 'Andenken', he could have superimposed, lightly, with just two touches, a 'savage' upon a 'civilized' code, maximizing the density and scope of his images.

### 3

Returning now to the syntax: What has become apparent is a recurring triadic structure in the syntactical movement, a structure embedded in single sentences, or disseminated — : Pyramids. There comes to mind the 'fiery spirit' of the beginning, line 3 (strophe 1), fire being represented as a pyramid, among Plato's geometrical figures for the elements. The fiery spirit is 'promised' for the mariners, as audacity. It is symbolically present in the 'mobility or principle' which animates the poem as it unfolds, as the reverie travels among the memory-traces and composes them into significant pattern. However, one should be cautious about deciphering this fiery spirit as the one that comes from the East and whose metamorphoses are the successive historical cultures. In Hölderlin's vocabulary of symbols, that great Spirit is a fiery and etheric one (and at this stage in his work it is terrifying). The double vision, switching East and West, in strophe 3, if it does occur at all, just might invite interpretation of *feuriger Geist* on this third level. But the context is such as to make such an allusion extremely faint.

Do pyramids appear in the last two strophes? My impression is that they do, but that their vehicle is no longer the discrete sentence as such. The triadic matrix is, rather, disseminated into the strophic organization, as the pyramid animates connotations, and as reverie deepens and unfolds still more richly its contents through these last two strophes.

Strophe 4. Two questions are asked, followed by two assertions (lines 1–5). The fifth line, after the period, opens a fresh perspective, with quite a jolt: *Sie* (= the friends)/*Wie Maler* . . . One might say that the strophe opens incoherently: 'Where are the friends? Bellarmin with his companion? Some are shy of going to the source; for wealth begins in the sea.' Incoherence is brought about by an eruption into the verse-design of a concern or anxiety from 'deeper regions' of the speaker's imagination than have so far been brought into play. It is not the questions that articulate incoherence, for the speaker has not lost the thread: 'It is good to converse . . . But where are friends with whom to converse?' No, the apparent incoherence is due to the densely connotative nouns *Quelle* and *Meer*. The *nämlich* of line 4 is a grasping only, as when one says 'You know?' The eruption is announced in the phrase *Mancher trägt Scheue*, and it is as if this has been eruptively said, as if now the speaker grasps for an understanding of what he was 'moved by great force' to say. *Mancher trägt Scheue* is quite peculiar, not normal phrasing. The word *trägt* (carries) possibly unfolds the prior image of breezes 'heavy with golden dreams', i.e., as those breezes are laden with dreams, so are some persons laden with diffidence about 'going to the source' (the adjective *träge* means heavy, sluggish). The 'wealth' that 'begins in the sea' would likewise unfold, in another dimension of significance, the 'golden' of 'golden dreams'. One possible gist would be simply this: Not many people want to go to the source, because they want wealth, and wealth is acquired by commercial activity at sea.

However cunningly the semeiosis is wrought as a continuum with different meanings, the effect here is of discontinuity in the syntax. *Harte Fügung* seems to be the principle, a jumping of semantic links, governing relations between these sentences. Nevertheless, if one simply telescopes the two questions into the single question they effectively are (the second only amplifies the first), a triadic structure appears:

(a)  Sentences 8–9 — two questions = one question, an interrogatory verb phrase.
(b)  Sentence 10 — *Mancher . . . gehn*, a disjunct amplification
(c)  a second disjunct amplification, in *Es beginnet . . . im Meere,* where what is being amplified remains debatable.

Next comes a more continuous amplification, from *Sie/Wie Maler . . . on* (sentence 11). There is the initial verb phrase, which is declarative — *Sie . . . bringen zusammen* (a). This expands into a two-tiered sentence, *und verschmähn . . . und zu wohnen* (b), which in turn expands paratactically into further qualifications — *unter/Dem entlaubten Mast, wo . . .* etc (c). The third leg of the triad has varied kinds of phrasing: prepositional, relative (two-tiered), and substantive (one plural and two singular nouns). The triad is disseminatory.

This is a point at which the syntax itself is most clearly the energetic principle which enables 'meaning' to arise out of, and also *as*, the verse-movement itself; and to configure as the very drama of colliding liminalities in the *Andenken* of the mariners themselves (no longer recollections of the speaker alone). For the speaker is with them in spirit. The disseminatory triad articulates precisely the spatial vastness of the open sea, into which the mariners have sailed. Yet, dialectically co-ordinated with that movement, the mariners 'bring together the beauty of earth'. The sense is elusive, for a meaning is being made, but not declaratively. This is not the kind of 'penny-in-the-slot' meaning deplored by Walter Benjamin in his essay on Surrealism. No, this meaning is being made in terms of an analogy involving (1) mental recollection of experience into pattern, 'as the painters do' when 'composing the beauty of the earth', and (2) a dispersal, as sea-space supersedes land-space and the *limes* is crossed. Yet, even in that supersession, or transgression, the land (earth) is itself a recollected element. The mast's unprecedented epithet *entlaubt* (unleafed) is itself a reminder that it was a terrestrial tree. Similarly, the strophe ends with a land image signifying another kind of composing: festive dancing of assembled 'natives,' whose dance motion is also a 'bringing together' — aesthetic enough — of bodies in celebration (*Feiertage*), such as the mariners at sea could be thinking of. (The passage invites reference to the elegy 'Heimkunft' (1801), where the festive reunion of the traveller and his family in strophe 6 involves the holy (*den Hohen, ein Gott*), as well as music (*Saitenspiel*), music which says that 'for which the words are absent'.)

In strophe 5 (sentence 12) the initial movement is that of a stricter triad:

(a)  verb phrase (*Nun aber sind*, echoing *Wo aber sind* of strophe 4)
(b)  amplifier (*Dort an der Spitz*, echoing *Dort, wo* of strophe 1)
(c)  Another amplifier (*Wo . . . und zusammen*, echoing *bringen zusammen* of strophe 4)

Here the very scope of visual reference has expanded across the land-sea nexus to become the disseminatory aspect that was previously a function of syntax. 'They are gone, there, where . . .' and the vast space enclosing the threshold between land and sea opens as the *Dort* directs attention to the point (*Spitz*) among the vine-hills, down which the Dordogne comes, and the two rivers, flowing *together* (cf. strophe 5) go into the sea. This is the great confluence that has carried, with the north-east blowing offshore, the 'men' toward 'the Indians' (no hint of double vision here). It is as if nature is doing what the poet does as recollector and the mariners do 'as painters'.

A stricter triad governs the last sentence also:

(a)  declarative verb phrase: 'The sea takes and gives memory'
(b)  declarative verb phrase amplifying and qualifying the antecedent phrase: 'What is more (or But) love too fastens the gaze'
(c)  declarative verb phrase again amplifying and qualifying the love phrase: 'What is more (or But) the poets institute what abides'

Here the *aber*'s are traces of the disseminatory structure; meanwhile the pyramid is clearest of all at this point, in the three successive verb phrases, two of which are successive qualifying declarations. Mounted on this syntactical triad specialists also discern another pyramid, that of Hölderlin's *Tonwechsel*, whereby, in poetry, there must be a dialectical variety of heroic, naive (or idyllic), and 'ideal' (or reflective, spiritualizing) tones. Here the sea-line connotes the heroic tone, the love-line the naive (because passional), the poets-line the 'ideal' tone. The alternation of these tones, or vibrances, marks emotional key-changes in a text, or transformations in verse-texture.

To sum up: this analysis is no doubt wanting in technical expertise, but its imperfections do not make it false. What I mean to show by it is that there exists a steady morphogonic movement in the syntax of the poem, an intrinsic formal *necessity* (as Kandinsky would have said). This morphogony has a definite pulse-like progression, which can be intuited in infinitesimals or larger phrase-sequences. Pulse-like, because the movement is like a steady opening and shutting, contraction and expansion. But the movement is not stable or regular, or even symmetrical. It is variable, and triadic, not duple, likewise. It is triadic in its tempo and in the changes of the tempo. In an exemplary way, the poem shows how parataxis — successivity with all its hazards — need not succumb to its inherent tendency to run out of control.

## 4

Where to go from here? It would be nice if a reader's delighted perception of the syntactical morphogony were to help him unriddle some of the semantic enigmas of the text. My sense so far is only that a triadic structure, and the varieties of tempo and focus that it generates, enable the speaker with one voice to proceed from the radiant sensory evocations into a penumbra of discrete, or more crudely 'private', connotations, as in the words *Quelle, Reichtum, Meer*, and thence to emerge at a threshold where the recollected scene and the connotations complete one another in the surprise of the whole last sentence. Straight-spoken as the poem is, surprise and enigma are two of its main characteristics.

In strophes 3–5, ordinary words become polysemous, their significations exceeding limits they had prior to this act of recollection, or outside of the time it has taken these memories to configure in this syntax: The discretion is extreme in the naming of Bellarmin and his companion. Who are these people? we might ask, if we cannot identify them as characters in Hölderlin's novel *Hyperion*. 'Now to the Indians the men are gone . . .': Where? we may gasp, if we cannot place Bordeaux and the rivers that flow into the Atlantic, or even if we can, for, these Indians, are they American or Asian? This loading of every available surface with depths evolved from memory's sensuous and intelligent work on experience makes the poem mysterious, but not a mystification: it is a poem of wonder, not of wilful obscurity. The reader is invited to overhear what a speaker recalls — re-*presents* — of a place; but the focal points in the reverie suddenly turn out to be placed in a divinatory perspective, to be otherwise than they might have been thought to be, before such images 'flared up' (as Bachelard says) on this threshold between the land and the sea that this mind is beholding as presence: between the past and the present, here and there, action (the mariners) and contemplation (the poet). It is peculiar indeed. The last sentence is like a meditation entered into while actually overlooking the threshold, not just recollecting it. At that threshold, all convexities of presence become concave and slant toward deeper meanings that a mind is in the very act of generating through recollection.

This is the sense of the mysterious 'fragrant cup full of dark light' (strophe 3). The image, by virtue of its syntactical relation to others, not of its isolated sense, shows the inherence of the waking in the reverie, the light in the dark liquid. Again: a threshold. Proust might come to mind — the wine desired is a kind of madeleine. The whole text exemplifies a truth formulated by Irving Wohlfarth in his commentary on Walter Benjamin's reading of Proust: 'Presence of mind doesn't connote empty alertness to outer signals at the expense of inner ones, conscious attention to the present to the exclusion of the unconscious past, but rather a simultaneous receptivity to their actual conjunction.'[2]

For the poem is not only 'about' a geographical threshold situation. It realizes in its movement an act of recollection, and it marks a threshold between poiesis as a remembering, and reality — a threshold at which the remembering is found to be the initiator of the reality, its ground and shaper. Hence Hölderlin can claim, in this context believably, that the poets do *stiften* (institute, ground, inaugurate) what is permanent. They do so because they make, as Hölderlin has done in this poem, of the oceanic flux of memory a rhythmic, syntactical, legible structure, a *Gestalt*, which is a focus on time, a focus which is itself a shape made by time.

## 5

What, then, of the last sentence, with its oft-quoted last line? The line has been weighed and measured, cited histrionically, analysed and explicated at will for many generations. It does lend itself to all sorts of sentimental abuse. Taken out of context, as a declaration of faith, or as a programme, it is overweening; but this is hardly noticed, although it is almost always cited out of context.

Excursus: The line prompts one to pick a bone with Hölderlin. Certainly it levels with a fundamental human anxiety in the face of fugacity and nothingness. But it also 'does' something else. The Protestant version of the idea of a fallen human will, of the subjection of human nature to its own dissolutions, gave rise to the doctrine, in which Hölderlin was educated, that redemption of the will from dissolution could only occur if an individual made an act of faith (the Pietist doctrine of *Umkehr*, the 'turnabout'), and thus disposed himself to be superintended by a predestining and absolute will of God. 'It is the permanence of eternity, constantly impressing itself upon the discontinuity of human moments' (Georges Poulet).[3] The doctrine had historic consequences in the groupings, or party-alignments, of the complacent 'Saved', who could only think in one straight line, their own, and who failed to conceive, dialectically, that without the Lost there can be no Elect. Even the Roman monolith, imperial or Catholic, with its *élites* and nations, presumed to exclusive authority, and excluded or had to subjugate other beings as being categorically 'inferior'. And so it goes on, even as regards the animals. Hölderlin's line reverberates with the Protestant pretension, but, altogether heretically, it reverses its terms, making 'the poets' institutors of the permanent, not 'God' and the Elect who put him on their side. 'The poets' not only presume to usurp what was the divine privilege; they also segregate themselves, as a visionary élite, — from their dissolute fellowbeings. This apotheosis of the poet was not uncommon among Hölderlin's contemporaries: the poet was, for Coleridge too, a Promethean demiurge. As new economic structures and moral decorums evolved new rankings in German middle-class society, the writer had to redefine his rôle. This redefinition was particularly painful in Swabia, with its authoritarian social structure, where, if you had enjoyed a clerical education, you had no choice but to conform, becoming a parson, a tuppenny schoolmaster, a profane private tutor, or a small-town lawyer. No wonder it could seem preferable to think of oneself not as a mere Messenger, but as the Emperor himself. Hölderlin's line carries to this day the sting of that compensatory impulse. His genius was straining to institute its own system, so as to oppose, and by opposing neutralize, the pseudo-permanence of a social system which harassed him, which he resented, and whose delusions he would by poetry erase.

He has agonizing doubts, even then. In 'Mnemosyne' his heroes are listed as dead (last strophe), as if the poet has to shoulder the load alone, enduring also language-loss (second version). At the end of 'Der Einzige' (second version) comes the shattering phrase 'zahllose gefallen', though here, too, 'some are safe/on beautiful islands'. The poem 'Wenn aber die Himmlischen' modulates this sorrow with an astonishing inversion of the humanly *tragic* situation in the image of prophetic beings 'who hide the abyss from God'. — As for Hölderlin's activist, as opposed to poetic, radicalism, scant as the evidence is, it points to his having been at least a sympathizer with the Swabian 'Jacobins'. His friend Sinclair had strong Republican leanings, but supposed Napoleon to be the man of destiny, the legitimate strongman of Revolution. Both Hölderlin and Sinclair, for all the furor, held political views that were deeply stained by the authoritarian — and ultimately theocratic — nexus into which they had been born. The Swabian species of the *Deutsche Misère* did entail paralysing conflicts and fears not unlike those that Stalinism variously implanted in Slavic dissidents today. —

## 6

Returning now to the interpretation of the line, we can cool our tempers by reading it at a much lower angle — neither metaphysically, nor socio-historically. In context, the line can mean that poets conserve such fugitive memory-traces as institute (*stiften*) a personal shape of time, which is given as this particular poem, in its imaginative structure. If that is what is meant, then the line does not say, even though it might still be felt to suggest, that poets say what should be, or are, the indelible, absolute paradigms of being. It says that the poets institute what abides in memory.

One can, of course, go further. Read in the context of poetic lore since classical times, in which Hölderlin was well versed, the last line radicalizes three commonplaces in one swoop: the one that names Memory as Mother of the Muses; the one that asks of poets that they should immortalize heroes, and lovers too; and the one that says God made his creature Man in his own image as creator. I think it has never been noticed that, in radicalizing the last of these commonplaces, Hölderlin retained in mind something proposed by the 'Magus' Hamann. Johann Georg Hamann had said, in his *Aesthetica in Nuce* (1762), regarding the Hebraic analogy of Man and Creator (Adam Kadmon in Hermetic and Kabbalah doctrines): 'Every impression of nature in man is not only a recollection (*Andenken*), but also a surety, of the fundamental truth as to Who is Master. Every counterreaction of man upon the creaturely world (*Kreatur*) is an assurance of our having a part in the Divine Nature, and that we are of His Kind.'⁴(It is a small coincidence that Hamann once says, too, that the title of a text is its 'nucleus in nuce': did Hölderlin opt for his title, in preference to any other, because he had Hamann's view of *Andenken* in mind?)

As he came to be, in his short astounding maturity, and knowing Pindar as he did, Hölderlin was not one to shrink from re-thinking the three commonplaces mentioned above. Yet, if his last line says, and resoundingly says, with its internal alliteration and assonance (b-b, i-i), that the poets institute what abides, it still seems not to say what it is that does abide. Is it the heroes, who risk 'the sea' that takes and gives memory? Is it anyone whose gaze is directed and steadied by Love? It might be both parties, if the naive ancient world were the place where recollection occurred. Heroes and lovers alike, the poets have commemorated them, making sure that for posterity they do not perish with the moments they made luminous. But the commemorated lovers and heroes do perish all the same. What abides must be a transmissible and distinct imagery of them, which does not perish, an imagery wrought, in the freshness of now, out of the fluid of recollection. That is not all. The last line cannot be isolated from its contexts of image and syntax. In memory the poets think of 'the sea', and this sea takes and gives memory. It is also the sea in which 'richness begins'. The 'richness' is not so much material wealth that might be acquired by exploration and commerce, as the fluid manifold of immediate experience itself. Reflecting upon that sea (or making that sea signify this by reflecting upon it in recollection), the poets then institute images, rhythms, syntagmata. With these they track a movement on its journey, from a forbidding source (*Quelle*), to the reflected and signified oceanic flux, where richness begins as times and tides fill recollection, out into the distillate of the poem. Not just the single poem: these plural poets compose from age to age a tradition which says what the rhythmic constants of this permanent movement are, and by this saying, they institute those constants, not only in personal recollection, but, more, in the dialectic of history, in history's own gigantic recollection: the slow pulse or long march of Spirit steadily transforming itself into temporal shapes. The poetic instituting is such that source, sea, and text do not fall apart. The poets compose tradition as a crystallization of all the sea-surge, a crystallization shimmering with signs that flex personal and historical meanings back to the point of origination itself. Or, at least, these poets invent signs that flex meanings back across countless thresholds in recollected experience to a manifold immediacy, out of which any individual recollection starts up, to be transmitted in a tradition which does not stop. It is here that one might see, I should expect, that the line read in isolation as a seemingly conservative statement, actually *in context* shoots a piercing look toward a future, and perhaps even questioningly shouts, like Odysseus Elytis' fabulous pomegranate tree, 'the dawn of a new hope'.

This contextual reading of the last line amplifies the simpler readings proposed above (personal shape of time, or com-memoration). If one winks at the binary conception of time recollected as change in permanence, but only then, one could also argue that the line contradicts the entire text which it concludes. It would do this, insofar as it insists on a twofold stability (that which abides as such, and the poetic instituting of the permanent), whereas what institutes the text itself, up to its limit, is a continuous cryptic wandering, an imaginative oscillation across numerous thresholds, thus nothing stable at all. Such a reading is not as far-fetched as it might seem. It is, at least, not insensitive to the poem's defiance of oblivion, of time as that which deletes or decomposes the very memories of which it is the medium.

A contextual reading of the entire last sentence can next be developed by asking: What does the last line *not* say? The line speaks not of the poet, but of poets. For Hölderlin, poets have to be, as 'die Geistigen', also 'weltlich' — spiritual people, but of this world ('Der Einzige,' first version). They mediate between spiritual and material (mundane) levels of historical consciousness. They read history as the unfolding of successive transpositions and transformings — revolutions — of the etheric and fiery spirit. Now the line does not say that the poets authorize a perishing of anything. Selective as they may be, in their deciding as to which memory-traces carry significance, they do not ordain the liquidation of 'insignificant' memory-traces, as Robespierre or Marat had chosen to do. On the contrary, their positive institution of what abides entails an exactly structured tracking of correspondences between ordinary infinitesimals (the significance of which might have been not thinkable before memory made a pattern of them), and the mighty flux of memory as a threshold between the *cogito* and the *incognito* ('Spirit'). We are close here to a conception of memory, in its poetic functions, as a threshold to those neural functions of the deep brain which emit, on occasion, to be conveyed by *mémoire involontaire*, eidetic syntagmata which are in turn representations of origin, shimmerings of the originative process itself. Andrew Marvell's heaven-sent 'Drop of Dew', no less, 'recollecting its own Light,/Does, in its pure and circling thoughts, express/The greater Heaven in an Heaven less', for 'Moving but on a point below,/It all about does upward bend.'

The line also does not say that poets mediate or channel into the volatile memory-world 'being' or any superhuman, extratemporal potential (idea, spirit, collective unconscious, etc).There is a hint, true, of the Platonic anamnesis here. But the line says that the poets *institute* (not detect) what abides; more, 'stiften' must imply an *immediatization* of the abiding (not, thus, a self-reflecting representation). The line also suggests that there is no other abiding in the oceanic flux which takes and gives the *capacity* to remember (*Gedächtnis*) or to dwell on memories so as to structure them with the originative poetic immediacy. One has to tread on eggshells at this juncture, because when Hölderlin says *aber*, here or elsewhere during this period (e.g., 'Patmos'), he means not so much 'but' as 'moreover' — or else he swings it both ways. The last two lines, of which the last of all does not gainsay the other, are saying: Love makes us fasten our (memory-structured) gaze on what we love, and it does this assiduously (*fleißig*); moreover, the poets, whose writing is *andenken*, authorize what is to retain the imprint of love's fast and ever-freshening gaze. So the poets inaugurate this love's profoundest intent: the intent to stabilize in freshness the 'dark light' of time in mind, that quivering medium which the 'sea' can only 'take and give'. This is not inconsistent with the advanced psychology of Hölderlin's period (e.g., Condillac, *La logique*, 1781, notably chapter 9); but the wording and images concretize and defamiliarize that psychology, 'switching the code' especially in the term *stiften*, as will be seen. The poets function here as initiators of the mind's *mouvemens* (in feeling and memory) which Condillac could trace to no cause. The poets intercept oblivion and avert disorders with which oblivion menaces the laral domain, just as forgetting and ageing disaggregate ideas, beneficial habits, and the unexplainable *mouvemens* that animate the individual brain.

# 7

This authorizing or instituting is not so recondite, once we come to think about it in the light of some ideas that were not foreign to

Hölderlin. We know that he was extremely sensitive to air (and other elements), and that he studied assiduously the windings of rivers, the tilt of hills, patternings of landscapes, the 'architectonics of the sky', air-pressures, cloud-shapes, varied effects of seasonal change — inscapes, forms embedded in matter. Now, in his introduction to *L'eau et les rêves* Gaston Bachelard proposed that two types of imagination operate both in nature and in mind. 'Shamelessly relapsing into some of the oldest philosophical categories', as Etienne Gilson noted in his introduction to Bachelard's *Poetics of Space*, he proposed that a formal imagination elaborates, complicates, and beautifies the displays of things, while a material imagination (not unlike Coleridge's primary imagination) is cosmogonic: it 'aims at producing that which, in being, is both primitive and eternal', and is 'attracted by the elements of permanency in things' (Gilson). As the author of 'direct images of matter', the material imagination is a kind of clandestine poet in nature. For Hölderlin, these ideas would have been congruous with ones he knew from Schiller's aesthetic writings: *Stofftrieb* and *der schöne Schein* — 'formal imagination', *Formtrieb* and *die Idee* — 'material imagination'. Yet, whatever might have happened to Hölderlin in France, in 'Andenken' he has revised Schiller's concepts, to make of 'idea' and 'nature' polarized but somehow dovetailed functions of a single originative fiat. The poets institute abiding protoforms of a *vis formativa*, over which their material imagination, acting through the ins-and-outs of poetic recollection at play, will cast a divinatory gaze, to capture those protoforms as language, that is, as analogue-structures which language alone can drum up. Hölderlin seems here to be envisaging the poetic fiat as one that completes the circuit (as it became in Hegel) by which 'Spirit' comes to recognize itself. If, then, 'was bleibet' means not only such memory traces as configure to shape the act of divinatory (but conscious) poetic instituting, but also 'primitive and eternal' (but unconscious) designs that are embedded in nature, then it must follow that poets give speech to an energy in which spirit and nature are consubstantial functions of a signifying power invested in that energy. The poetic mode of gnosis, moreover, does not merely read the signs that phenomena deliver, for it consists, that gnosis, of originative acts of language. The composition of those acts, in image and syntax, is not made random by recollection, rather the random is absorbed, as recollection *weathers* the composition, much as a stone, formed by the dance of its molecules, is gradually shaped by climatic forces which write into it the signatures of time. Thus it is too with the 'gods', as Elias Canetti has said: 'nourished by worship, starved by not being named, remembered in the poets, and only then eternal.'[5]

## 8

The notion that poetic gnosis is quite specific, different from other kinds of knowing, is a debatable one, even when it does not so privilege poetic intuition and poetic language as to mock interpretation. Secret but knowable interactive regularities common to mind and nature, such as the Ionians dreamed of: some poems make all too free with them. But I am anxious here not to overinterpret this poem by rummaging among overtones. I would not want to impute to Hölderlin thoughts without any basis in the atmosphere of *this* recollection (e.g., that mind and nature are isomorphic, not just convergent). Yet it might seem, in the perspective I have been proposing, that he streaks ahead of Goethe (whose poems up to 1789 he knew) to Mallarmé. Goethe does appear to have credited — by an extraordinary act of faith compatible with his kind of vitality — credited the celestial with a decently objective cosmic plan. To that plan, human beings may contribute; but only on the rarest occasions, when everything is propitious, can human beings, in a manner of speaking, claim as he does in his great poem of amorous wit, 'Wiederfinden,' which Hölderlin would not have known, for it is dated 1815: 'Allah braucht nicht mehr zu schaffen,/ Wir erschaffen seine Welt' (Allah need no more create,/We it is create his world). Mallarmé doubts that we can know or say any such thing. We can and do only invent, as the poet of the supreme *ouvrage* invents 'the hymn of the connexions between all things, harmony and joy, like a pure whole grouped in some dazzling circumstance' ('Le livre, instrument spirituel'). With such imaginations, such fictions of design, we direct our attention, guided by the poem, back to the azure void at the inception of mind, a void out of which every individual complexion of sense, memory, and reflection randomly erupts upon the palpable. Thus the Faun finally claims that he does have the key to the whole dreaming-waking spectacle: 'Je tiens la Reine!' He has the 'queen' of the faculties, in Baudelaire imagination; he has the nucleus of Desire, embedded in imagination's elusive projects. Hölderlin's last line, read in the context of the two preceding lines, does not only rehearse the music of the Faun's flute; it also touches the middle string of Wallace Stevens's eventual 'harp':

*What am I to believe? If the angel in his cloud,*
*Serenely gazing at the violent abyss,*
*Plucks on his strings to pluck abysmal glory . . .*
*Forgets the gold centre, the golden destiny . . .*

*Is it he or is it I that experience this? . . .*
*These external regions, what do we fill them with*
*Except reflection, the escapades of death,*
*Cinderella fulfilling herself beneath the roof?*[6]

In 'Andenken' there is no redeeming Prince: Hölderlin invokes no
angel as guarantor of duration and fulfilment, he does not invoke
Holy Writ (as he does at the end of 'Patmos'), nor does he invoke his
etheric gods. His notion of what endures comes very close to the
'duration based of affective memory', which Georges Poulet detected
as the gist of most eighteenth century French secular thinking,
Rousseau included (and the latter's 'Take away his memory and his
love will no longer exist' — *La nouvelle Héloise*, iv, xiv — might well
underlie Hölderlin's ending). If there is a metaphysical aspect to the
poem, it is woven invisibly into other aspects. There is the presence of
the past in the transparency of the text as a paratactical web of
wondering signs. There is the commemoration of imagined friends,
not poets, but takers of other risks, who, they too, compose earth's
beauty in their minds, as men of action. There is the dilation of plain
words to embrace the distant horizons of meaning, diurnal and
nocturnal, palpable or in memory's depths, the Bordeaux scenes or
the remote mariners. The metaphysical, divested of the thematic part
it customarily plays in Hölderlin, has become the voice of an
unearthliness calling through each movement of the poem.

## 9

What I am finally after is the sense of the poem's vibrance between
abstruseness and directness, elasticity and straightness, 'style' and
rectitude, a vibrance corresponding to its geographical, emotional,
and otherwise semantic liminality. With all due respect, it is not
enough to treat the poem as a cryptogram of an ontology, or to
explicate the text as a cluster of intuitions enigmatized into images, as
Heidegger was doing.[7] The images are not reducible, either, insofar as
the *harte Fügung* arrests any tendency toward the softly conceptual or

the seraphic. The intentness of the speech is that of an imagination drawn fiercely and wondrously taut over its own fulminations in nocturnal otherness. It is not ruminant speech, maundering or self-indulgent. The triadic structure in the syntax restrains every stretch, varies voice-tones from bold to halting, from observant to contemplative, from oracular venturing to evocation of this specific scene beheld and held fast, in memory, but with a freshness of the first immediate response. In the tonal variety there is a restraint which is no stoppage, but an exact balancing of energies, between artifice and improvisation, monumental and spontaneous, patterned and drifting speech, grandeur and simplicity, while not an inch is yielded to the wizenings of a 'theme' or to the postures of a 'classicism'.

How did this come to be so? Hölderlin was fighting back his madness. The poem by no means masks blandly some frightful antithesis that lurks between its lines. On the contrary, its tensions signal a defiance, defiance of a consuming void in which foul and pure are chaotically jumbled, a void in which intelligence is stranded, a 'flaming solitude/Envisioning all, without creating it'. That is the void in the Mexican poet Gorostiza's devastating 'Muerta sin fin' (1939), a poem which reverses almost every sign — and value — to be found in Hölderlin's. Against madness, Hölderlin's voice in 'Andenken' is that of an imagination which has invented a range of vocal gesture that responds as vitally (and not with irony) to shocks as to undulation, as subtly to catastrophe as to the impulse of control. The whole gesture, or *Totalhorizont*, masters, in a single consecutive utterance, not only a perplexing variety of threshold situations, but also an awful awareness that, whether or not one has a part in 'Divine Nature', whether or not one is 'of His Kind', liminality alone could be all that abides. From that awareness the voice takes rhythms that are definitive but never final, which convince, but, even when the wording is conclusive, reflect no effort whatever to persuade.[7]

Aristotle said: 'The act of recollecting differs from that of remembering, not only chronologically, but also in this, that many animals have memory, but of all that we are acquainted with, none, save man, share in the faculty of recollection. The cause of this is that recollection is a mode of inference, and the process is a sort of deliberate investigation.'[8] In Auden's poem 'In Memory of Sigmund Freud' (1939) there are lines which happen to echo Hölderlin, adding to Aristotle an essential missing link: wonder. Recollection is a sort of wondering reconnaissance, a wondering and deliberate investigation:

*But he would have us remember most of all*
*To be enthusiastic over the night*
    *Not only for the sense of wonder*
    *It alone has to offer, but also*

*Because it needs our love . . .*[9]

# Baudelaire: Chevelure and Pentagram

The short paper which follows was written for students in March 1981, as a contribution to a seminar on Symbolism, at the University of Texas. I have kept the annotative format, in view of the fact that this inquiry was informal and experimental. (The paper led to some grappling with differences between non-linguistic, linguistic, and poetic varieties of symbolism in proto-historical, medieval, and recent times.) The 'analysis' was originally typed in three columns adjacent to the text, under the headings 'psychodynamic', 'sound-profile', and 'grammar'. Here the comments appear in boxes below each stanza, even though this interrupts the text, adding to it the aspect of a columbarium, or, worse, a zoo. The summary and sequels do not attempt to deal with the conflicts out of which the poem was 'generated'. These conflicts would lend themselves, by reduction, to a number of rubrics, I expect: male oedipal autocratism, fetishization, erasure of the woman as person — she has become a mere producer of the hair which the poet exploits to envision a luxurious alterity, and so forth. Yet the conflicts in question are creative ones; and creative conflicts should not be mistaken for logical, psychological, or psychosocial confusions. Having mistaken the one type of conflict for the other, some critics then proceed to exact from the ramified scripts of the unconscious, by deciphering and regulating them, insights which make the original author seem to have been wrong-headed. Had the author been capable of such insights, no text at all, or a quite different text, would have been the outcome. Unmistakable in the creations that bear the stamp of deep conflict, as Baudelaire's poem does, all signs point to 'the magnificent here and now of life in the flesh', as Lawrence has it, in his *Apocalypse*.

## La Chevelure

O toison, moutonnant jusque sur l'encolure !
O boucles! O parfum chargé de nonchaloir!               } 2(+)

Extase! Pour peupler ce soir l'alcôve obscure
Des souvenirs dormant dans cette chevelure,
Je la veux agiter dans l'air comme un mouchoir!         } 3(−)

| psychodynamic | sound profile | grammar |
|---|---|---|
| explosive<br><br>intentional | plosives (b,p)<br>and dentals (t,d)<br>softening into<br>open-mouthed<br>vowels in<br>line 5 | exclamatory<br>(4 apostrophes)<br>projective |

La langoureuse Asie et la brûlante Afrique,
Tout un monde lointain, absent, presque défunt,
Vit dans tes profondeurs, forêt aromatique!            } 3

Comme d'autres esprits voguent sur la musique,
Le mien, ô mon amour! nage sur ton parfum.            } 2

| contemplative | liquids(1,r) —<br>symmetrical<br>placing of<br>contrasting<br>vowels (voguent,<br>nage) | assertive (3rd<br>person)<br>in extended<br>exclamation<br>interpolated<br>exclamation |
|---|---|---|

J'irai là-bas où l'arbre et l'homme, pleins de sève,
Se pâment longuement sous l'ardeur des climats;       } 2

Fortes tresses, soyez la houle qui m'enlève!          } 1

Tu contiens, mer d'ébène, un éblouissant rêve
De voiles, de rameurs, de flammes et de mâts:         } 2

liquids: delicate
differentiation of
vowel-series in last
2 lines. A liquid,
plosive, and labial
consonant-frame
orchestrates now
line 5 of st. 1

| intentional<br>challenging<br>expansive (into<br>detail of surfaces) | | projective (future)<br>imperative<br>assertive |
|---|---|---|

*Un port retentissant où mon âme peut boire*
*A grands flots le parfum, le son et la couleur;* ⎤ 2

*Où les vaisseaux, glissant dans l'or et dans la moire,*
*Ouvrent leurs vastes bras pour embrasser la gloire* ⎤ 3
*D'un ciel pur où frémit l'éternelle chaleur.*

*liquids (r, l): rich vowel diapason, opening and closing e.g. pur/frémit/chaleur*

*assertive, each phrase charged with qualifiers (où . . . ; glissant, où . . .)*

*Cheveux bleus, pavillon de ténèbres tendues,*
*Vous me rendez l'azur du ciel immense et rond;* ⎤ 2

*Sur les bords duvetés de vos mèches tordues*
*Je m'enivre ardemment des senteurs confondues* ⎤ 3
*De l'huile de coco, du musc et du goudron.*

*contemplative — surface (azur)*

*emotion sensation*

*plosives/liquids Low vowels set off by high ones, e.g. enivre, huile.*

*assertive (2nd person plural)*

*assertive (1st person singular)*

*Je plongerai ma tête amoureuse d'ivresse*
*Dans ce noir océan où l'autre est enfermé;* ⎤ 2

*Et mon esprit subtil que le roulis caresse*
*Saura vous retrouver, ô féconde paresse!* ⎤ 2

*Infinis bercements du loisir embaumé!* ⎤ 1

*intentional*

*expansive (into detail of surfaces)*

*liquids interlaced with fricatives (v,f). Low vowels: noir, roulis, retrouver, féconde, loisir*

*projective (future) — je plongerai . . . N.B. complementarity of body and mind in action*

*Longtemps! toujours! ma main dans ta crinière lourde*
*Semera la rubis, la perle et le saphir,*
*Afin qu'à mon désir tu ne sois jamais sourde!*    ⎤ 3

*N'es-tu pas l'oasis où je rêve, et la gourde*
*Où je hume à longs traits le vin du souvenir?*    ⎤ 2

| | | |
|---|---|---|
| *explosive/ intentional/ challenging (afin que)* <br><br> *conjectural interiors of feeling* | *liquids. Some softer plosives (b, p) and dentals (t, d). Guttural aspirated into h of hume (= quaff)* | *exclamatory (3rd person)/projective, plus one qualifier* <br><br> *interrogative, plus two qualifiers* |

*Psychodynamic: moiré* effect of rapid temperamental shifts. Expansive movement involving externals and interiors in a complex web of linguistic and psychic relations ('correspondences'). Periodic contraction, as attention returns to the source of the stimulus, hair.

*Sound profile*: orchestral complexity, with consonance. A harmony ('unity') wrought by foregrounding of liquids with low vowels. Rhythms flexing, spinning out, contracting, rippling, varying (with grammatical groupings of lines) in the 12-syllable, 4-stress frame.

*Grammar*: variety of phrasing, with many shifts, some abrupt, in the sequence. A variable but consonant field of speech-events. The rhetorical texture is such that its density reminds a reader constantly that this is a *poem*: self-reflexive text, with its coherent surface (the experiencing of hair by touch and smell), and its deep multiple volume (responses, metaphors, subjective interiors).

*Hair*. For a study of cultural significations, see Mary Douglas, *Purity and Danger*. Cf. also the poem 'La chevelure vol de flamme' by Mallarmé, and Debussy-Maeterlinck, *Pelléas et Mélisande*, especially Act 3, Scene 1: 'It's so soft . . . as though it fell from heaven . . . It lives like birds between my fingers.'

*Stanza form*. Spanish quintilla, rhymed here abaab. Baudelaire adapts it to the Alexandrine with chiefly masculine rhymes. Some rhymes are more sliding than regular, e.g., *couleur-chaleur, enfermé-embaumé, tendues-tordues, saphir-souvenir*. Overall effect: the rhyme scheme sets limits over which the restless expansive movement of the stanza flows forward and back again to closure (opening, lines 1–2, expansion to closure, lines 3–4, reopening to closure, line 5, e.g., in stanza 1). Rhythm and rhyme jointly sustain the flow and recoil of imagination rushing to and from its pretext, hair. Marine imagery (stanzas 3, 4, 5) is rhythmically realized in the flow-ebb dynamism of the stanza form. In brief: perfect formal integration of the equilibrium-in-motion, unity-in-multiplicity, of the motifs; complex 'translucence' of the 'One' in its multiples (cf. Coleridge), as the sensory-imaginative experience of the hair is VOICED: an 'other' world is evoked by a recomposition of the signs of 'this' world, into a consonance, which 'conjectures' that in language itself lies the way to an ulterior (spiritual) bliss, akin to (and perhaps consubstantial with) the bliss of sense and imagination voiced in this text. As 'hair' comes to symbolize the whole shuddering and swaying web of desire, memory, will, thought, dream of the voice that speaks, so too does that web symbolize the ultimate 'other'. This conjectural factor (involved with the rhetorical tonalities which announce the poem as poem) actually *inhibits* the thought that the 'other' is latent *only* in language, only in thought, only as artifice.

## 2

The foregoing is a schematization of some thoughts I had while wondering how Baudelaire's poem comes to present such density of surface and diversity of mood in a design which integrates all elements. It seemed to me that the grammar was one key to the question. The study of the grammar led me to consider how grammar enacts psychodynamic attitudes; and the study of those attitudes alerted me to the patternings of sound, ways in which they voice the attitudes and generate a consistent, or coherent, *tone*.

Later, I started to wonder why the stanza form was chosen, that is, the quintilla. Even if Baudelaire did not deliberately opt for it, after coldly weighing various choices, before writing the poem, how did the quintilla come to suggest itself to him? It is not a stanza that he uses ordinarily. Was he practising a quite specific 'sorcellerie évocatoire' by using it for this poem?

Then it occurred to me that there is a traditional five-fold sign: the pentagram. This sign, as employed by magicians, represents the 'earth spirit' (see Rembrandt's painting of the magician, and the classic passage in Goethe's *Faust I* — 'schon glüh ich wie von neuem Wein . . .' 'rote Strahlen [zucken] mir um das Haupt'). The sign represents all the creative forces in nature. It has horizontal and vertical directions, but must be sharply distinguished from the hexagram, which represents the confluence of heaven and earth, the integration of celestial and terrestrial forces. The earth-spirit's sign is a notoriously dangerous one: when drawing it, we have to leave a corner open, for spirits to exit through, in case they get trapped:

The sign's verticality signifies an aspiration toward the celestial, but it stops short of any interlocking of the celestial and terrestrial matrices. Does Baudelaire's poem reactivate this sign in language?

Now I began to look 'through' the images of the poem, in order to test their values: whether their axes had celestial or terrestrial fields of reference (or allusion), or else vertical and horizontal directionality. The marine imagery could be considered terrestrial, I thought, in so far as it is structurally horizontal in the heaven-earth (or air-earth) polarity, whereas any word in the poem, any word or phrase, which answered to an etheric quality, could be considered vertical.

First, then, I charted the sense-fields, to which, line by line, the text draws attention (five-fold: eye, ear, touch, scent, taste). Having done this, I analysed these fields into their respective air-heaven/earth-sea components. The following chart shows the results.

| *sense* | *directionality* |
|---|---|
| stanza 1 | |
| line 1:  eye | earth (physique of hair) |
| 2:  eye/scent | |
| 3:  eye | |
| 4: | |
| 5:  touch (agitation) air | |

stanza 2
line 1:    touch (temperature)        earth (*Asie, Afrique, forêt*)
   2:
   3:    scent
   4:    touch (agitation)/ear        air/earth-water (*voguent, nage*)
   5:    scent

stanza 3
line 1:                                earth (*l'arbre, la houle*)
   2:    touch (temperature)
   3:    touch (agitation)
   4:    eye
   5:    eye/touch (temp-           air (*voiles, mâts*) interlaced
       erature — *flammes*)       with earth (*rameurs, flammes*)

stanza 4
line 1:                                earth
   2:    scent/ear/eye
   3:    touch (agitation)/eye
   4:    touch (agitation)          air (*d'un ciel pur*)
   5:    touch (temperature —
       *chaleur*)

stanza 5
line 1:    eye                         air (*cheveux bleus —*
   2:    eye                         *azur du ciel*)
   3:    touch (*duvetés*)
   4:    scent                       earth
   5:    scent

stanza 6
line 1:    touch (agitation — *je*      earth
       *plongerai*)
   2:    eye
   3:    touch (agitation — *mon*   air (*esprit subtil*)
       *esprit que le roulis*
       *caresse*)
   4:                                air (*infini*)
   5:    touch (agitation)/scent
       (*embaumé*)

stanza 7

| line 1: | touch | earth (minerals) |
|---------|-------|------------------|
| 2: | eye | |
| 3: | ear (quasi-negative) | air (in associations |
| 4: | eye (faint in *oasis*) | arising from *esprit* of |
| 5: | scent/taste | stanza 5, modulated |
| | | now into *hume*, as |
| | | breath-spirit in action) |

The following observations might now be made: (1) in each stanza, both elements are present, earth and air. The semantic axis rotates from one to the other. (2) There is a slight preponderance of 'horizontal' (earthly) directionality, as befits the sign which presides over the text, the pentagram. (3) A submergence occurs, of some air-heaven-vertical-etheric signifiers, as they pass into the associative series which connote sensory-earthly elements, e.g., the last two lines of the poem, where 'esprit' is submerged into 'hume'. (4) A 'deeper' reading depends on your ability to detect, on *structural levels*, significations which may seem random or merely impulsive on the 'surface' of the text, e.g., the tacit presence of 'air' in the adjective 'infini(s)' in stanza 5. (5) The 'symbol' hair is made co-extensive with the ensemble of the poem by being contextualized, and densely so, in a web of rhythms signifying confluences of earth and air under compulsion of the earth-sign.

### 3

My next question was this: Did Baudelaire consciously control the patterns of imagery and their sense-values, in this poem, in order to invoke, and by invocation resuscitate, the magic powers that are traditionally enshrined in the pentagram? How conscious was he of the pentagram as a 'model', or might he not have been so Faustian after all?

If he was conscious of it, if he was using it as a model (a geometric one, at that), then the poem shows us a significant transposition of *traditional* symbolism into an intense personal *symbolism*. We would then have to qualify the view of such critics as Lloyd Austin, who argue that Baudelaire marks a break between perennial *Symbolik* of the type which has been transmitted down the centuries by esoteric doctrine, and, on the other hand, the 'purely human' symbolism, personal and idiosyncratic, which arrives on the literary scene with

Romanticism. (This break is discussed in Angelo Philip Bertocci's book, *From Symbolism to Baudelaire*, 1964. It was Paul Valéry who first suggested that Baudelaire's symbols (e.g., hair in 'La chevelure') are not symbols of the older type, but, more like Eliot's 'objective correlative', structures which visualize and dramatize complex personal feeling and sensation.)

Certainly there are symbolisms of the personal type in Baudelaire's poems. Possibly, in 'La chevelure', we have an exceptional case of a resurgence, into a personal frame, with or without Baudelaire's conscious connivance, of a symbol of the older type. Possibly, too, even symbols of the older type, in order to become valid at all, had and have to be reanimated by intense personal engagement, and are otherwise merely available models for mental process, inert and latent models. The latter process of reanimation has been discussed, of course, by Eliade. It is continually impressed on students of the Kabbalah, who, intent as they are on personal development, seek beyond the act of reanimation, to 'unify' the Four Worlds of Creation in Travail.

The fact remains that the Baudelairian shift implies a specializing of poetic language. Human speech is here aspiring to a level formerly reserved for a divine language, the latter being *occult in the perennial symbol*. Poetry is a kind of divinatory language, which can spell out a reconciliation of eternal and temporal values, such as we read about in Coleridge: the poetic symbol as a threshold at which universals and particulars coincide.

Thus we might recall Bertocci on 'La chevelure' (page 155 of his book) — though he is not thinking about pentagrams:

> Such a poem not only is symbol in the Goethean sense, having its origin not in an idea, but in an object of perception which opens toward some paradisial bliss. Not only does it contain a metaphor that is focal, massive, repeatable, 'la chevelure', through whose properties *as developed in the poem* beyond a mere heightening of the observable, the bliss is conceived. The component symbol *covers the expanse of and coincides with the poem itself* ... The 'radical' metaphor generates a poem.

In so far as the experience of the symbol is thus voiced, in the ensemble of the text as divinatory speech, we shall find poets and critics alike soon (after Baudelaire) wondering about symbolism as a purely linguistic event, or, rather more often, about what it is inside language that makes entire syntagmata and tonalities coalesce in patternings which 'divine' values *other* than the cognitive and ethical values that depend upon language to become at all distinct. Thus, in Rimbaud and Mallarmé, there is a divinatory exploring of linguistic 'interiors', engaging the total personality of the poet, and volatilizing that personality into flying tissues of metaphor, voicings of an 'infinity' which can be released into imagination by refigurings of the speech-norms that have trapped it, or have obliterated it. Rimbaud seeks to 'reinvent life', Mallarmé to etherealize it to a vanishing point, from which then life rebounds (from the infinite) back into the immediate and so can be relived in a purified state. Such, at least, is the gist of 'Quand l'ombre menaça de la fatale loi', and it is part of the gist of *Un coup de dés*.

As for the present little monster of an essay, it rests its case, regarding Baudelaire and the pentagram, in the following thesis: The symbol in 'La chevelure' is not an adjunct, isolable or even transferable *component* of the poem only. It is coextensive with the poem, as a kind of divinatory speech, which reanimates an ancient symbol which it still allows to rest in a tacit condition. Yet it is the ensemble of the poem and its mode of composition that 'ordain the permanence' of that ancient symbol, for the poet is the imagination that remembers and insists on that which is to be remembered. . . . 'Was bleibet aber, stiften die Dichter'.

What now can be said to remain, as Hölderlin's project is metamorphosed into Baudelaire's pentagram? It just might be — somewhat further down the nineteenth century — Mallarmé's 'compte total en formation'.

# Mallarmé: 'Le tombeau de Charles Baudelaire'

The essentialization of the poetic word in Mallarmé's practice has seduced commentators into presuming an abstractness to be his strongest claim to glory. To be sure, the purging of 'direct' reference, the hyperboles of 'secondary terms', his intricate 'algebra of metaphors', and his insistence, no less, on 'the elocutory disappearance of the poet, ceding the initiative to the words', are signals of a genius which wonderfully rarefied the orchestra of ideas that accompanies French poetic tradition. Also he knew perfectly well what new harmonic system that orchestra had to explore in his own epoch: a subtle system, intended as a deviation, or radically disgusted aversion, from the 'reportage' that was threatening to reduce French everywhere to 'rudimentary' discourse: 'l'emploi élementaire du discours dessert l'universel reportage' (for decades past, it has been not unreasonable to call this reductive process 'cretinization').

Yet the tendency to isolate Mallarmé as a mathematician of poetry, and to make innocuous, by dehistoricizing it, his revolution of the word, as well as an academic proclivity to exchange one field of reference ('the concrete') for another ('the abstract'), should be regarded with some suspicion. Embedded in Mallarmé's abstruse ethereality there is a corporeal aspect, and this indicates that he did not naively propose to sever ethereal or abstract planes of lyric speech from those which, in language generally, were 'blunt or immediate'. Well and good, he does say: 'An undeniable desire in my time is to separate as though with different properties in view the twofold condition of speech, blunt or immediate here, there essential' ('Variations sur un sujet'). Notably for an English reader who may value highly the prose tradition in poetry, there is no denying this razoring separatist Mallarmé. As abstract as any of the great revolutionary troublemakers, he went straight for the essential, it might seem, liquidating the blunt or immediate, or at least dispelling the reek of reference with Buddhist incense: 'The poet is an aptitude of the spiritual universe to see and develop itself through that which used to be me.' What I would like to propose in these remarks on one poem, is that the blunt or immediate is not liquidated, except on one level, that of reference, while on another level, that of voice-gesture, it is fully articulated, with an immediacy, indeed, that reference lacks. Even on this level, the blunt or immediate is not so much liquidated as turned to face another way. It is not shunned but transformed into the very motoric (neuro-muscular) source of speech acts. It is, if you like, retrieved to its well-head.

Such retrieval is not as rare as thematic literary criticism has made it seem to be. Similar sound-sense linkages occur not uncommonly, and among poets of vastly diverse sensibility — in Eliot ('Marina,' for instance), in Keats, and in Góngora. To show where I stand on this, let me cite a small and valuable discovery made by Donald Carne-Ross. He observes that in Góngora's 'Polyphemus and Galatea' the cameo of the nymph Galatea rising from the grass as Acis appears, contains an image of 'unusual physical energy':

> La ninfa, pues, la sonorasa plata
> bullir sintió del arroyuelo apenas,
> cuando, a los verdes margenes ingrata,
> segur se hizo des sus azucenas.

Galatea, rising up, 'made herself a sickle of her lilies'. She detaches, as other commentators agree, the lilies (of her body) from the grass. It is an image in which the secondary terms of an analogy take on a singular perceptual life of their own, made possible uniquely by the stretch of these words in their context. Carne-Ross observes: 'Since sickling is a vigorous business, we are surely invited to contemplate the moment when the white flowers fall beneath the blade.'[1] We are invited also, he goes on — to the delight, surely, of any student of Marcel Duchamp — 'to see the abrupt transformation of the still, white surface of Galatea's body into an agitated complex of planes as she not merely gets up but jumps up'.

Now let me suggest a bridge from here to Mallarmé. Góngora's line 'segur se hizo de sus azucenas' is a brilliantly perceptive tonal miming, with seven sibilants, of the sweep of the sickle and perhaps also of the rustle of Galatea's silken lily limbs as they — what? Jump up? Isn't there something wrong here? Shouldn't the lilies, shorn, be falling down? Has Carne-Ross realized the content of his discovery to the full? I think not, for the image is activated by a detail absent from his cubo-futurist explication. The image has caught the fugitive instant in which the green lily stems are decapitated and the white lily flowers fly up. The sibilants frame a vowel series which is looped but rising in pitch, from *u* to *a*, epitomized in *(a)zucenas*, and this series tracks the sudden elevation of the white flowers, Galatea's body. If one reads along the sound-sense braiding of the Góngora line, so as to visualize exactly where the sickle cuts, one has a model for the kind of muscle to be encountered, as I hope to show, in the voicing of Mallarmé's 'Le tombeau de Charles Baudelaire'.

## 2

### Le tombeau de Charles Baudelaire

Le temple enseveli divulgue par la bouche
Sépulcrale d'égout bavant boue et rubis
Abominablement quelque idole Anubis
Tout le museau flambé comme un aboi farouche

Ou que le gaz récent torde la mèche louche
Essuyeuse on le sait des opprobres subis
Il allume hagard un immortel pubis
Dont le vol selon le réverbère découche

Quel feuillage séché dans les cités sans soir
Votif pourra bénir comme elle se rasseoir
Contre le marbre vainement de Baudelaire

Au voile qui la ceint absente avec frissons
Celle son Ombre même un poison tutélaire
Toujours à respirer si nous en périssons.

Probably a reader's attention is taken at first by the conspicuous *b*s of the first quatrain. Certain vowel qualities occur, however, in among these plosives, to modulate their force. *La bouche, un aboi*: if you dwell on these sounds vocally, you detect in *la bouche* what I shall encode as a (z) sound: the throat is closed on the *ou*, the lips are open. *Un aboi*: here the plosive is followed by a (y) sound: open throat, as in English *ouah*. The first line begins with two other vowel qualities in rapid succession: le *temple enseveli* — these back (nasal) vowels, closed-throat e-sounds (*emp, en*) I shall encode as (x) sounds (they are close to certain *o* sounds). Thus, in the first line, after we have read the whole poem several times, we detect a patterning:

x     x         z      y y  z

Le temple enseveli divulgue par la bouche

Now I am going to argue that this patterning of successive vowel-qualities pervades the text: closed-throat sounds, open-throat sounds, and closed-throat, open-lip sounds. The exfoliation of the whole tonal ensemble is made possible by this concertina patterning. An epitome occurs in the last two lines:

y    x x       y       y        y

Celle son Ombre même un poison tutélaire

z  z    y    y    z  x  y  x

Toujours à respirer si nous en périssons

The concertina patterning is found not less, though it is less conspicuous, in the vowel sequence of line 7:

Il allume hagard un immortel pubis

What now could these sounds 'signify', if anything, in their semantic context? A movement, I suggest, in the very muscular activity of speech, from strangulation and nausea, to exhalation and qualified refreshment. The strangulation is audible in the first line. The exhalation is completed only in the last line, which, even then, contains strangulation sounds: *toujours*. This movement is diffused throughout the poem, and it is coupled with another type of alternately exfoliating and contracting sequence: modulation from back to front vowels (*o, ou,* etc., to the sharp *i*). This sequence is distributed among phrases as well as words: *enseveli, abominablement, essuyeuse, immortel, votif, voile qui, frissons, respirer si nous en périssons.* Within this sequence, too, there are fine modulations of the *o*, with varied consonant framings: *abominablement, idole, torde, opprobres, immortel, dont le vol selon, votif, contre, frissons, son Ombre, périssons.* The *o* is, indeed, put through a whole gamut of vocal permutations. Lines 5–7 and 9–11, however, locate the *o* in sequences comprising front vowels of a lighter quality, higher pitched, giving the effect of a key-change. This is especially notable in the phonetic tension between line 9 — *Quel feuillage séché dans les cités sans soir,* and line 11, which oscillates, thanks to the anomalous position of *vainement,* between lower and higher registers.

Another peculiar feature of the vowel-consonant relationship appears in the *o-m* linkage, which is more often that not attended by a *b*. The *o-m* relationships may be close, or stretched: *abominablement, flambé comme, torde la mèche, immortel, contre le marbre, Ombre.* If one reads the ensemble with attention to those relationships and all their subtle shifts, the concluding *Ombre* does come to sound like a tonal-semantic nucleus, or 'parole essentielle', which is diffracted through the ensemble. But here, ushered toward this climax by the *comme elle* phrase of line 10, here alone it is definitively foregrounded. It is as if the title of the poem, itself an epitome of the strangulation/exhalation movement ('Le tombeau de Charles Baudelaire'), had been encoded by diffraction into the text as a tonal ensemble. To invent *à reculons* a Joycean *parole essentielle* — since Joyce passed through the *ombre* of Mallarmé — the vocable encoded might be TOMBREAUDELAIRE. Nor is the *ch* of Charles absent from the ensemble, though it desists after line 9 (*feuillage séché*).

What I have called the concertina patterning of the voicing and of its distinct phrases (the latter audible one by one), is all-of-a-piece with the syntactical and semantic features of the poem. Not for nothing is the poem, after all, a 'sonnet', in which vocal activity as such sounds out what it signifies, in which an argument is harmonically structured.

### 3

In the literal translation that follows, the main clauses are italicized, amplifiers or qualifiers are bracketed; reasons for this will appear later. I offer some glosses, after the translation, as well as a hideously reductive paraphrase:

> *The buried temple divulges through its mouth*
> (Sepulchral, of a sewer, frothing mud and rubies)
> *Abominably some Anubis idol*
> (All its muzzle aflame, like a ferocious barking)
>
> *Or the new gas may twist its shifty wick*
> (Recipient, as one knows, of insults undergone)
> *It illuminates, (like a) haggard, an immortal pubis*
> (Whose flight, from lamp to lamp, spends all night outside)

*What parched leafage in the cities without votive*
*Night will be able to bless like it* (settle again
Against the marble, vainly, of Baudelaire,

In the veil which encircles it, absent, with shivers)
*It, his Shade, even* (a tutelary poison
Always to be breathed although we die of it)

Line 7: *hagard*/haggard: a predatory bird that hunts in hedges.
Lines 10–12: the Shade is the *la*/it, absent from the veil which
encircles it with *frissons*: the dry leaf is implied to take flight, like the
immortal pubis, before the shivering veil (unmentioned wind), and to
settle (*se rasseoir*) against the marble. An uncanny paronomasia also
asks here: What writings can bless as the shadow falling from
Baudelaire's language can? (*Feuillage* derives from *feuille*, a sheet of
writing paper.) *Au voile*/In the veil: Is this an image of the wind that
transports (as in Dante) the 'Shade' and which also by implication
blows the leaf and surrounds it? I believe so. Is it not also the
transparency of Baudelaire's 'marble', his transparent but obdurate
and monumental language, over which his Shade may preside?
*Vainement*: the parched leaf (nature) drifting against the tomb (artifice)
finds neither shelter nor revival, nor can it (nature) bring to humans
the blessing (deadly ambiguous) which only the shade of Baudelaire
might bring, or his vision, albeit bedevilled, of the sacred in 'cities
without votive night' (in which night is not consecrated).

Paraphrase: Quatrain 1: Baudelaire's tomb is imagined as a temple,
but from that temple is divulged an underworld god with a flaming
muzzle (Antiquity). Quatrain 2: From modern gaslamps, which some
detest, issues, fuelled from underground, the light which illuminates
the streetwalker (Modernity). Tercet 1: As the illuminated *immortel*
*pubis*, as streetwalker, walks for ever in the desacralized city, so
nature, however shrivelled, might, but does not, bring a blessing
(Profanity). Tercet 2: Only Baudelaire's Shade can bless, the Spirit in
his language — we breathe its diffused deadly poison, but that poison
may be protective (Ambivalent Sacrality of the Poetic Word).

**4**

With regard to syntax, the text actually has a simple structure of main
clauses alternating with amplifiers or qualifiers. What makes this

structure semantically difficult is the presence of problematic, or let us say irreducibly enigmatic, tensions — of contrast and conflict — between the words that constitute it (e.g., mud and rubies, immortal pubis, tutelary poison). In addition, there is not much of a visual scene, or the scene is not visualizable in such a way as to allay the perturbations of the reader's mind and set his 'emotions in right tune', as Milton says. Even where the semeiosis might be visualized, the tensions between terms are so stretched or twisted as to be almost occlusive (e.g., Anubis idol/new gas, immortal pubis/parched leafage). Not until the tercets does the syntax itself become baffling.

Some of these relationships can be intuited, once it has dawned on the reader that there is a ghostly paradigm (of negatives and positives) that plays upon this spume of correspondences. Thus, Anubis is an underworld god, and gas is a fuel piped from underground. Consistently, fusions and tensions are voiced in oxymorons: between organic and inorganic, natural phenomenon and urban artifice, depth and surface, sacred and profanized elements (the former negatively valorized). When fusion proper (as in *gaz récent*) does not occur, then contraries are spitted on one single prong. Over these tensions presides, from the start, the oxymoron Anubis, with his human body and jackal head, totem figure of Paris-Egypt. And the poem is floated across crypts and silences: thus, in lines 8–9, one might suppose that the immortal pubis flitting from lamp to lamp, across the gap of silence proper to the Petrarchan sonnet between second quatrain and first tercet, is 'like' a dry leaf blown by a wind. But here we have not a 'rudimentary' simile, we have a cryptic shift which breaks the frame and opens a new perspective, in which the syntax becomes baffling. The shift is entirely cryptic, and above all it is perplexingly sudden: the rudimentary grammar of likening has been scorned, the connection is hinted at only phonetically, in the *ch*-voicings of *découche* and *feuillage séché*, faintly framed by the internal rhyme of *selon* and *Quel*.

This tensed semeiosis, with its analogical leaps and agonized, twisting contrasts floating over the crypts and silences, is manifest from the start, as is the concertina patterning in the voice-gestures which it lexicalizes and syntagmatizes. The *buried* temple *divulges*/ through its *mouth* . . . of a *sewer*/frothing *mud* and *rubies*. Tensed semeiosis develops largely in the main-clause armature of the text. As far as I can see, it occurs in only two amplifiers, the first and last — in line 2, and, lastly, doubled in 'a tutelary poison/Always to be breathed although we die of it'. The concertina patterning, the harmonics of the semeiosis, occurs in amplifiers as well as main clauses.

Other riddlings and twistings in the text might be explored, even though it has become a rash act to treat of more than one Mallarmé line at a time. I shall confine myself to one (metathesis), after turning over — toward an interpretation — the following proposals: (1) The poem is an orchestration of the sounds given in the title, even if the soft gutturals (*ch*) desist after line 9. (2) The 'rhythmic creation' here has a specific physiological movement, or arrangement, of the vocal chords and oral muscles. It is a movement from strangulation and nausea, to exhalation and qualified refreshment. The strangulation is audible in the first lines, alternations proceed through the text as an ensemble, and the exhalation is completed only in the last line. (3) The instrumentation of this movement can be read in two principal aspects; (a) the phonetic aspect comprises what might be called phonetic metatheses, or dislocations, such as are found in the quasi-anagrams *Abominablement Anubis* and *respirer si nous en périssons*, but there are many other subtle loopings and sequences of sound; (b) the semantic aspect is dominated by singular oxymorons, or by shifts and twists which spread their significance beyond single figures — shock-juxtapositions, agonized contradictions.

A closer look at the tercets now might show the following: in the first tercet there occurs a syntactical metathesis affecting the position of *vainement*. Normally this word would come before *contre*, not between *marbre* and *de Baudelaire*. The metathesis lifts up the word, to give it a distinct profile; but this small peculiarity provides a key to the verse-design as a whole and is congruous with the phonetic and semantic shifts and twists elsewhere in the text. A comparable twisting (a kind of diffused metathesis) in the semantic aspect, begins with the second tercet: *Au voile qui la ceint absente* — the veil encircles a being (*la*) who is absent and has not even been designated yet, whose naming, suspended since line 10, occurs only in line 13, as *son Ombre*. The suspense, as this spring uncoils, enables the sound sequences to form a pattern here, in conjunction with the open-throated *celle*, thus releasing *Ombre* at a *stretto*, a narrow intersection, of the closed strangulation sounds and the open exhalation sounds — *celle son Ombre même*.

One can read *son Ombre même* as 'his Shade, even', or one can read *même un poison*, 'even a poison'. It seems too that this *même* shifts metathetically up into the penultimate line from the last, where it would otherwise have given the sense to be gathered in any case: *même si nous en périssons*, even if we die of it. This shift also prevents *même* from interfering with the consummate braiding of phonetic and semantic twists in the last three phrases, a playful-horrific epitome of the poem's whole thrust, in which four tonal combinations can be heard in counterpoint:

> un poison tutélaire
> Toujours à respirer si nous en périssons
> — *aire/-érissons*
> *poison/respirer/périssons*
> *tutélaire/toujours/nous*
> *respirer/si/périssons*

### 5

Now for one or two suggestions as to what kind of 'reality' Mallarmé's sonnet grapples with, and to its method. In a celebrated phrase, Mallarmé designated the task of poetry as 'the orphic explication of the earth'. We need not agree, or we might agree that he was designating only one task among several. Either way, the sonnet implies a poetic method which reflects the designation. A sound-pattern unfolds (explicates itself) variously throughout the poem. This is a different procedure from any by which a verse-patterning is confined to single phrases, or to rhymes in sequence, without rising to any whole tonal *convocation*.

There are many implications to this *Durchkomponierung*. Let me consider three of them. First, the great poetic dream of the universe as One Being which unfolds or explicates itself incongruously into the Many. In order to compose the Book of that Being, Mallarmé contended with hazard. Hazard must be denied, or at least restrained, in so far as it interferes with relations between the Many and the One. Its locus in verse is the very verse-sequence itself. That sequence may lapse toward blind matter, rudimentary speech, blunt or immediate. The very *successivity* of verse (the term was made significant by Tynianov in his treatise of 1924) has to be restrained, and its 'semantic material' is indeed 'deformed' (again Tynianov) by such repetitive but varied patternings as arise from rhyme, rhythm, figures, and so forth.[2] But Mallarmé in the Baudelaire sonnet goes one step further: the restraint of hazard, of successivity, of all variables that might interfere with the exfoliation of the verse-design as a whole, is as far as possible assured by the vocal *Durchkomponierung*.

The voice itself has so radically recomposed the semantic and phonetic variables, recomposed them into a total so sufficiently approximate, that the text is proof against any variable that might be random.

I say 'sufficiently approximate total', because Mallarmé was ultra-perceptive of the forces at large which may break up any *compte total en formation* (*Un coup de dés*). But his kind of verse-design is such that it 'completes this isolation from speech', as he wrote in 'Crise de Vers', while it does yet realize to the full the symbolic and organizing sovereignty of the poetic voice — 'denying, with a sovereign stroke', as he says, 'the chance remaining in the terms despite the contrivance (*artifice*) of their alternate retempering in sense and sound . . .' It is worth noting that Hölderlin's conception of the 'tragic poem' (1799: 'Uber den Unterschied der Dichtarten') coincides, at certain points, with Mallarmé's, most noticeably in this area where poetry and metaphysics coalesce, where the poem, even in its infinitesimals, is conceived of as renegociating relations between the Many and the One. Another area of coincidence is that in which Hölderlin stresses provisional rupture or contrast as a necessary moment in the self-recognition of the One in the Many, which the inspired poetic artifice can enact.[3]

This brings me to the second implication: contrast, or frame-breaking, as a means of converting sequence into simultaneity. The oxymorons in Mallarmé's sonnet are, in conjunction with the voice-patternings, 'contrivances' (still *artifices*) designed to restrain successivity. The tensed semeiosis of hard-edged contrast restrains any lapse toward mere loose successivity. The vocal *Durchkomponierung* is a sort of symbolic simultaneity. It cannot immobilize the successive phrasings, but it can restrain their momentum. The symbolic simultaneity of an overall sound-pattern (not merely local, phrase by phrase) enables the hard-edged contrasts to make their contrapuntal impact on the mind with a *demonic suddenness*. (Even without that suddenness, they exert a kind of *traction*.) The orphic explication of the earth as a Many exfoliating from a One has distinct procedures for evoking, or invoking, what might be 'real'. Here it invokes the real in the form of an illuminated corporeality, that of the vocal patterning (instrumentation). This voice, in response to its reality, creates the complex of 'fictions' to which it is 'consecrated' and this reality is anything but solid or external, blunt or immediate. Rather it is essential, in its movement, to cite Wallace Stevens, 'a shade that traverses/A dust, a force that traverses a shade'. Yet it is simultaneous: one flesh modulating through all its complexities and incongruities.

The third implication has to do with the poetic voice. For Mallarmé, and not only for him, it is certainly not a merely local or subjective voice that wants to confess something, or is looking for something to confess. It speaks in vocal gestures that arise, with sounds of strangulation and exhalation, from feeling that might reasonably be called primal. Yet it spans the vast distance between the primacy of physiological process, or of the ego's entrapment in a body-image, on the one hand, and a macrocosm in which an ancient temple coexists with a sewer, an immortal pubis with a shrivelled leaf (or inscribed page? yes, but not a figleaf). And in the radiation of that voice certain singularities conspire phonetically to articulate a paroxysm of horror in the presence of an evil (whether metaphysical or not).

My sense here is that even irreducible contrasts, including contrast between successivity and simultaneity in verse-design, have no 'authority' unless they make a text a radically voiced and thus corporeal event, for the poet and for the reader. In Mallarmé's sonnet, it is a structured vocality that gives authority to his twists and contrasts and riddlings. Without that vocality, here, there would be no textuality at all. Primal vocal gestures give rise to oxymoron, paradox and the very syntax of contrast. Vocality is the authority that implants radical insight into the text, weakens the magnetic field of reference, restrains successivity, and shapes that insight with an incorruptible contour. If, in definable ways, Mallarmé was 'ceding the initiative to the words', here that ceding was no passive transaction.

# Some Old Hats
# from the History of Imagination

*. . . verschwiegener Tänze geheimnisvolle Bewegung*
Goethe

**1**

On the surface of the table at which I am writing there is this very small object. By saying 'this object' I mark it off from the generality of objects, while making no claim as regards singularity, or strangeness. It is such an ordinary object, in fact, that I could not reasonably see it as amounting to anything much at all. If I were to measure it, it would certainly be something. If I were to classify it, I would perhaps think it out of place on the table, at least on this table. A rational person might lose interest in this object even before he came to consider what purpose it could have: Can I use it? To what end does it lie there, on the table? Is it materially serving some end? Was it there an hour ago? What is it made of?

I might well think about this object in these ways, even if I judge it, as a rational person, to be insignificant. All the same, the object does not exist in a vacuum. I know, too, that I am perceiving it, or I was, even if my perception of it is subservient to, if not sooner or later erased by, my aptitude for considering it in terms of magnitude, use, purpose, class, typicality, and so on.

As a rational person I can tell myself that there is a relationship between this object and my thoughts about it. Is this relationship vital? Do I respect the object for its own sake? Hardly. I want to pass beyond it and think my way through its isolation. I want to burrow through it, think it away, into a synthetic paradigm where my reason can feel at home, if a paradigm for particles which synthesizing has, more or less, erased can be called 'home'.

What if I were to look at this same object in a way which is not perhaps foreign to reason or contrary to it, but which is sometimes at odds, quite catastrophically so, with the logics on which reason is said to insist? With this other look, I might view this object with contempt, or with curiosity, or with shifting careless moods anywhere in between it and the me who looks. But I would interpose such responses with as little self-interest as may be. I would be evaluating the object, inevitably, but by means of different criteria from those of the rational person this same me was a moment ago. My look would admit inconspicuous shades of emotion. It would emit a host of ethereal responses (hence the reduction of self-interest). My field of vision which contextualizes this object being alive with Leibnizian 'little perceptions', I would want not to violate the object in its purity. Those little perceptions are like pleasure-atoms and I would like to keep them playing out the fluid threads which have by now relieved the object of its isolation.

I might, for instance, actually rejoice that the object in its purity is puce. I could at the same time be wondering if this colour really is what they call puce (was I wrong?). I see, too, that it is cool, this object, no, but seeing it as something not quite round but altogether still, I might already have inferred that it is cool. There is a dent which saddles its top edge, a green fleck. The fleck is something I hadn't noticed until now. The object is about as large as a middle fingernail, smaller than a rabbit's eyeball. A host of possible affinities crowds into my thought, as I try to evaluate this 'pure' object, as I place it in the various contexts of experience which it is proposing to me. Seeing it now more clearly, I feel the more relieved of myself, thanks to the ethereal responses it happens to provoke.

Reason was pulling away from the object, once certain categorical criteria had been exhausted. Imagination may play with more contexts (not categorical criteria) than it can ever exhaust in any given meeting with an object. As regards 'evaluating' the object, the next thing is to catch the moment when the contexts that spring from imagination harmonize around the object and raise it into singularity. Out of indifference it is raised into singularity, as sea by song is raised, through the sky-contrast, in the third stanza of Wallace Stevens' 'The Idea of Order at Key West':

> If it was only the dark voice of the sea
> That rose, or even coloured by many waves;
> If it was only the outer voice of sky
> And cloud, of the sunken coral water-walled,
> However clear, it would have been deep air,
> The heaving speech of air . . .
>             . . . But it was more than that . . .

Back to this unviolated object. Reason tended to enshrine itself in an indicative, imagination in a subjunctive grammar. The one — a rhetoric of deletions moving toward an affirmative enclosure of its object, only to discard the object in the end. The other — a rhetoric of questioning enjoyments which only deviates from the object in order to have it spring back into a more free enjoyment, a more open field, a more expansive singularity.

With imagination I respond to the object's intrinsic physique. I carry forward a game of classifications, by serially relating this object to others I have experienced: saddle, green, fingernail, eyeball, rabbit. Yet, at the same time (so not as an afterthought), my searching for the identity of this object is a searching within and not beyond its physical properties for formal affinities with other objects: no less, with other sensuous qualities, such as coolness, rotundity, volume, puce, green, its humble reception of the lamplight. Eventually I might decide that it is shaped like something I saw as a child, on a Greek farm, or was it in Bulawayo — anyway, somewhere between Cornwall and the Levant, via Africa: something being disentangled from the entrails of a sheep.

The spontaneous rays of imagination showering down upon and around this object may, if I should ever try to put together some intrinsically interesting words about it, flex in quite different directions. The writing-out of an imaginative field may involve searching revisions and transformations of any pretext, of the content and timing of the first bundle of responses. Further, it is the otherness of any such object or pretext that, often enough, engages the fullness of an imagination. Once hit on, or admitted, by imaginative perception, this awesome otherness may mark the presence of an object that has no name, or one whose conventional name seems to be a blank. All possible fields then converge on an intangible, a vanishing.

This particular object is called a kidney bean. It is thus called because it is like a miniature kidney. Its difference in size from an average animal or human kidney might intrigue a mathematician, or a rational person who suddenly notices what it is called. What intrigues a person who looks at it with a trace of imagination is its formal kinship with the kidney. The perception of this affinity enables such a person, as it enables anyone at all, to acknowledge that this bean is not broad, French, or mesquite. But whoever first transferred in English the cognomen 'kidney' from the animal realm, he had a trace of imagination. So did the person who, in Staffordshire, before

Shakespeare's time, called dandelions chimney-sweepers, on account of their resemblance, when in seed, to chimney-sweeping brushes. That person made a perceptual leap, what is more, and while doing so he conjured up this small name from a small set of affinities.

The namer of the bean was attentive to shape and colour, also to texture, with its shine and smoothness. These qualities entered the name they had provoked and a cosmos of formal correspondences fitted around that name. If he later thought of numerical ratios and protein and dinner, fine. If he had thought of the latter first, could there ever have been a Sistine Chapel, could the moon have been perceived in the icicle at the end of Coleridge's corridor of mirrors in 'Frost at Midnight'?

## 2

One can be fairly sure nowadays that any theory of imagination will have a personal bias, a theory like that of Wallace Stevens included, even though the perspectives of his theory converge on a kind of poetic ontology. It may have been in the 1760s, however, that a German painter in Rome lighted upon the legs of an actual chimney-sweep as ideal models for his portrayal of the legs of the warrior Achilles. Whatever personal bias he had, that artist was crushing it into the pattern dictated by old instructions. He had been taught that ideal forms, perhaps even ideal forms of military legs or dandelions, had already appeared concretely in the world, and that you only had to find them, not initiate them by an imaginative act. Having found an ideal form, you only had to copy it, in order to manufacture a perfect painting. The 'idea' of beauty as a germinal essence of things had assuredly, it was thought, radiated itself into the visible world. Art demonstrated mimetically the inherence of ideal forms in the phenomenal world. It showed what could be identified, what could be found perfect, and what was copiable by hand. The work of art, which mediated spectacularly between mind and nature, facilitated a glimpse of the golden flower at the heart of things.

Later, once the mediative role of art had become suspect, a different configuration of beliefs comes into view. In mid-nineteenth-century France a poem came to be written, in which a female corpse rotting beside a road is presented in painful detail. The writer showed (because the poem was ruthless and 'deadly accurate') that the ghastliest subject achieves meaning, against expectation, and wrought among the antagonisms of disgust, when an imagination realizes itself in a contest with ugliness. A new value system, with unideal coordinates and a broader receptivity to both nature and atrocity gave rise to what Octavio Paz much later called the distinctive feature of modern poetry: 'dissonance within analogy'. Certainly interchange between mind and nature has now become tortuous. The aura of the golden flower might, after all, have been the phosphorescence of a fungus.

For the old painter, the circuit of the ideal had already been completed in the best of all possible worlds. To enter that circuit and work it into a painting you first eliminate obvious contradictions, or you 'beautify' them somehow. With his fresh and horrific immediacies Goya changed that, and so did the immediacies of the French Revolution. For the poet working upon his passionate imaginings in the 1850s, the circuitry of the ideal was somewhere else, or it had been broken. It was imagination now which, with its critical component, with its passionate intimacy, as 'queen of the faculties', could put it here again, or mend it, seeking out dissonance, not shrinking from it.

Imagination, for the post-revolutionary poet, proposed images in contest, massive images or miniatures, webs and architectures of images, rhythmically interwoven or constructed, and it was this imagination that *initiated* the circuit, on a canvas or in a text, not what *concluded* the circuit.

Shed whatever trammels we may, he thought, and fly toward a supernatural beauty, beauty as it is imagined into being is an aura inhabiting the image created by the artist. In addition, the imaginative creation constitutes a mode of knowing and judging which differs from that of reason or 'moral sensibility'. Goethe himself, around 1800, had moved away from the chimney-sweep's Achillean legs, to emphasize the sovereignty of the artist's conception in a world of constant morphological process. But Goethe also did keep a fine old-fashioned distance, preferring the fact of aura to the opium of the immediate, and feeling, more often than not, that the 'empirical world' was a monster with a thousand heads.

## 3

It is this new emphasis on the primacy of imagination that ushers back into the minds of a few singular artists, writers, and thinkers after the Napoleonic period the ancient theory of correspondences: Chateaubriand, Goethe, Hoffmann, Poe, Nerval, and Baudelaire.

Contrary to the older theory, however, and most particularly after Hume's dismissal of the 'argument from design', it was now not possible to say, without seeming absurd, that all possible objects of perception correspond by virtue of substantive resemblances (a bean is not a kidney). Notwithstanding Pliny's idea that the moon nourishes the oyster, it is 'mere' metaphysics now to regard the whole rainbow of creation as a self-resembling universe of sympathetic particles.

It had become possible to say, however, that the mental factor called imagination can make coherent rhythms out of its own radiant substance, its own projective power. To its passion for rhythms in kinship imagination appropriates the semblances of such objects and emotions as do resemble one another in their formal qualities (this bean looks to me like a kidney, these are Achillean legs).

Correspondence could no longer mean that forms which look alike are identical in substance. That notion, deeply rooted in older theory and in the stratum of the brain from which comes what Owen Barfield has called 'participatory consciousness', had certainly once controlled beliefs. It had even been carried into physiognomy (Lavater), astronomy, and medicine, right into the sophisticated eighteenth century. But no, substance was now in doubt, universals also; likewise the argument from design as to God's manner of spelling himself out into his creation. Yet this theory of correspondences did retain a threefold interest: it answered a deep human need to harmonize the heterogeneous; it might be able to do for the world of free and sensuous intelligence what typological exegesis had done for figuring out the fluctuations of sacred history; not least, it could help in recodifying the 'aesthetic function'. That function had been relegated to a humble sphere, vastly inferior to Reason, during the eighteenth century. But now, upon entities with formal affinities, imagination could be thought to project, as a special mode of ideation, its organizing power. Even if it still could not fathom nature or abolish hazard in the lapsed material world, that power could be seen as an active regulator of any individual's field of consciousness.

As 'queen of the faculties', imagination initiates meaning. It is with this imagination that in Chapter 3 of Flaubert's novel Salammbo meets the moon, terrible, changeful, immaculate, and is told by Shahabarim a myth of origins. It is with this imagination that Stephen Dedalus is shocked into complete lucidity by the mystery of the birdlike girl he watches gazing out to sea, whose image, as he contextualizes it for recognition, makes his body glow and his limbs tremble. True, these epiphanies spring the trap of common time. But the principle they reflect is stated in two of Baudelaire's mid-century sayings which suggest that imagination does unfold in history: 'The whole visible universe is a storehouse of images and signs to which imagination will give a relative place and value . . .' and 'everyone is the whole world in miniature and the history of an individual mind represents the history of the universal mind on a small scale' (*Salon of 1859*, and *Richard Wagner and Tannhäuser in Paris*, 1861).

## 4

How might Baudelaire have looked at the kidney bean? So intimately and scrupulously that it became, in the glow of his bodily imagining, and without much detriment to its local character, a nodule among millions of other nodules in the great mobile web of relationships between sensation and forms that constituted his moral universe and his 'symbolic mind' (as Valéry calls it in his *Leonardo* essay).

The artist's imagination, above all, was here not asked to isolate the legs of the chimney-sweep from the rest of the chimney-sweep. Imagination was not a needle for stitching together the severed limbs of an already perfected 'whole form'. It was a relic, still radio-active, of the original cosmogonic process, embedded in man, even though the originative process itself was otherwise out of sight. It was a power of ideation that could deliver limbs from their illusion of separateness, recreate their original wholeness, and generate new wholes, microcosms of meaning, made out of the innumerable tensions, nuances, contrasts, and contradictions which are life's irreducible stuff.

Certainly in Baudelaire, to whom the theory of correspondences was regulative, in Kant's sense, not pragmatical, this new and old imagination was a vehicle of the contradictions. The paintings of Cézanne, whose favourite poem, to Rilke's delight, was Baudelaire's 'La charogne', later came to be coherent pictorial sign-textures, in which the inherent oneness of the chimney-sweep is optically explored, under the guidance of the brush, by the viewer. The chimney-sweep, as a physical and aesthetic whole, all of a piece, comes to be self-sufficient, in a world of balanced aesthetic proportions, and in a complete figuration of analogues in conflict. The picture as an aesthetic universe (or multiverse) is just such a manifold of finely nuanced contradictions as is the moral or physical universe which the picture 'symbolizes', and in which the bean and the sweep are dramatically involved. Briefly, this imagination re-awakens primordial dynamic images from the dream they normally enjoy beneath the *somnium breve* of ordinary life. It arouses the archetypes.

## 5

Between 1750 and 1850 there occurred a transfer of initiative in the realm of aesthetics — from Reason to Imagination. (There was and still is stiff resistance to any such transfer in the moral and epistemological realms.) The transfer began with the first wave of the Romantic movement, which had little time, or too much eternity, for the kidney bean. It continued with the consecration of subjectivity in the wake of the French Revolution and the Rousseau epidemic. A stratum of confessional language glazes the intricate maze of a new self-consciousness that writes itself into the undermind of Europe during and after the Napoleonic Wars: Byron, Shelley, Hugo, Lamartine, de Vigny — all in their time egomaniacs of crisis.

What had happened with Goethe's enormous subjectivity? Distilling it (during the 1790s) into self-consciously 'classical' figurations, he moves away from the legs of the chimney-sweep to a most pensive concern for the morphological coherence of the whole chimney-sweep, as an intrinsic unit in the incalculable sum of the universe of divine-human relationships. The legs may symbolize the whole man; but the whole man, if he can be aesthetically dignified, is asked to symbolize at least one point of intersection in the towering hierarchy of evolving creatures, or a knot in the aesthetic universe, with all its moral and physical coordinates, such as fossils and stars, plants and the jaws of sheep, types, and chaos.

What makes patterning in subjectivity possible? Precisely an innate aptitude of the symbolic mind: A bridge, a caterpillar, a cup, an apple, without loss to their intrinsic structures the symbolic mind recognizes their formal affinities and valorizes them according as these affinities correspond to certain shapings interior to its own composition — the arcs of emotion, enclosures in which dwells a void or a transformative energy, a hollow into which a fluid trickles, a fugitive solidity, a certain colour or fragrance. One group of morphological affinities will come to terms with another, or collide with another. When a collision occurs, slow or abrupt, a new complex is catapulted into consciousness, more and more reality is appropriated — intangibly — as this or that pattern splits asunder, as limits change their positions, a curtain of glass beads rains against the binding of books it shelters, even though outside the street is for once washed in sunlight.

Such an aptitude for noticing things need not be named. But already in August 1797 Goethe is remarking on the possibility that 'symbolizing' is for him a matter of urgent personal necessity. It is an exercise which enables him to momentarily outwit the 'millionfold hydra' of empirical reality, the monstrous fluidity of phenomena.

So he symbolizes, selectively, according to his most finely nuanced contextualizations. He observes that the symbol selected to be a magnetic field for his thought can only move across thought by acting, as if *transitively*, upon his consciousness. A curious reciprocity, with vague unconscious underpinnings, between receptivity and projectivity, his yin and his yang, is then set afoot — as the legs of the chimney-sweep fuse with the sweep's whole symbolic identity, and likewise when the bean is specified by name-transfer from entrails.

## 6

Next, however, comes the conversion of reason into ideology. Briefly, with the advance of industrialization, as the technological crust thickened, and with the new doctrine of Positivism moving away from a revolutionary toward a conservative posture, during the 1830s, reason does reinforce its analytic frontier, but, as a calculating instrument, it locks into and insists upon *positions*. Simultaneously, with its revision of earlier readings of time as sacred history, historicism comes about — 'a product', Eliade calls it, 'of the decomposition of Christianity'.

Socially the world is not 'getting any better', because getting is what the new bourgeois have hoisted to the top of their value-system. Commercialism is possibly no worse than ever it was, but it is more pervasive, and so competition is more severe, survival a more wretched matter. Moreover, the new wealth and new production methods alter profoundly the materials and the diffusion-rate of objects in the market: Haussmann's iron scaffoldings, and La Paiva's onyx commode. The world of French artifice is flooded with novelties and crudity, even if the cuisine, at least, underwent some genuine refinement at that time.

The new imagination — sometimes it looks like a ramshackle bulwark with which a few writers, against the majority, desperately sought to prop up the structure of belief, which was collapsing under the weight of the new commodities, the new buying power. I mean by belief not an ecclesiastical weapon, but an essential healthy function of the psyche in the midst of the 'fourfold Creation in Travail', of which the Kabbalah tells us. It is a capacity for thinking about time as the impetus of the unseen, time as a secret unfolding of a trans-historical reality. The Imaginary, the Invisible, The Life of Pure Forms — these had made cultural history possible; but a slow and imperceptible shift in the angle of their vision now deprived most people, embedded in historicism, of any wish to discern them. A dense mass of beanshoots gone-to-seed in ideological ramifications was burying the golden flower. But imagination, in the new understanding, might function as a solvent, to make less important and more transparent the immense wardrobes, the plenipotentiary helmets, the palaces, teeming cities with unnatural vices, superhuman buildings with skeletons of iron, with which the European psyche was equipping itself, into which it was now reifying itself. Imagination, subversive and revolutionary, a convulsion of the psyche *in extremis*, now sought to restore, by undoing the colossal artifice of alienations, the balance of power that had been upset by the Death of God.

## 7

The bean has begun to palpitate as if it were a real kidney; lest I be mistaken, it proposes to me that the aesthetic function, actual in art, is not to be confined — as it was in most eighteenth-century theory — to the 'sensuous world'. The bean proposes that this function, as a creative, projective, and ideative *frenzy* of the nervous system, exceeds in scope, complexity, and energy all the regular functions of consciousness. Those functions, for all their dignity, might be mere precipitations from the volcanic depths in which the aesthetic function mysteriously moves. Yet by no means does the bean place out of sight the social functions of the work of art.

This bean proposes that the eighteenth-century primacy of *ratio* over *aisthesis* (perception) might have been a shield against that very frenzy. But it was more likely just one aspect of what Robert Solomon has called, in his critique of the white western mind, a 'transcendental pretence'.[1] That pretence had ideological ramifications. Upon the latter perched, high up, socially privileged persons such as princes, ecclesiastics, and obedient executives. At the tree's foot clustered in filth and trembling the sensuous folk, among them their humble sheep, and kidney beans, and chimney-sweeps. Industrialization was soon to ravage them, body and soul.

But the wicked bean also proposes that Kant's laborious critique of the theoretical privilege of reason, and his revaluation of *aisthesis* as a sovereign function in the *working* of art upon intelligence, made it possible to conceive of the relation between mind and the super-sensuous ('Absolute' or 'God') in a heterodox way. That relation was not a logical or rational one any more. It was an analogical relation to which Kant was pointing. Even if Kant was more concerned with aesthetic judgment — 'taste' — than with imaginative creation, he did inch open the door upon the latter: upon the idea of imagination as the fountainhead of the analogies. (As a young teacher in Königsberg, Kant had shown an extraordinary gift for realizing sensuously mere ghostly schemata such as maps, for mentally *living* what he read in books — an aptitude of genius described with vigour by Balzac, in his account of the childhood of Louis Lambert.)

Imagination: a calculus of the infinite. A space in which, barely supported by any recognizable matter, yet, like space itself, inseparable from the matter and time that are its own radiations, the ladder of analogies reaches from the good and evil grounds of sense, to the supersensuous incognito. Or: imagination, so conceived, reaches to the archetypes, which are always waiting for it to give them sensuous texture, sensory scopes. Its inventions must be 'smelled, felt, heard' (Rimbaud, *Lettre du Voyant*).

Hegel opened a rather different door. Though he opened it wide, it gave less access to the actual methods by which imagination makes credible its mobile fictions. Rimbaud's 'Le bateau ivre', on the other hand, marks a clean breakthrough. It is a prodigious reinvention of the (archetypal) aquatic symbolism of the ancient world: water decomposing and creating, the abominable polymorphous mass of sheer Potency which, terrifying and nocturnal, ebbs and flows against the underside of any least Act — 'Est-ce en ces nuits sans fond que tu dors et t'exiles,/Million d'oiseaux d'or, ô future Vigueur?' Baudelaire, Rimbaud, Mallarmé — each in his own way breaks open his time by creating images of origination, so recreating a lost *eschaton*, the impulsion of a Paradise into the present, even though the Angel of the New may flee before it, backwards, in horror, knowing that History could never for a moment endure Paradise.

Come back, sighs the chimney-sweep, to the question of alienations and reifications. I am perplexed when you say that imagination, during the Second Empire, became a dazed captive of excessive semeiosis, iron-skeletoned buildings, wardrobes, and helmets. Well: as eighteenth-century science had concerned itself with the clockwork of the planetary system, nineteenth-century *citoyens* of the new economic nexus, having artfully gathered what Revolution meant, concerned themselves with the clockwork of the predatory system.

The first concern had at least allowed for ideas about other worlds, alternative realities, nestled into the surface of alien stars, like Poe's Al-Aaraf awaiting translocation to this wrong world. The second concern allowed for less in the way of alternative realities, or 'open' spaces. Utopian constructs abounded, nourished by advanced and often hermetic eighteenth-century models, but their actualization in Europe was prohibited by the police, the military, the new bankers, the new nationalist vanities, which adopted the pretence of providing a total reality. (America promised more hospitable ground.) The climax was the massacre of the Communes in Paris, May 1871. In the mid-nineteenth century opacity, imagination had already internalized the alternatives, and in some respects it had tended to de-socialize them. The other world is 'within', within, for instance, the imagination, no, the language, of Gérard de Nerval, as an other being, angelic or not, *alaukika*, as they said in Sanskrit, whose flutterings in the net of consciousness may or may not obey motivations arising from levels deeper than those of the reptilian brain.

This interior alterity is the haunt of the Imaginary, and it devises new styles for the aesthetic function. The Romantic ego, inflated, heavily foregrounded until about 1835, with its grammar and syntax emanating from the vocal first person singular, begins to recede. The immensities of interior alterity displace the fractional ego to the perimeter of the text, or beyond. In Baudelaire's 'Le voyage', the *moi* of Baudelaire is like that of Pascal's 'world' or of an orchestra — its centre is everywhere, its circumference nowhere.

Perhaps this new orchestral objectivity paralleled imagination's offensive against the predatory forms which economic behaviour was assuming. The predatory ego, as in Balzac, had to be turned inside out, or decalcified in some way. The first person singular develops in poetry an aptitude for invisibility, or else for multiple masking. This was also, either wittingly or spontaneously, an offensive against the 'creative' pretensions of technology. Technological invention from 'models' is distinct, says the new imaginer, from imaginative creation out of 'the haze' — that is the adequate term, provided by Goethe in his two great poems 'Dedication' and 'Amor as Landscape Painter', and it has more recently been used by the contemporary Arab poet Adunis, in his 'Modernist Manifesto'.

In polyphonies based on finer sensuous and emotional nuances than ever before, the marvels of interior vision might be voiced, just so long as the voicing is what makes poem and style integrally one. The morphologies of alternative reality might be magically enacted as language, condensed and cryptic. The very privacy of the finer cryptic style, with such delicate incandescent textures and unpredictable movements, seeming to come not from a person but out of language itself, might enable subjectivity to resist the commercial-technoid malaise. Poems might function as apotropaic spells, to dissolve the fatty tissue threatening Europe's heart. But I don't know that any such *intentions* were ever expressed. Nor do I know how Darwin might have figured in France at that time.

Some late eighteenth-century reasoners, like Lessing, had already seen that 'dehumanized science' and the profit motive might collapse the heart of values, human values, in Europe. The trouble was, and remains, that this dehumanization, so-called, made worse and more widespread the monstrosities of which the human predator is capable. Force is queen of this world, not reason, said Pascal. We remember, in vain, what horrors are acted out not only when reason sleeps, but also while it is crowing most complacently, to announce another day for the dismembering of angels and chimney-sweeps.

So imagination, 'queen of the faculties', with all her values conjectural, took the field against the well-equipped but muddled armies of lethargy and organization. I do not know if 'Ratio Artifex' was the motto on the latter banner. On that of imagination the motto was double: 'Je est un autre', and 'Je tiens la Reine'; one might fancy some heraldic figures also, a rampant kidney bean, dexter a chimney-sweep, and the hoofs of a faun couchant. Somewhere else, Napoleon III on horseback was riding helplessly, between Bazeilles and Givonne, to be specific, his grey face rouged, for he was Emperor and had speeches to make, wrong battles to fight, in the wrong war, as usual.

From imagination's emblem we might read one thing. Any non-chimerical spiritualization of the sensible universe is foredoomed to be a long struggle, slow and painful, beset with nullity. Yet from the nullity, exercised by the struggle we extract images and maps for another enterprise, nameless, even more slow, even more painful for some. For others it may pass too quickly; it may ask of the individual more insight and energy than any single imagination can summon. Yet it is in individual fictions, according to Mallarmé, that an unknown other being, animal and musician, alive among the roots of consciousness, calls out with an uncertain voice:

*Naïf baiser des plus funèbres!*
*A rien expirer annonçant*
*Une rose dans les ténèbres.*

# Neighing in the Wind
## on Hermann Hesse and Ralph Freedman's
### *A Pilgrim of Crisis*

Hermann Hesse became quite well known in Germany as early as 1904, when his short novel *Peter Camenzind* was published. Since 1945 his renown has spread across the world, yet in spite of his 1946 Nobel Prize his work is somehow not admitted into the canon of 'great' twentieth-century German authors. Germans, at least, would be amused nowadays, or mildly astonished, if a foreigner were to mention him along with Thomas Mann, Hofmannsthal, Rilke, Kafka or Brecht. This is not only because readers now aged fifty or sixty and upwards may not have read him since adolescence. Nor is it because the sceptical generations now between thirty and fifty have largely avoided him. Nor can it be entirely because his prose is too readable to be thought difficult enough to be important, although it is probable that younger writers today have not read him at all, let alone learned anything from him. It is partly because the canon has no place for a writer whose work, though a coherent whole, is so curiously mixed. It is sometimes cloying, sometimes profound, then quixotically unironic, then at once brisk, mysterious, and topical, and at other times, if not in his last two fictions, what Germans patronizingly call *pubertär* — and most of this in a prose that has a mercurial texture all its own.

The mixture does not seem to have vexed either American Hesse scholars or youth-culture fans who adopted him ten years ago. Nor has it embarrassed the Japanese readers (thirteen pages list translations in Joseph Mileck's massive bibliography), or the Italians (thirty-five items in Mileck), or the Persian, Spanish and Swedish readers. Most literary historians and critics outside Germany have taken the mixture in their stride. Ralph Freedman's new biography[1] shows that he does much the same, certain subdued doubts aside. It also shows, amply, how the mixture arose: out of a collision, in the tempestuous but wistful character of an exceedingly long-lived author (eighty-five when he died in 1962), between oddly blended family traits and the bloody flux of this century.

Hesse was halfway through his twenty-second year when the century began. He had been by no means a standard child of the south-western German Pietist missionary family from which he came — because he resisted, from early childhood on, the ruthless 'breaking of selfwill' that Pietist culture demanded. So he was sent away to a boarding-school when he was six, and his education thereafter was confused, to say the least. He would conform for a few months, then break out, run away, or be sick and despondent. He had a terrible temper. At one stage he was parked in a school for backward children. His parents, rigorous but not unkind, found him ungovernable; and yet, as a boy, Hesse seems to have found authority intolerable only as long as it frightened him into feeling guilty. Which was, inevitably, most of the time. No pleasure, in that world, and everything outside of work and worship a cause for guilt. Even much later, Freedman remarks, he was incapable of enjoying anything wholeheartedly; elsewhere too, Freedman writes of Hesse's 'constant sense of physical and emotional deprivation'. An odd fish to be found, much later, in the midst of the 1960s Aquarian pleasure-culture of unregenerate young North Americans. But perhaps not so odd, if they found in Hesse a voice of understanding, the guru who understood what they were up against: the dog-collar, the hard heart, and behind these the bayonet.

At the age of thirteen Hesse resolved to be a writer. He wrote his first two books when he was an apprentice bookseller, first in Tübingen, then in Basel. He was a priggish and stilted young man, but perhaps no more so than most of his genteel Wilhelmine contemporaries. No sooner had his first successful book appeared, *Peter Camenzind*, than he married a woman nine years his senior, and settled into a 'wilderness' sort of life at Gaienhofen, on Lake Constance. Maria Bernoulli came from an eminent Swiss family and was a gifted pianist. She had three children by Hesse, all boys, and eventually, after long depressions, she went mad. Her episodes and remissions followed Hesse through a large part of his life. It was not until he married Ninon Ausländer, nineteen years his junior, and his third wife, in 1929, that he seems to have met his match, or at least not deceived himself by substituting an image for a person: of the robust thirty-six-years-old Maria he had written in a letter home that she was a 'delightful, petite, black-haired, wild sweetheart of a girl', and 'a little girl who reaches only up to my beard and yet can kiss so powerfully that I almost suffocate'. These details are not trivial, for they illustrate Hesse's constant inclination to edit, or reduce, the 'world' of his experience to a psychically loaded image or idea, with which he could then play imaginatively. Precisely the same reduction occurred after his thoroughly discomforting trip to Indonesia and Ceylon in 1911.

The Gaienhofen years shaped Hesse as a mildly disturbed, but polite author of Swabian small-town tales and of two novels about desperate but rather dreary artists. He was successful, second-rate, and trapped. The change came in the middle of the First World War. At the start, he was no more opposed to the war than Thomas Mann was. He hoped that Germany would win and save European culture (the gist of German national myth at that time). Yet his anti-militant posture soon came under attack. He dutifully reported for the draft (though living then in Switzerland) whenever his card came up, but was always sent away because his eyes were weak. He did not like it when his wartime journalistic statements, which emphasized (conventionally enough) spiritual purification through suffering, raised a vicious clamour among jingoists. He worked long and hard hours in Berne, obtaining books and printing literary booklets that were sent to German prisoners of war in France — hoping still that 'culture' might prevail against mud and carnage. A partial breakdown brought him into the charge of J. B. Lang, a Jungian psychiatrist; the two men remained close friends until Lang's death in 1945 (his notebooks were unfortunately destroyed by his widow). Lang was the model for Pistorius, the church organist, in *Demian*, the fiction written 1916–17, which appeared pseudonymously in 1919 and launched Hesse into a trajectory that could hardly have been predicted from his previous work.

Yet Hesse does not quite belong among those writers who extracted from the war, besides horror, disgust, and irony, a distinctly altered outlook, a vocabulary purged of cant, and a new poetic architecture. Doubt as regards any pretention to dignity and nobility — that is one experience Hesse confessed he drew from the war. Also a heightening of the colour, tempo, urgency of his prose, could be taken for a sign that he too now believed all the idylls were over. But this is not quite the case. Hesse's utopian fantastic impulse was not subdued but quickened, and its shattering against the historical world was recorded now with just that more intensity. What did change Hesse, or what he came to create, was a new narrative form, in which his polymorphous interiority could be reflected. This was the fictionalized monologue, with a figured bass of images (later he called this his 'private mythology') that recur in modulations and, from book to book, explicitly or tacitly organize the fields of events.

Hesse was one of the first European authors to be psycho-analysed, but analysis was never purely clinical and always broken off. He duly became, during the next twenty years, a self-analytical novelist whose fictions orchestrated psychic crises of his own, and, rather mysteriously, thousands of readers could find their own troubles reflected in those of his protagonists. Published in 1927, *Steppenwolf* — the biographical context is nicely investigated by Freedman — was his most mazey and spacey monologue of the 1920s. It is a book in which most of the *idées reçues* of cultural and psychological crisis during the 1920s are anatomized, and its structure has been explored by various critics. Yet however remarkable the book is as prose, the Steppenwolf poems that Hesse wanted to be printed in the book are quite one-dimensionally vapid. What, indeed, is one to make of this acrobat of self-exploration, whose oscillations between self-esteem and self-disgust, psychological daring, imaginative acumen, morbid ferocity, and intent moralizing, make him resemble a being who might have been begotten by Isidore Ducasse on (say) Maria Edgeworth?

Hesse's new kind of eminence of the 1920s did not protect him. Somehow he was always in trouble, it seems, almost as if he had to fabricate troubles in order to test himself against them, in order to justify himself. No, not quite, because his existence was also fortunate in many ways, not one-sidedly ill-starred in the way that Kafka's was. Hesse became a Swiss citizen in 1924, but his income depended on royalties from Germany (hence, later, his *relief* when the Nazis did not burn his books). He wrote narratives, but they were neither realistic nor mythocentric — the main modes developing in the 1930s. He married Ruth Wenger, with her cat, doggy, and parrot — but saw precious little of her after two months of cohabitation. He lived for a time in Zürich, grindingly sick, and then learned to dance the shimmy, drank heavily for and to the joys of carnival, and had long nocturnal talks with Lang ('sharing depressions'). Even before he was fifty he felt he was dying of old age. Though tending to passivity, he was too contemplative to be simply sensual, and his cerebral sensualism, being rather low-powered, shocked only fools and prudes. If not a practical man, he had a sharp sense for money. If not a sensual man, his image of the artist was otherwise: Klingsor — the erotocentric, vital vagrant, exposed to all the joys and horrors, wasting his substance in unreflective life, then incubating experience, then hatching it in an essential, abundant, ravishing image that transcends all sense and all intellect — a curiously philistine, or at best Romantic notion. Basically, too, a confessional writer, his self-revelations are (to us now, it should be said) mostly moderated by a discretion which used to be the mark of civilized persons. Hesse never was the untamed self-eviscerator whom Henry Miller and Timothy Leary thought they were shepherding into the Scene. Briefly, Hesse was never truly an outsider, he was 'liminoid', his work a soft threshold, between epochs, between cultures, between opposed compulsions of his own psychic riches and his singular (but not powerful) intelligence. A Manichean *malgré soi*, he was a 'deeply civilized man' of the old school; so he could feel, the more painfully, civilization's discontents, yet he thought of those discontents as wrongs inflicted by fate, rather than as effects of wicked and long-standing injustice, or as the social exoskeletons of people poisoned by fear and greed.

The rhetoric of Hesse criticism, even in its earlier stages, was strained and sometimes thunderous, because it endeavoured to make a highbrow author out of an essentially upper-middlebrow one. Ralph Freedman's first detailed biography of Hesse in English is, in regard to his manner and his judgments, reminiscent of much that has gone before. On the positive side, Freedman does map all sorts of fascinating connections between Hesse's life and work, showing of what stuff the successive self-portrayals were made. If his focus dulls, it is because he tends to rate each of Hesse's fictions as highly as Hesse rated it himself. Since each was cathartic and left its author feeling high, dry, and relieved, until the next slide into misery, Hesse's own ratings were not only exorbitant, they also seldom lacked a note of glib self-praise. When Freedman might seem to have his doubts, he tucks them almost out of sight. But some inconsistencies are surprising. For instance, *Narcissus and Goldmund* is introduced as 'one of the most revealing but also one of the most beautiful novels Hesse wrote', and then twenty-one lines later is judged as 'this sentimentally con-structed medieval allegory'. If Freedman means the term 'sentimen-tally' to have a positive sense (as retrospective reverie) he should have told us how, and, specifically, on what grounds, he would presumably not agree with readers who find the text cloying and the whole book, excepting one or two splendours, a clear case of *Edelkitsch*. Later, after a most positive account of the genesis of *The Glass Bead Game*, and of its shift from 'image' to 'geometry', with 'dialectical intricacies', comes the wellnigh shattering epitome of that last novel as 'an arid, intellectual work whose harmonies remained theoretical and whose characters were puppets'. Yet one could not say that Freedman harbours a love-hate relation to his subject. Far from it, his treatment is largely reverential.

Here I found another difficulty with this 'definitive biography'. Freedman explicates, with biographical details, Hesse's personality and writings in their own terms exclusively. He seldom if ever moves those terms out of the context, in order to elucidate them in a critical way. (Hence his monotonous insistence on such words as 'within', 'inward', 'inner', and 'interior'). So he declines to sharpen or deepen his view, or the portrayal of his subject, by changing the intellectual, psychological, or social contexts. This reverential method does have some heuristic value. On the other hand, it strains the reader's patience when the biographer's values (or his clichés) reiterate those of his subject, when there is no contest, no drama, no friction even between surfaces. I felt this most particularly when Freedman is speaking of Hesse's 'poses'. He usually says, for instance, that such-and-such a feature was 'by no means only a pose', and then he goes on to some implication of some kind, soon to repeat (e.g., p. 214) that Hesse's 'new life was by no means only a pretense'. Why doesn't he sail in and question the entire tendency toward self-inventing stageyness that marks every phase of Hesse's work, every modulation of his histrionic self-image? What kind of a man was this, if his simulations were so lacking in panache and so stricken with *mauvaise foi*? These are crucial matters — after Sartre's injustices to Baudelaire and after the entire Existentialist problematic of good and bad faith. The problem here is that Hesse's sentimental and solipsistic aspects do often tiresomely overshadow the more incandescent aspects of his personality and work, manifesting themselves in limp stereotypes, clichés, and other forms of low-energy escapism. Hesse was tormentedly aware of this and large tracts of his work display it.

Now the North American Hesse 'legend' (a compound of ignorance, faddishness, and manipulation) did change the context, but without doing any better. One problem here is that, with a Hesse prised loose from his German value-frame, American fans could read (or 'scan') him as a spellbinding phantasmagorist, a wizard of poetic suggestion, without feeling their way into the traditions that supported him. Even more vexing is the fact that non-German readers could not see how Hesse's sentimental and solipsistic aspects connect the writer Hesse with all kinds of German psychosocial malaise, all kinds of morose philistine paltriness, all kinds of self-pity and self-aggrandizement. Precisely the otherworldly utopianism, whether or not combined with deep Indian equations between self and world, was eccentrically part of a broader context of wishful thinking that inched the German middle class via hero-worship and 'inwardness' into hideous self-deceptions and eventually into Nazism. The floating irrationality that American fans adored in Hesse can be benign in some social mixtures. But, as a German phenomenon, historically speaking, it was part of the set in the theatre of tribal compulsions in German class-psychology. Nazism tightened the endemic authoritarianism and directed the tribal compulsions massively — while whipping up the common pathological hatred of any 'others' — into policies that were a lethal swill of complacency and terror. To change the 'culinary theatre' metaphor somewhat: Hesse never was able to grasp the connections between irrational flights of the solo mind and the thermals of mass-hysteria.

I'm not saying that Hesse was an irrationalist like Hamsun, or like Lawrence, although some of their notions, in or out of context, have been thought fascistoid. In fact, for all his quasi-mystical traits, Hesse did not fluctuate into irrationalism, least of all into its terrorist fringe. Quite the reverse: his task in the 1930s was to wrest the utopian impulse, the *idealism*, away from its manipulators, and to enshrine it in an unassailable imaginative form (*The Glass Bead Game*). How he did this is shown in some of Freedman's better pages. What I am saying — I hope without echoing any old Marxist cant — is that Hesse's political indeterminacy, and his haughty liberal-parochial gentility, as regards the 'real world', were typical of the German middle-class mind as both initiator and victim of Nazism, and that his phantasmagorias should not be blithely viewed in isolation. Also I am saying that his sympathetic biographer does not change the context so as to strip away the clichés and reveal the psycho-mechanics of Hesse's *Edelkitsch*. As for the horror of such a writer's impotence, Freedman may not dramatize it comparatively, in a European context, but he does here deserve credit. He tracks with expertise the ambiguities and timidities of Hesse's stance *vis-à-vis* Germany in the 1930s, even after the 1938 *Anschluss*, and in that expertise there is a rare blend of insight and charity.

In the area of literary evaluation Freedman and I would further disagree. I am not bilingual enough to be dead sure of my ground as regards some traits of Hesse's prose. But I am sure that Freedman's rhetoric is so typical as to be worth dwelling on, for a moment. He does not make the contextual leap because his native German, despite long years in the USA, gives him to think and write, especially in the first two-thirds of his book, in an English that is Germanicized, sometimes heavily so. He relies on lexical and phraseological stereotypes, for one thing, and this for me raises doubts as to his ability to see through Hesse's own (putatively) frequent clichés and cloyings. Here I must be brief, so I shall focus on three aspects: metaphors, vocabulary, and phrasing.

First, metaphors. There is a marked tendency toward mixed stereotypes, which may be due to Freedman's reluctance to visualize or to etymologize. Thus: 'crisis in the poet's eye found its resonance in the minds and hearts of his readers' (p. 6: two stock metaphors clumsily mixed). Again: 'bolster the outward trappings of an artistic life with actual accomplishment' (p. 104: the same problem). And this: 'the figurative mole . . . dug beneath the well-kept gardens of his life . . . yet, paradoxically, opened gates to freedom' (p. 132). Fourthly: 'He had crossed the Rubicon of his life . . . the vault of *Siddhartha* had been reopened' (p. 230: not a mixing but a clumsy juxtaposition with phrasing all wrong in 'Rubicon of his life'). Questions of vocabulary arise where there are similar fumblings. Some of these occur through faulty translation. Examples: ' "God give" (should be *grant*), wrote the dubious (should be *doubtful*) mother as she was preparing his blankets and sheets, "that Hermann will discipline himself and improve in diligence and manners" ' (p. 40: some involuntary comedy here). 'No less an expert of (should be *in*) unconscious longing than Sigmund Freud praised *Peter Camenzind* as one of his favourite readings' (from German *Lektüre*, but it should be books, p. 117). 'Now the *Hausfrau* is home again, not yet fully recovered but cheerful and dear' (p. 125, quoting Hesse: in all contexts *lieb* is translated as *dear*, but *nice*, *friendly*, or *kind* would often be preferable). 'I have picked up carbon (should be *pencil* or *charcoal*) and paintbrush for the first time in forty years' (p. 187). 'Hesse was impressed by the charming, still (should be *quiet*) and serious bride Frida and the sober in-laws' (p. 195). Of one-word errors due not only to mistranslation I cite three: 'testimonial to romantic art' (p. 87); 'apotheosis', the true sense wickedly violated (p. 335) when Freedman writes, 'the years of composition encompassed the Nazi years in Germany to their apotheosis in World War II'; and on p. 394, just where it is least wanted, there appears the bastard malapropism 'multivarious': 'multivarious perception of colourful nature'.

Clumsy phrasing, apart from some odd misprints and many academicisms such as 'molded a form commensurate to . . .', or 'emerged between covers', 'create a healing novel', or 'erotic functioning': 'Maria's musical passion allowed her to enjoy these friends a good part of the time, although they retained (with the obvious exception of Ilona) a distinctly masculine coloration; (p. 136: why not 'although most of them were men'? Or has Freedman forgotten he wrote 'friends' and not 'friendships'?). 'A sturdy farm wife' — Freedman is paraphrasing an episode in *Klingsor's Last Summer* — 'allows the great painter to work in her yard . . . Later she follows him into the mountains; her approaching footsteps are heavy with sensuous meaning' (p. 206: the original says that the footsteps are strong and regular, but not heavy, and the original is not even involuntarily funny. Nor, incidentally, does Klingsor 'bed' the woman 'under the pines', but on the grass, and the local trees are chestnuts). 'It (*Siddhartha*) clearly bears the earmarks of Hesse's attempt to transform himself into another person while preserving the essential core of his being' (p. 235: an editor could have corrected *earmarks*, but only a finer auditory sense could have prevented 'clearly bears the earmarks'). And with a bang not a whimper there appears on p. 255 the following wow of a misprint: 'Comparing his own with his Ball's marital troubles, he wrote with a rare touch of humour . . .' (quotation follows) — the reference is to Hugo Ball, but where are the brackets? For good measure, I detect a heavy German accent in phrases like 'friend Finkh', (p. 92), 'gardener Hesse' (p. 159), and 'publisher Samuel Fischer' (p. 237).

A copy-editor could have drawn Freedman's attention to some of these oddities. But the Germanic flavouring, as well as the fumbling, are to some extent inseparable from his whole cast of thought. I could find hardly any such traits in the last third of the book, but cannot say whether this was because I was adjusting, or if Freedman's language was purging itself as it went along.

Freedman is fundamentally a benign and loving biographer. He has explored and read his subject indefatigably, and he writes with finesse on several difficult aspects of it, notably the 1930s political contexts of *The Glass Bead Game*. Even then, I felt that he was on occasion fighting the dragon with a tuning-fork. Hesse was, even more than most writers of his time and now, a monomaniac. Out of his monomania he constructed an individualism which has been highly attractive to several generations of younger people. Yet between the monomania and individualism there is a dark linkage.

The benign side of this link is formulated quite nicely by Freedman on his next-to-last page: 'Throughout the many decades of his life, Hesse had lived as a self-conscious artist who viewed his function as that of a painter not of mores but of the inward features of man whose glory and suffering were beyond time ... The uncertainty with which Hesse has been charged was, in fact, a sign of his humanity, of his need for and his success in reflecting the inner visions of those around him.'

What strikes me, while reading Freedman before he reaches this (ah yes, rather owlish) formulation, is precisely Hesse's inability to empathize, his devilish opacity, which he projects into the minds of all his protagonists, and his compulsion to deflect everything into his own ego-frame, almost vampirically, without any particular interest in 'the inner visions of those around him'. In his writings, these traits are fully documented in every fiction from *Peter Camenzind* to *Journey to the East*, fictions oppressed, as their protagonists are, by a twofold failure. The protagonist cannot achieve, let alone sustain, communion with the subjective worlds of other persons, and, if he can at length be animated and 'saved' by the healing flow and touch of proto-images governing deep levels of his own self, he does so in isolation or by marginalizing all externals, persons included.[2] The exhausted protagonist in a world impenetrably dense has to edit that world drastically, in order to make the slightest sense out of it, even in order to achieve belief in his own identity. Likewise Hesse in his life vampirically edited his world, in order, so it would seem, to inflate his ego even if he could not animate his self, except in moments of grace, hermetic moments, perhaps those of actual writing. Freedman himself remarks (p. 226) on 'Hesse's usual habit of exploiting publicly a carefully edited picture of himself as the artist defined by his private agonies'. It is in this context that the supposed 'Zen' Hesse of the American legend, the magic hallucinator, has to be seen. Freedman provides all sorts of details for his context, but wisely refrains from forcing them into a scheme. Yet one could figure out how such a scheme might work, if one were to hazard, admittedly via various short-cuts, a more one-sided formulation — 'points', as Freedman would say, 'without counterpoint'.

One could select some details and call them typical. Hesse, aged 32, in 1909 goes to a health spa, and leaves his wife Maria, their child and the new baby, in the care of a maid. He was undergoing a crisis, mental and physical, but also, as Freedman writes, he himself needed to be 'a subject of compassion. In this way, Hesse realized a deeply felt need to take himself out of the everyday into a rarefied life where the ailing person is cared for and made the centre of attention' (p. 141). And from this time onward, Hesse is to be found ailing in a spa, once or twice every year. In the autumn of 1909, Hesse goes to visit the aged author Wilhelm Raabe, and in mid-November writes to him, after an appendicitis operation, that he awoke at noon on the second day after surgery to hear the bells of Frankfurt ringing in unison for him. Actually they were ringing for Schiller's Memorial Day, but I can detect no humour in Hesse's remark. During the next few years, with Hesse frequently absent from Gaienhofen, Maria sinks into the depression which eventually takes her into an asylum. When under attack for his (ambivalent) stance *vis-à-vis* the First World War, Hesse defends himself by self-justifications cushioned against lofty appeals to a spirit of international brotherhood; after the Second World War, many letters and essays (supplanting now all imaginative work) are again self-justifying attempts to explain his reluctance to condemn Nazism outright. After his father's death in 1916, Hesse was thinking, as he wrote in a later essay: 'They have never understood him. Nobody. Not even all his friends. Only I understand him fully, for I am just like him, alone and understood by no one.' During the exhilaratingly productive months following spring 1919 there are numerous 'friendships' which 'counterpoint' the life of the solitary Hesse in the Ticino (his wife is now mad, his sons live somewhere else). Yet it is questionable how far Hesse's supposed genius for friendship went toward real communion (as it probably did in his affection for Hugo Ball and Emmy Hennings). The quality of his friendships is a sensitive question indeed, and Freedman hardly probes this issue. One might suspect that Hesse did use friends as screens upon which to project himself, experimentally, in his various 'poses', just as he 'used women' (here I quote an unblushing Freedman), without being receptive, so it seems, to their actual separate and subjective realities. 'Reality,' he wrote in 1925, 'is an accident, a bit of life's débris'.

The equation between self and world which ends *Siddhartha* might just be a lyrically glorified, sublimely transposed (or displaced) version of such hubristic monomania as this. In 1925 Hesse writes to Emmy Hennings: 'I remain always alone and can never penetrate the great void that separates me from other people.' By that time he was living apart from his second wife, the 'singing student' Ruth Wenger, with whom he lived for two months after marriage in 1924. That marriage seems to have been not only absurd, but also a sign of extremely poor human judgment on Hesse's part (just three years after the difficult completion of the wisdom-book *Siddhartha*). He needed Ruth to look after him when he was ailing, perhaps. When her own illness is diagnosed as TB, he writes to his sister Adis: 'It is really funny that Ruth's passivity toward me at the very moment I was about to go on strike against it takes on the form of this illness, so that now she has been relieved at least of any responsibility for caring for me a little.' Freedman comments, two pages on (p. 265): 'He had, he wrote Emmy, suffered less from Ruth's illness, Mia's [Maria's] madness, and his concern for the children than he had from his eyeaches' — because the eyeaches impeded his writing.

The double vision of self as miserable sufferer and humorous onlooker in *A Guest at the Spa* certainly provided a greater elasticity, more abundant space, in the world/self and body/spirit relations. But all experience remains marooned among the caprices of the desperate (split, 'verzweifelt') ego that supplants the world of others. Hence, in the Magic Theatre of *Steppenwolf*, Haller's vision of life as illusory play; but hence, too, the altogether implausible other characters in that book, Hermine, Maria, and Pablo, who are mere husks, puppets, without a scrap of fictional substance, let alone 'truth to life'. Hence, moreover, the song and dance about ' "reality" and its horrors being *overcome* (my italics) by reflecting the self in the "immortal" or "eternal" self of the artistic consciousness' (Freedman, p. 273). Not reality is overcome, but one creative individual's despair about it. As that individual discovers his 'inner space' of images and rhythms, reality is piped away, to become a figment, first believed to be a luminous projection of the 'immortal self', then soon absorbed vampirically by the irreducible, desolate, vain ego, and then dismissed with loathing. The scandal here is just that the pretences of the ego, always clamouring for psychic food, induce a 'poetic reality' which is not substantial but substitutive, an escape, down an endless corridor of mirrors, thus no real escape, but the paralysis of self-entrapment. Hesse noted these escapist features, not in *Steppenwolf*, but in his next fiction, *Narcissus and Goldmund*: 'In reading Goldmund the German reader can smoke his pipe and think of the Middle Ages and find life so beautiful and sentimental, and need not think of himself and his (own) life, and his business transactions, his wars, his culture, and other such things' (letter of November, 1930). In passing let me say that Kafka, whom Freedman summons at this stage as a witness in Hesse's favour, imagined through his own sufferings a diametrically opposite version of ego-negativity (as evil), and that, if

Hesse was influenced by Kafka at all, he took him along, in *Journey to the East*, in a direction that would not have suited Kafka at all.

As a last detail, just as *The Glass Bead Game* — ' "an island of humanity and love" in the midst of the killing and satanism' (Freedman quoting Hesse) — was appearing to Switzerland, after Suhrkamp had had to reject it in Berlin, Hesse wrote regarding the August 1943 air raids on Hamburg: 'In Hamburg I, too, lost a thing or two. It was a city from which I received most of my letters for years. In the past not a week went by without a letter from Hamburg.' How casual! It is not cynical. But had this man no imagination of what those fire-storms had done to people? Not a word does he utter that might allow one to find in the ageing, weary, polyarthritic Hesse, as a human being, genius of the kind that Alexander Dovzhenko, himself tormented by Stalinists, said was needed, at the time of the Nuremberg Trials: 'New German geniuses are needed — not just one, but many — to shine a pure light on mankind, to bring about a creative joy that would be able to fill the abysses of evil that the German people have created by giving birth to Hitler. Does the German nation have the strength for such a venture? I kneel. I kiss the ground where our soldiers passed in battle as they fought and died by the millions to save that goddam old whore Europe.'[3]

Of course, *The Glass Bead Game* was a shining of that light. Of course, too, Hesse for years on end wrote letters to all kinds of people, dispensing much-needed counsel (in a way reminiscent of Polonius). Certainly the sketch of Hesse as monomaniac, combating evils of individuation but shrinking from social evils, is too selective to be anything but provocative. Yet, as a hypothesis, it is not unsuggestive. It points to dubious areas where 'individualism', as a vague posture, is a mere charade of opaque egotism, self-serving vanity, parochial ignorance of what other human beings are like, and certain other paralytic disorders of imagination. It points to even more dubious areas where freedom of expression is at stake. For if 'subjective feelings' — a writer's facts, as Orwell pointed out — are consistently taken as supercriteria of truth-to-life, then the genius of subjective feeling may have a high old time while the Karamazov syndrome takes over, anything goes, not now because God is dead, but because the world is my toy and language my playpen (or pigpen).

In consequence, both world and language are subjugated to the ideologists, to the political, commercial, and media manipulators, who neutralize all 'islands of humanity and love', just as in the first place those islands were fabricated by literary minds incapable of seeing pot and kettle before them — 'skotomizing' the world, as neurologists might say. The hypothesis also warns. If the ingenuity, energy, and revolt which inspired significant art earlier in this century peter out in forms of opaque egotism (here I see Hesse as a transitional figure), the danger arises that foregrounded ego-drives alone might be mistaken, as they often are now, for 'creative' activity, whereas in fact they are accidental to the poetic imagination. Those drives are not a feature of the real artist. They are a contamination from the automatic philistine world, from which the syntax of creative process radically deviates.

Whatever reservations one may have about Hesse, a question remains: Do the recent books about him annex his work now to Academe? Does Freedman's biography transform the wished-for Hesse into a tame professor's poet? Or do there remain, beyond rather damp disputes, areas of his work, or of his legend, which will continue to radiate positively through the lives of readers all around the world? There must be, of course, and different people will read him as they please. Tacitly Freedman's biography shows how misshapen the American legend has been, or still is; explicitly it adds to serious study of Hesse but is unlikely to change its general complexion. For me there is a chirping, still to be identified, that comes from among these documentary tombs, just as there is a durable but *abstruse* Hesse to be disengaged from the defences he built into his writings and around them. All the seraphic talk of his being a pilgrim, wayfarer, a magician, a sage, and so forth, tends to reflect only the sedentary and cerebral habits of readers who fancy Hesse so. Yet he certainly was what Germans call a 'seeker'. In his thirties he used to advertise himself as a 'quiet' or 'secret' lyricist. If only his poems were not so insipid, this might offer a clue to his abstruse side whence that chirping comes. His naivety is perhaps what deserves to be noticed now, and understood. It is a trait that the intellectualizing overkill of much professional Hesse criticism has till now obscured, more than other traits. Freedman, symptomatically, does not mention Hesse's affection for his contemporary, the great naif Swiss writer Robert Walser, whose fame was zero compared to Hesse's. To Walser, very late in life, Hesse sent a conspicuously unpatronizing postcard to say he had been reading him again. Walser received it in the lunatic asylum at Herisau, where he had been living for many years. The simplicity of that postcard might have warmed his heart.

There was, in and under everything, something wild about Hesse, something of the ungovernable child of Pietist missionaries. He kept it alive, sometimes in grotesque forms, sometimes in luminous ones. And there was in him, too, something of his Swabian intellectual ancestors, whom he came upon quite late in life: great God-hounded deviants, dreamers, and delinquents, from Albertus Magnus to Hölderlin and Mörike, each peculiarly rapt in his vision of the One in the Many, the Many in the One, and some of them coming apart in pursuit of that vision. What is it, after all, that Hesse's protagonists seek, if not naivety reborn as illumination through grace? And something more: not the subjugation of reason to any system, but a just peace between the naif and intellectual claims of consciousness. Just you listen, he says, listen actively, there it goes now, 'the wooden horse is neighing in the wind'.

# Seventeen Hiccups
# on the Question of Novelty

*For G.K., who rescued the eighteenth-century
candlestick from a junk heap in East Berlin*

## 1

Dead ends of desperate dreams — the words that blur in politicians'
mouths; manifestos, mute diplomacies, or new slogans in old
rhythms, fists beating on air: the brew in the pot keeps on cooking, the
same old elements go into the works, the same secret recipe: human
meat, with every trace of incarnation punched, drilled, whisked,
strained or drained out of it.

## 2

Territories. What Germans call *Galanteriewaren*, though use has
erased the erotic tint of that word, are called in English *novelties*, and
especially in the USA *notions*. In a novelty shop you see what these
notions are: whistles which uncoil when you blow them; sequins;
masks horrific or funny; souvenirs and explosive cigars; floppy plastic
spiders; wigs, lots of wigs. How did the word *notion* ever migrate into
that territory? One might infer that a notion, some new but vague
thought, is largely or initially, at least, an amusement, a gesture of the
play principle. Aphrodite presides, from an immense ironic distance,
over the baubles in the novelty shop. Emerson, not a bit amused,
turns away, hardly interrupting his transcendental walk, racking his
brains for 'a thought so alive that, like the spirit of a plant or an
animal, it has an architecture of its own, adorns nature with
something new'.

## 3

On the other side of the street: the antique shop. In the North
American provinces, but not only there, antiquity and junk are

bedfellows. Collectors now value at $7 an early variety of Coca-Cola bottle, mass-produced. In Berlin, a small tintype (1860s photo) may sell for as much as DM 80, and dealers cannot distinguish a tintype from a daguerreotype. Tintypes in the USA cost about 75 cents nowadays, daguerreotypes of the plainer kind about $30. Within specific territories the old things jostle one another and want to be identified. Once identified, special, rare, they acquire 'value', just so long as identification spawns a market. In New York a few years ago there was a craze for old pisspots, to be used at dinner, ironically, for soup. The craze put the price up by several thousand per cent. Mischievous millionaires! Feasts of 'economic shit'!

## 4

Patina is the frontier across which certain classes of things pass from use to collection, from one value territory to another. Patina may be intrinsic or extrinsic: a function of the object's chemistry, and then again a glow radiating from the mind of the person whom the object attracts, whom it amuses, on account of its rarity (or cash value, or investment value). Even then, collection is only a narrow strip of territory among others, a sort of Polish Corridor, with a population of hovering objects, objects with changed or changing functions.

## 5

Americans also enjoy 'conversation pieces'. These are objects old enough for their use to have become obscured; the object is placed conspicuously, visitors notice it, ask about it, and so a conversation starts, which may lead anywhere. The old thing has a secret it cannot keep. The revelation of that secret leads to revelations between people. The past speaks, through the people, living again, thanks to the conversation piece which animates discourse, and then resumes its place. One symbol gives birth to others, the others being the terms of the conversation. Maybe something new is born, an important relationship. Here, at least, people may avoid the debasement that was affecting the word *notion*, as well as the vulgar ironic elevation that affected the function of the pisspot. Many other formalities mediate the delights ushered into existence by the new. What city directors call 'growth' — urban sprawl — entails, on the other hand, a stereotyping no less vacuous than that caused by the withdrawal of *alternatives* from societies that are ideologically policed.

**6**

And so on. The real issue here is that novelty is an unstable perimeter of notions or objects, and that this perimeter marks a fluctuating outer fringe of some deep and constant pulse in the human psyche. The pulse, like an appetite, can survive intact through fits of orgiastic or ascetic behaviour which alternating cultural epochs prescribe for its encouragement. It is a passion for invention, an irrepressible urge to innovate; it is resistance to the stupefactions of habit and circumstance. One cannot isolate ideas about novelty, I suppose, from the greater psychosocial dynamisms which transform nature's *élan* into countless cultural facettings. Novelty has no certain, no fixed frame of reference. It is a morphogonic force, volatile, fugitive, at once occult and pervasive.

**7**

Is what we call 'new' an aetherial substance, or a spirit, not quite substance yet? You might say it is delicately linked with the concrete liberties that figure so large in the drama of evolving self-consciousness in the human species. It configures in that drama with freedom of speech, choice, struggle, self-determination — all those notions displayed in the window of dynamic liberal thought — and most especially with the infernal voyage, as Hamann called it, of self-knowledge (*Höllenfahrt der Selbsterkenntnis*). The 'new' even seeks refuge, together with its fellow notions, exceedingly fragile individual concerns, in certain institutions. ... Even then, what if all this radiance of a pleasure principle only sustains us so that, having eaten this planet, we shall go on to others and eat them too, for life's sake?

**8**

The new is a rare bird, on the filth-encrusted bottom of whose cage we are dancing gloomily around. It is a phoenix no sooner identified than shot, stuffed, and put out for show, soon barely distinguishable from the pterodactyl or the dodo. Or does such a conception of the new fit only into an ancient framework, where tragedy was still true, still a fact of life? After all, tragedy displays the struggle of the new to survive and procreate, for it is the ritual enaction of a struggle for self-renewal occurring in the entrails of godhead.

**9**

I suppose that Dada was born wearing already the scars of this knowledge, launched into the accelerated time of this century. Hence Dada's affinity to the Trickster Spirit Eshu (among the Yoruba, in Nigeria and Brazil). Hence its constant quarrelsomeness, its cavalcade, from city to city, of metamorphoses and deviations. Wulf Lepenies says that this acceleration of time was reflected in the changing design of natural-history books in the mid-eighteenth century. A 'new' vision, of reality temporalized, a vision of great consequence, transformed prevailing habits of mind which had favoured fixed systems, spatial configurations, and generally absolutism. The new actually reforms phenomena by reforming the ways in which we think about them and cope with them. But the new seldom leaps into existence. It moves at a snail's pace, more often than not, toward existence, and then, sometimes unnoticed, disappointedly the other way, into the apocryphal, or else hobbling like Büchner to Strasbourg, like Rimbaud to Ethiopia — anywhere to escape from the stink of evil that others breathe without anxiety. Its efforts to slip into language are symptomatic of this. The creative impulse in the singular subjectivity grounding the new, the pressure toward perception of a truth beyond deception, does there reside in it a purity, a resolve, an unerring absurdity, such as might disengage it, as the younger Nietzsche disengaged it, from the universal semeiosis of distortion and self-deception?

**10**

Does nature come up with anything new? Very slowly, so slowly that we can seldom observe her means of production. It is part of her coquetry, no doubt — always doing things behind our backs, always 'going on'. Or else, in her millions of imperceptible patternings nature renews herself. In the new phenomenon she appears — as a spectre; but in the process of self-renewal she is flesh. That process may be objectless and undirected, so it is here, in the very process, that we might detect the substance of which, on the bottom of our bird cage, we are shadows. Constantly we confuse process and product. Fetishizing the product we cloud the source, or we poison it. How to keep the source of self-renewal clear and flowing? Products proliferate, reaching deep into the present, while feelings, the personal and the social feelings, get stuck in the mud of fifteenth-century farmyards.

## 11

Memory plays us false, which is fine, as long as memory's fictions are generatively and morphologically true enough. Or we neglect memory, neglect (another vital organ) history, we *skotomize* (neurologically speaking), not seeing what is there, because indifference or fright or absence of imagination deprive us of adequate metaphors. History, spates of which look so horrible backwards, might look better the other way around. So we try to turn it forwards, not recognizing, either, that novelty only repeats horror, unless it has sprung from the source (pure? innocent?) . . . What is it in *aesthetic* experience that washes clean the windows of perception? The good novelty, the sensitive notion, as pure construct, seems to filter corruptions out of the source, or out of the systems which are nourished by the source. If only we had time, we could be practical and sensitive enough. We could learn to see the web of process, the vibrant web, through the glitter of gadgets.

## 12

In 1911, after eulogizing the new fashion in trousers for women, Robert Walser conceded that he liked skirts on women too. 'Anyone who loves, esteems, and admires women's legs as I do, can consequently, it would seem, only concur with such a fashion, and indeed I do concur with it, although I am actually very much in favour of skirts too.' My scepticism regarding novelty (trousers) is no more unusual, I suppose, and no less perplexingly bourgeois, than my curiosity about old things (skirts). Not only things, I should say, but all sorts of customs and rites of antiquity also, like feasts and dances. When I was about twenty, I saw an old coin on the green baize cloth of the brass-stall in the market-place at Cambridge. Something about it fascinated me. Something in me wanted it to be me who took that coin in hand. After that, most of my pocket money was spent on coins, Roman, like the first one, until at sixteen a variant of the same passion somehow switched my attention to old books.

The obscurity of the objects gave me good feelings in their presence. I loved to identify them. Their age was also a source of good feelings. It had been the same — but not quite the same — with the neolithic flint scrapers I had picked up from fields in Norfolk — every Sunday afternoon, combing the ploughed fields for flints. The good feelings came from a sense of contact, through wind and rain, with the human past. When the feelings came to me, they touched my imagination. This did not increase my stability as a person, rather it suggested a direction, and I became excited, viscerally and mentally. I was no longer imprisoned in the present moment, in a specific time. Perhaps it was self-renewal which such contact with old things, and the identification of those old things, brought about. One's being seems to expand through time: backwards into antiquity, real or possible, while France was falling, and outwards (though it may seem to be inwards) into real or possible dimensions of an inclusive personal world — while Dornier 215s drove me into a ditch that flanked a Romano-Celtic pottery site. The old thing helps you to have such feelings of kinship with something invisible, and to explore your *Selbstgefühl*. There is a particular beauty to old used artifacts. The beauty is perhaps touched by nostalgia but not limited by it, not deformed by it. An old spoon can certainly survive the grip of feelings that I put around it. To me it transmits a *form* of life. An old candlestick can be a birthday telegram singing from the sane surface of life, a bit of its modelled and gleaming topsoil.

## 13

When in 1931 the new Citroën track-vehicles, travelling from Beirut to Peking, passed through Herat, a breakdown caused a curious incident. The scene was a quasi-medieval foundry, in the bazaar. The Afghan smith, who had been asked to make an earthen mould for an aluminium casting, suddenly doubled up as if seized by stomach cramps. His neighbour, a man in a yellow turban, who was jealous, had cast a spell on him. Two of the expedition's mechanics, Ferracci and Collet, then advanced toward the magician, waving a blowlamp 'in fiery circles'. The magician fled, the cramps stopped, work could begin.

What happened in Herat possibly epitomizes the contest for the soul of that region, including Iran, which has actually been going on since 1925 when the Turkoman Kajiar dynasty was succeeded by the Pahlevi one. It is a contest between Islamic religious conservatism and secularizing modernism. The epitome is being explicated in the present conflicts (March 1980). These show how entrapped in its one-dimensional notions of modernity US foreign policy has become (how unresourceful, compared with Ferracci and Collet.) Entrapped — by the technological needs of a domestic system which include fuel for its 'new models', on which depends in turn a vast labour force, which in turn, again, and in its own terms, is becoming more and more conservative. On the 'other side', the revolution in Iran looks like a new Laocoön, entrapped in coils not to be pictured as pipelines but as recrudescent tribal passions with paranoid features.

### 14

Collisions between old and new: the shockwaves released by the Citroëns driving through largely unmotorized Asia are now stronger than ever. How fortunate my little collisions were, how sheltered, among old coins and books. Changing the frame again: how propitious the meeting in Stravinsky of Ragtime and Bach. But in the political area the collisions have been catastrophic, not 'tragic' at all, but deathly, even the sacrifices beaten into the mud of literal-mindedness. In some parts of the world it looks as if time has become for now so cramped in historical overlayerings, that it has lost its capacity to spirit the beneficial new into public existence. 'The angel would like to stay', wrote Walter Benjamin, of Klee's *Angelus Novus*, 'awaken the dead, and make whole what has been smashed. But a storm is blowing from Paradise; it has got caught in his wings with such violence that the angel can no longer close them. The storm irresistibly propels him into the future to which his back is turned, while the pile of debris before him grows skyward. This storm is what we call progress' (translated by Harry Zohn).

### 15

Even in a relatively coherent society the levels of human reality intersect at odd angles and are stratified across loops and slopes. Those angles, loops and slopes are different warps of time in which people actually live, participating in the same epoch only tangentially and under sexual compulsion and economic coercion. Transfer this model to a country as complex in its temporal warps and ethnic strata as Brazil, and you see how extremely variable (time-variable) even European societies are, within their recognizable 'styles'. Assuming that some stability is a good thing, the dangers of destabilization arise from the thrust not only of raw atavisms, but also of sentiments which, though civilized in themselves, lend their energy to public schemes that are dim in conception and in effect pernicious.

**16**

Happily, even if some deep strata enshrine a palaeovirus of madness, this non-fusion of the time warps, or time tracks, in so-called developed societies, has a creative dynamic of its own. It leaves room for play, at least. Even if all sorts of separatists are found in that room — where fanatics are apt to make fools of themselves — the room adjoins a territory, too, in which human beings can consort with animals, trees, clouds, feeling the liberating magic of the planet. Unhappily, non-fusion is ignored by history-makers, especially so in a technological age. Their thinking cannot accommodate it. Two reasons for this occur to me at present. First, no economic nexus can remain intact without homologizing consumers as synchronous entities, with identical or similar needs. Second, any such accommodation of the non-fusion factor would subvert political command of those velocities of change which agents of power select as being 'viable', 'advanced', and thus paramount.

Or have those agents been selected by nature? What might she be preparing behind their backs?

**17**

Asynchronicity is the key, I am guessing, to any significant renewal, as act or event, personal or social: asynchronicity in cultural and cross-cultural stratifications, as in those that give shape to any developed individual person. Is asynchronicity a time-model corresponding to the space-model of molecularity in current theory of the social dialectic? If the two models do correspond, from their practical articulation new methods might be derived, for the undoing of misfortunes inflicted by the polyp of totalitarian thinking, by the engines that enforce conformity. But it is altogether enigmatic, how the rare bird called 'new' can escape before being crushed, when the strata, enormous fluxions of time constantly solidifying into blocks, crash and grind against one another.

# Louise Moillon's Apricots (1635)

She has allowed the absolute standpoint of a twenty-year-old woman to be consumed by a heap of apricots in a long basket. The apricots in their basket are on a table, the front edge of which is paler than its remoter edge; and here on the front edge there are drops of water, five of them, at one of which a fly is sipping. The spectacularly detailed little fly is wearing wings of a delicately veined fabric.

The other drops of water, various in size, are in that perfect condition which precedes eruption or evaporation. They, in their way, though transparent, are as radiantly corporeal as the apricots.

To the left of the group of four drops of water there is an apricot that has been sliced open; the kernel is still attached to its hollow in the one half. To the right of the fly's drop, there are two apricots, whole, and across them a leafed twig is placed, while attached to the flyward end of the twig are two dark purple shining fruits, probably plums.

Every visible apricot has a bloom, but only on a few is this bloom so noticeable as to be almost an aura. The basket which contains the apricots is made of dark, aged reeds. The apricots stand, or rather they configure, against a background which is black, opaque, impenetrable. Is it really a heap of apricots? Their golden and rotund volumes are casually consorted; it is not so much a heap as an ordering of apricots. Some are resting, each one at its own tilt or angle, on others which are lodged in the middle of the heap, and still others can be seen as a third and remoter group, closer to the darkness. The tripling of the picture space, darkness upward and behind, golden rounds in the middle, and in the foreground the pale brown table surface and edge, is apparent also in this terracing of the apricots.

It is thinkable that she ordered the apricots in this fluid recessive way, each apricot with its twin rondures meeting in the tender sweep of its crease, even though not many display this crease, so as to discourage any donjuanesque counting of the apricots; but also in anticipation that someone, sooner or later, would be certain to count them, someone would ascertain that there are twenty-nine apricots in the basket, and that the number twenty-nine is one of those that are not divisible without a rupture of number into fractions.

There are, however, eight apricots that are so placed as to show the crease, nine, if the apricot on the far right, outside the basket, and on the surface of the table, is included. Also the apricot farthest to the left, but only second highest in the heap, diagonally across from the other, has a crease that is set at a contrastive angle to that of the lower right-hand apricot. The two halves of a circumflex accent, drawn apart, anchor thus each extremity of the left-to-right diagonal from heap to table. It is thinkable that she put her own cocked eyebrow, interrogatively, into the picture.

What is more, the fluid recessive triple-terraced heap of twenty-nine apricots rests in a lining, or nest, of leaves. This nest is hardly noticed at first. Each leaf has sharp, staggered points, six or more. The group of leaves across the top of the heap is not so fresh; no crisp points. These leaves, against the opaque dark background, look wilted, they are contaminated, perhaps by the darkness: one of them is only half a leaf, the absent half has been eaten away, and another has a distinct black hole in it.

Apart from a subjection of certain leaves to an alien and tainting mouth, what can be felt? The spikiness of the leaves around the apricots warns any mouth that all is not so sweet and velvety as one might suppose; as one might suppose, on seeing with one's mouth, even before the eyes have come to the matter, that the seductively edible, creased and golden fruits are for all the world like virgin quims, waiting to enjoy and to be enjoyed. She is saying: Don't you be so sure, these curves are analogues of us, curved ribs, which even our creator could or would not lean upon to make straight. But as a woman she was saying also to women: In you, bodies, there is the presence, a treasure; too soon a leaf goes limp, too late the spikes bristle against the intrusive prick, the eyeballs —

Because the subject is so familiar, you might hang this picture in your kitchen for a year or two and never notice, never really care. The one care might be for the drops of water and the fly. She spent more time lavishing her skill and attention on them, than could ever have been encompassed by any actual co-existence of theirs on the forward edge of the table. Here, too, the accent of her eyebrow, putting a question. Or the diagram of a prolonged insight, a frenzy transfixing an instant, makes the presence violently manifest, as wonder. No, that cannot be it, that cannot be exactly it. A noun phrase or two cannot reflexively represent what she perceived and created as a complex hypotactical sentence, dominated by an as yet uninvented verb-series.

Green and gold, spiked leaf and vulnerable *mons*, the tainting dark and the dance of apricots across the kitchen, forgotten, explored, what happened, Louise, you were a Protestant, in the Cevennes I have seen the museum of the desert where the atrocities inflicted upon your people are commemorated. Actually your eyebrows circumflexed a mystery which we have still not chattered away: Is the presence real, do intervening mediations obliterate it, have we not yet invented any language for it? Is nothing immediate? When it happens, now, and someone coming into the kitchen suddenly winces at the shock of a new cell originating in his brain, that sharp shock, is it paintless and nameless? Or is it graduable into ontological regions, subtle removes, the provinces of difference?

Bless you, do not see wounds as apricots inflicted on the darkness, no, I meant to put it the other way. Place yourself otherwise; be vigilant, but without anxiety, which means — do not interfere with it, let your folds unfold to envelop that force, though it is terrible, mind your reed basket is ventilated and does not dry out. The basket exists for the ordering of apricots, it is the cage of ribs in which each one of them contends for its time, the apricots, which are not weightless, they press against one another, and only the drops of water, really, fly up, evaporating. The fly, the fly is a heavy being, a twinge in the bruise. Of that bruise the two plums are telling, also otherwise, soothed by the twig that is laid horizontally across them, a touch. But look: where the twig was torn off, a flitch of white shows, another wound, the lowest factor, in the right-hand corner, a little curl of white, or a snarl, ridiculously completing all the curves of all the apricots.

Again, begin to read the apricots. Because the deeper tones of gold are among those on the right, and these tones are in an ironic concord with the darkness of the ground, you will respond to a compulsion to reverse the mechanics of any European text — and see from right to left. The creases in the apricots obligingly shift their angles that way also, relatively clockwise. Yet, having made this reversal, you wonder why you made it, why you did not read from the relatively stronger illumination of the apricots on the left, why you did not swivel your eyes then slowly to the right, following an anti-clockwise jerking of the creases toward the deeper tones, unbinding the spell of time.

Precisely that act of wonder suspends any absolute viewpoint — with nothing lost to indeterminacy. This is the threshold across which

Keats listened to the nightingale, and on which he constructed, for wonder, a Grecian urn, which also had three groups of figures, deities, or mortals, or both, in frozen ecstasy around it. Louise put her fly on that threshold, in relation to the absolutes of levity — the tight-skinned drops of water; and to the collapsible, heavy, fugitive fly corresponds, in other mythologies, the prince of all metamorphosis, the frog.

Her liminal fly, her to-be-absolute water-drops, her present apricots, and this great bruising darkness — all the visible, little, fugitive bodies enact in a configuration the magic of an oneiric etymology. 'Abri' — shelter, dark shield, death a refuge, at least, and 'cot' — a more minuscule non-lexical non-seme could hardly exist. There could be no lighter consonant, no rounder vowel, than in the sound of 'co[t]'. It has no gravity of signification at all. Yet that non-word's oneiric axis generates a small whirl of shadowy relatives: Rabelaisians might find that it verges toward a word now lost, 'cotal', meaning penis; 'coter' is what surveyors and engineers have to do, measuring land for buildings, plotting a site for a construction; and 'cotir' — sometimes for rustics, even if this one did not know it until this very instant when he looked it up — means 'to bruise', as a fruit is bruised.

# An Allegory of Erato

*. . . qui n'admirera que notre corps, qui tantôt n'était
pas perceptible dans l'univers, imperceptible lui-même
dans le sein du tout, soit à présent un colosse, un
monde, ou plutôt un tout, à l'égard du néant où l'on
ne peut arriver?*

Pascal

It was only later that she looked at herself as if for the first time and
called herself a dish, but she came into my life and now there's
nothing I can do about it. I had seen her before, seen into her face,
notable eyes, seen her long thick golden-brown hair, several times she
had found me looking at her. I was glad because one day she might
come into my life, and she did, with a backpack of green nylon
swinging from her left hand, as she strolled along the platform.

When she smiled, the slant of her eyes became steeper, but to
equalize things, between innocence and ruefulness, she had ever so
slightly drawn the corners of her mouth down. Even after eleven
hours in the train she was a dish. We walked across three wide streets,
then down a narrow one and up some stairs into an old café. I
remember several dark columns, vast mirrors, it was happiness,
winter, evening, and later it was night. I did not know how she felt,
bewildered, or curious. She wore only striped panties. We lay in this
room together and looked around. She said it was like the middle of a
blueberry, for a bluish light was filtering in from somewhere.

Since that night the dish has been for me an obsession. Here she is ,
walking. The long noisy street led to the agricultural exhibition not
far from the radio tower. She walks in a lazy sort of way, tall, southern,
and she throws back her hair with a shake of her head. I see her
combing her bangs out, gazing into a mirror, opening her mouth she
inspects her tongue, white teeth, and she puts a finger to her round
chin. At the exhibition we see several hundred cheeses and many
kinds of meat. We look for the cows but cannot find any. We walk

away and climb into a taxi. Now I hardly ever climb into a taxi, but, if I do, I remember the absent cows, I remember the chin of the dish and the fingertip she is putting to it.

Another time, among machine sculptures, she is wearing a long black borrowed dress and incongruous boots: like ski-boots, discoloured suede, with hooks instead of eyes. Someone had thrust a bunch of violets into her hand, but she held the violets down at her side.

Neither the violets nor the sculptures meant anything to her, she said. We came back to this room, she lit a big candle she had brought, and we talked about the world. Behind her there are five pictures of old sailing ships, one with a pennon inscribed ENGELBERT. When she took her dress off, she was still wearing the striped panties. For a second time I noticed her orange socks. Between her lips bubble gum made a tiny balloon, and every balloon burst with a tiny splat. Splat . . . From any perception of the purity of that instant I shrank back, as if she had leaned across to bite me. I shrank back, anxiously thinking (hence the defilement) that the pneuma enshrined in the tissues of that small pink expanding globe, even before it was distended to the limit of its endurance, had been wasted.

To kiss the dish when dancing with her in a disco was something else. She dances in a way that is thoughtful but bewitched. She dances best in her old blue-jeans, tossing back her hair, looking you in the eye, then kissing with her eyes closed, slanting large eyes under strong circumflex eyebrows.

When her eyes open otherwise, there is such mercy in them that you have to gather your lifetime up to hold the gaze. Once I saw only one eye flash silver blue with a sideways glance, after we had made love and come together. Goddesses have been made out of that look. So she has occupied my mind, the dish, steering it away from everything else, month after month. The trouble is that while the dish occupies my mind little else can get into it. This infuriates the dish, for she is free. She is not to be imposed upon. She has a different kind of understanding, all presence. It seemed impossible that she should ever saunter into a past and be gone with it.

Soon after she had come into my life, I asked myself: Has she any imagination? I wondered if she might have none, because everything she did or said was direct. I was wrong, it was a devil's innocence that prompted me to think that soul is not direct. When the dish opened her Greek immortal mouth in the mirror at Bacharach and said: 'It's not a big mouth, but look, plenty of space inside,' or when, being photographed in an automat, she pulled faces and made her mouth look like a frog's, then, too, then I began to know about the soul of the dish.

There have been other proofs. She sat propped in an open window high up overlooking the Rhine at sunset and sang, without the flicker of an eyelid, the Lorelei song to some people on a terrace below. She wept when she read a letter from a friend in trouble. She attacked me hammer and tongs for seven days and nights, stripping me, she thought, of every fantasy I might have had about her, the goddess and that stuff. Swallowed up in the bushes of a nocturnal park we tore off our clothes, rolling naked in the leaves. When I think of her in the moonlight among the leaves, then I know she has imagination, or when, back from a run, she sings to her guitar, or asks how do I get under her skin, how do I do it, then too I know it, she has soul.

Why this obsession? We have met four times, or is it five? Between times, I have been travelling, together with a beautiful girl, who loves me; and everywhere the dish is not, I see her before me, the slanting eyes in their wide hollows, the curve of her cheek, the golden-brown hair flowing, the tufts in her armpits. I hear her plain low voice, I smell her scent, remember how she moans, the sharpness of her speech when she attacks me, the warmth of her tongue. She doesn't love me, not now, at least. She once wrote me a letter, saying that for the first time ever in her life, now, she was telling someone: I love you. But something is wrong, she is too strong to give herself, no, nothing is wrong, the dish does not trust me, she is wise, she keeps her distance, doesn't want this maniac to inflict his contradictions on her, having enough of her own as it is. The obsession could be the wild twisting flight of desire as it hurtles across that distance; doing so, it only makes the distance greater. I could wish that these were games. I am thinking of a person, or of a poem: 'When Spring comes, everywhere there are peach blossom streams./No one can tell which may be the Spring of paradise.'

Of the dish I am jealous, and not jealous of the beautiful girl who loves me. Why? The weight of an obsession alters the regular shapes of feelings, without inching their doors open a crack upon the chaos they come from. A is crazy about B because of X, where X equals A's image of B, which may be X plus or minus B. A wants to capture B's aura all for himself; desperately he wants to possess this aura. He becomes jealous when he suspects that D or E may enjoy, or be tormented by, the same image. A is also jealous because he knows that he can only capture the image in the aura, never the reality of B, in all her mutability and truth. Even the aura, being fugitive, may never be captured. So B escapes, frantically A pursues her, his image of her, that is, which might never, in the last analysis, equal B at all, it is only a trace of some being he has detected in her, a latent being, a snatch of a melody she never heard in herself. Or the image is nothing, the trace nothing but a whiff of something that A has lacked, for which he has craved, as long as he can remember, longer, for memory is not bad nourishment.

There is no last analysis. There is an irreducible irreversible nonconformity: What A pursues is not this, not that, but always other. B knows this, in her bones, she makes no mistake, she escapes across the border, every time. Good for her, but not for A, not for him. What she wants is to be truly herself, she says, and, if wanted by anyone, then wanted as a person who has something to do in this life, to be criticized, to be put in focus by that criticism, someone you can feel free with or close to, take it or leave it, to be desired for herself alone, that's what she wants. To be understood, she says, just that, no Spring of paradise, no dithering up and down the streets and airways of Europe, no rainbows, no goddesses, not even a honeypot in a park after midnight. But I could never find it in me to understand: as if her being were a word for which there was no spelling whatever.

Immensities of starlit night are forgotten by two who can exchange one look across time, or in the lamplight of a tavern. In that forgetting lies the misery of an exchange that is none, because neither can read between the looks the script that is written in kerosene and suspicion. A is deluded if he thinks that D or E may project the same image of B as he does. In his stupor, or simplicity at best, A fails to see that his image is an exoskeleton of his own unanswerable desires. With tooth and nail, as A knows, B will resist any move of A's to reduce her to his figment, or to the status of a relay station for the signals his demon sporadically sends him. See me for what I am, she says, plain ordinary, hateful, confused, hot and cold, depending, not this skin, this dish, though I can't blame you, she says, standing naked before a washstand mirror early in the day, I'm quite a dish, but I don't know you, you don't know me, desire simply comes and goes, and for me there is nothing much comes of it, unless you gradually get to know a person as a person, me, I'm real in all my changes, you can't figure me out by putting me in a box, what do you think it all means otherwise, only these scattered moments, beautiful sometimes, but this up and down, I can't stand it, why don't you just go away? Three moments later she is embracing A, in the bed, for he has buried his head under the sheet, and sobs: 'Goodbye, body, I am being born.'

On another bed, in a blue room, not far from the great river, there was another embrace, the bodies of A and B together, one stream, an embrace like no other, everything fitting, arms and mouths, legs and thighs, knees, elbows, but nothing tight, all airy cool, and a lightness in it, the touch of acrobats in midflight, sustained for a moment, until, fools, they broke it up and went down the stairs for a meal.

At present I don't even know if the dish is alive or dead. She was alive when I was crouching over a letter to her in a dark Danish café several centuries ago. When we were together I had felt her life glide into me, not as an interference, but as some permanent, precious, and strange thing. I received her life then, even if now she is dead. If she is dead, nobody but I could have done it, nobody. But in the letter I only said that the coffee had a sheen, like a clock face on a remote tower, that I could see no clock hands in it, no divisions of time, no hours but one, vast, like a space, and motionless, yet light as a sigh, and hoping this reaches you.

What are they made of, these signals, these penetrating rays that human beings transmit to one another? Love, a great and terrible spirit, can materialize through hosts of tricks. My trick is to love more by imitation than by understanding. A few details, glowing distinct notes, a single look, then the play begins. When the dish and I do fall apart, it is because she feels that it is I who am calling all the shots, playing all the roles. Yet, given time enough, we can be at one in both ways, we can imitate and understand one another, we are channels through which what is between us freely flows, and then I can tell no difference between understanding and imitation, for there are better differences to respond to.

Nor, when I imitate, when my imagination starts to fly, lofted by an image of the dish, can I sharply distinguish between the dish and my image of her. What am I capturing, her aura, or mine? Wanting the dish, I want her to be in myself, that hard energy, coolness, elasticity, what is it, I have seen it in small casual gestures, an eyelid flickers, a finger curls, it is some element I have lost sight of in myself. At least, some of the time it is missing, not always, how could I otherwise respond to her at all?

Missing the dish is what makes me the maniac she has told me I am. No question: I am more of a maniac when I am where she is not. What I make of her, could I induce it to live inside me like daylight, and would I then be luminous, contained, would there be in me a radiance like that which I see when I see her or merely think of her face? I doubt it. Deep down inside me there is this triggerman of mine, insatiable, a maniac of the unknown, who invents the unknown, in order to get at it, who feels, in the unknown, the movement and tension of desire itself.

My only depth, this desire. The rest of me, come to think of it, is flat, schematic, like the universe of a terrorist, or of his progenitor, the colonialist. Seeing the surfaces all around me, extensions of my own ghostlines, I tell myself: Tens of thousands of years and still, now more than ever, perhaps, the ego, shut out, or believing itself to be, impostor, beats everything flat, to find a way in, achieve a deathless insight, its golden Agamemnon mask, and how frustrating to be so inflexibly hooked on penetration, it must be wrong, it has put the world wrong, any response that thrills through two beings must come from something else, a receptiveness creates it, a turning inside-out, plantlike, or a touch is relayed — and is the lock sprung? Now, even this talk of mine — flat. My jaws work, I feel a link snap, I slide in one breath to the limit of what I can say. Wholesome words, once they spelled out the body's living truth, history has lost its voice, that's what flattens me, no, brushes me aside, my rigmarole a raving from the gutter, unaccountable frenzy, a featureless thrusting want.

A tarpaulin spread over two sticks: the writing: — a flat sort of shelter. But the desire, what to do with it? In times past it could break out of me, doing no harm, never shucking consciousness, couple with this particular rock, that smell of fresh hay, a sound far-off, I could send out my triggerman to fathom the small studious eyes of a blowfish. Even in the language we share, what can the dish know of this? Would it not have been better to look a shark in the eye? She has given herself to it, in high spirits. Then she stands back. No deal, she says; later, all of a sudden, happily, 'You're a gem, you're in!' But what's in it for her, she asks. Doing so, she sends me this signal, and there's nothing in me to contradict it: If you want me in yourself, make me out of yourself, not out of selected bits of me. Is that difficult, or is it nonsense? Either way, she has been sensitive. It was not unjust of her: she had caught me redhanded, not thieving from her, but using her as a medium, and I should have been feeling a way toward her, dispassionately. I should have been simply receptive to her as a being, absolute, other, in her own right, as an independent subject, with a great distance, call it freedom, between what I could see of her and her whole configuration. When there is no other to be conceived of without the one, and when, once identified, the other becomes the one, you have no contradiction, for you have no freedom, only the lock, which will not be sprung.

Yet it was a surprise to her when I simply listened to what she told me of herself, her people, her foods, her games and thoughts, her animals, and doubts, her skills, as if I was only somebody who wanted to listen and knew how to listen. Later she was asking: 'Well, is there any mystery left between us now?' There is, even if you are dead, dish, even then there is a mystery, it is not a thing that talk can diminish, listen to it now, rustling deep down inside my imitation head, this mad pomegranate tree.

Hundreds of miles and a sea away from the dish I saw a girl run down the beach, shaking her hair back and plunging into the first wave. I knew it could not be the dish, and in a moment I was ambling over to see if it was. In some other age I could have put her there by a magical act: participation in her being, an exchange of forms mediated by the sheer power of the image that breathes and dances in my mind. All you can put there now is imago. The being is resistant, living elsewhere, another configuration, occult. Mythic union has been and gone, eventually it bored imagination stiff. A loss, for if imagination has nothing impossible to play for, it can engender no new substance.

What then. If. If only. If but this . . . And sorry it often is, in its delicate fibres, but potent, God knows, this flesh, hard as nails. Did God once so magnetically love his creatures that he was loving in them himself? If he too was a self-multiplying magician, ringing every form and atom with the force-fields of his own give and take, then the dish and I might still be there for his pleasure, and for his cross-purposes. Dish, remember the dry leaves that stuck to your hands, the dark rushing of that river, the candle you were going to put outside my door. Remember the dinner plates crashing to the floor at Syrtaki, the Macedonian dancing for Easter, how Niko and Elias capered all over the splinters. Upstairs, afterward, with the blackbird starting to sing the dawn in, I lay on the carpet, don't forget, blasted with drink, and wept, because I have done nothing for the poor people, because children are murdered in riots of rotten idealism, and because all the books do nothing to stop evil in its tracks. That is the despair your beauty unleashed in me, dish. It goes out in all directions, when I am where you are not.

Again I am impossible, whether it's you I embrace or this limbo of want in me, where nothing is rooted, but out of which, here and there, a complete moment may sprout, the lotus. Still more remote, we might find joy in one another's being, or else collide in caprice. Not for us the knifelike divine objectivity even with duller human edges. Not for us the devil's indifference. Some wounds there are that can't be closed, they can't be, or else the world might stop breathing. Out of wounds like those a mystery still manages to trickle, different, real.

In Corsica there is a place called Porto, a cove framed by mountains of red rock. Huge cliffs plummet to the sea, yet when you look at Porto from a distance the mountains weigh nothing: their bases are swathed in a light blue mist, which floats them upward, or like enormous animals they have splashed into a sea of nothing, and the splash permanently bathes their bellies. The dish has never seen this, but she may have seen something like it, in one of her dreams, or when she stood up, early one morning, in the hills below Digne. 'Tremulous snailhorn perception of beauty' — a Chinese painting, not exactly, for Porto, except on the map, is neighbour to nothing, the sea near nightfall one colour with the sky, sun a blur or radiance buried in the sea, mountain crest melting into opal mist that fetches up from unexplored deep valleys, a bell sounds, faint, an oar splashes, a bus romps along the narrow winding cliff road, and it was here, held up for a time by a flat tyre, walking to the sea, that I felt my heartbeat was stopping, any moment now, no strength left, this was it. A blaze of sun. I had no past, no future, I was thin to transparency, one last breath, not enough, not even enough for a soap bubble, any moment now, I had no thought, not even for my beautiful friend, there beside me, not for the dish, of whom I had thought day in day out for six months, no thought of myself either, I was this void, I was this void which Porto traps in its rocks and light, I was one with it, imitating it, but nothing, a mouthful of jelly at most, an eye, glancing across, enormous eucalyptus, silver blue sheet of sea on the far side of a knoll, and into the air, breathless, I said, last words, 'I am afraid', then sat down on a rock, amazed that everything was still going on, amazed that children came past, ready for a swim, a dog with his nose up, a man tinkering with his boat, he spoke to me, hatless, but still I am alive, one two three days afterward, alive, not frightened, so tell me, dish, answer me now, I cannot compel you, listen, it cannot hurt you, tell me if it was not you thinking me in Porto, obliterating me, answer me now, or did I do it, can we meet in no place but nothingness, are you alive or are you dead?

# Acknowledgments

Several of these essays have been published previously. Acknowledgment is made to Suhrkamp-Insel Publishers for permission to reprint 'On Translating Poems by Goethe' (Introduction to Goethe, *Selected Poems*, Boston, USA, 1983); also to the editors of *Chicago Review*, where 'The Pursuit of the Kingfisher' first appeared (vol. 28, 1977, 4); to the *New York Review of Books*; to *Poetry* (Hong Kong); to *Scripsi* (University of Melbourne); and to *Poetry Nation Review*, where several essays first appeared (in nos. 3, 10, 16, 22, 26, 28 and 32).

# References

## Introductory Afterthoughts

1. Robert Byron, *First Russia Then Tibet* (Macmillan, 1933) p. 58. For *vases*, below, see p. 93.
2. Leonardo da Vinci, *The Notebooks* (New York: Modern Library edn., 1957) p. 233.
3. Victor Turner, *Image and Pilgrimage in Christian culture: anthropological perspectives* (Columbia University Press, 1978); also *The Ritual Process: structure and anti-structure* (Routledge & Kegan Paul, 1969; Penguin, 1974).
4. *rare freedom of the particle*: Loren Eiseley, *The Man Who Saw Through Time* (Scribners, 1973) p. 101.
5. *a secular art*: William Carlos Williams, cited in Karl Shapiro, *In Defense of Ignorance* (Random House, 1960) p. 168.

## On Translating Poems by Goethe

The essay was written as an introduction to Goethe, *Selected Poems* (Boston; Suhrkamp Insel Publishers, 1983). Readers without German are referred to studies in English by Barker Fairley (1947), Karl Viëtor (1949), and Richard Friedenthal (1965); also to Stephen Spender's introduction to *Great Writings of Goethe* (New York: NAL, 1978) and David Luke's to Goethe, *Selected Verse* (Penguin, 1964). Two other instructive books are W. H. Bruford, *Culture and Society in Classical Weimar* (Cambridge University Press, 1962), and Wolfgang Leppmann, *The German Image of Goethe* (Clarendon Press, 1961).

1. *Carl Einstein*: 'Obituary: 1832–1932', *Transition* (Paris), 21, (1932). Eugene Jolas's English translation from the German is the only extant version of this text.

2. *Believable modern English idiom*: see Donald Carne-Ross's incisive remarks on modern translations of old classic poets, especially Góngora, in his essay 'Dark With Excessive Bright', *Instaurations* (University of California Press, 1979).

3. *Extempore*: John Keats, *Complete Works*, H. Buxton Forman, (ed.) vol. V, (Glasgow, 1901), p. 43.

4. *Thunder, raindrops*: Eliza Buckminster Lee, *The Life of Jean Paul Frederic Richter, preceded by his Autobiography* (Boston: 1864), p. 249.

5. *Dissect the lyrics*: Ezra Pound, *Make It New* (Faber, 1934), p. 338.

6. *Linearity and undulance*: 'Preface 1876' in Walt Whitman, *Complete Poetry and Selected Prose*, James E. Miller (ed.) (Houghton Mifflin, 1959), p. 440.

7. *Transcreations*: See 'Post Scriptum' to his book of Portuguese translations from *Faust*, and essays: *Deus e o Diabo: No Fausto de Goethe* (Sao Paulo: Editora Perspectiva, 1981).

8. *Violence within*: Wallace Stevens, *The Necessary Angel* (New York: Vintage, 1951) pp. 7 and 36. One touches here on the *oneiric* domain of Goethe's work, its mantic dimensions, its *arcana*, much respected by some Surrealists and depth-psychologists.

9. *Older translations*: Source — *Poems of Goethe Translated in the Original Metres* (1882) (earlier editions go back to the 1850s), with versions by E. A. Bowring, Theodore Martin, W. E. Aytoun, and others. My revisions have been slight in some cases; 'Dedication' and 'The Bride of Corinth' needed heavy restoration. Henri-Frédéric Amiel (*Les étrangères*, Paris: 1876) and O.V. de L. Milosz (*Chefs d'œuvre lyriques du nord*, Paris: 1968) achieved a few striking successes in French. Amiel's version (wholly forgotten, I think) of 'Song of the Spirits over the Waters' is unique for its rendition of the phonic qualities of the original, and it is odd, since it has rhymes, whereas the original does not.

10. *Mens teutonica*: in *Cousin Pons* (1848; Penguin, 1968) translated by H. J. Hunt, and in a passage that speaks volumes, e.g., '. . . the urge to find psychic meaning in material trifles which is responsible for the uninterpretable works of Jean-Paul Richter, the tipsy fantasies which Hoffmann has put into print and the folio volumes which, in Germany, ward off access to the simplest questions and delve down into unfathomable depths, only to reveal a *mens teutonica* at the bottom' (p. 34).

11. *Aquinas and Dante*: cf. chapter 7 of Philip Wicksteed's brilliant, stylish and seminal lectures, *Dante and Aquinas* (London: Dent, and New York: Dutton, 1913).

12. *Gleim*: see Max von Boehn, *Deutschland im 18. Jahrhundert*. vol. 1 (Berlin, 1927) pp. 494–5. Boehn misdates the event; I am grateful to Gregor Sebba for referring me to the source for the correct date, 1777 — Biedermann, *Goethes Gespräche* (1909–11).
13. *Bespeaks a great confidence*: Donald Carne-Ross, op. cit., p. 140.
14. *Part of the natural continuum*: quoted from David Luke, op. cit., p. xxx.

## For Márton, Erwin, and Miklos

Written at the invitation of the editors of the Hungarian literary review *Uj Irás*.

1. Francis Ponge, *The Voice of Things*, translated by Beth Archer (McGraw-Hill, 1972).
2. George Seferis, *Collected Poems 1924–55*, translated by Edmund Keeley and Philip Sherrard. (Jonathan Cape, 1969).

## Pai Ch'iu's Arm Chair

The translation of the poem is by John McLellan. It appears in *An Anthology of Contemporary Chinese Literature/Taiwan 1949–74, vol. 1 — Poems and Essays*, edited and compiled by Chi Pang-yuan and others, National Institute for Compilation and Translation, Taipei, Taiwan, Republic of China (University of Washington Press, 1975, second printing 1977). Pai Ch'iu was born in 1937: *Death of the Moth*, 1967, *The Sky Symbol*, 1970, *Chansons*, 1972.

1. Osip Mandelstam, *Selected Essays*, translated by Clarence Brown and Robert Hughes (University of Texas Press, 1977) p. 37.

## The Pursuit of the Kingfisher

1. Franz Kafka, *The Castle* (Penguin, 1957) p. 173.
2. J. Z. Young, *An Introduction to the Study of Man* (Clarendon Press, 1971) p. 136.

3. Emile Benveniste, *Problems in General Linguistics*, translated by Mary Elizabeth Meek (1966; University of Miami Press, 1971) pp. 224–5.

4. Dorothy Eggan, 'The Personal Use of Myth in Dreams', in *Myth: A Symposium*, Thomas E. Sebeok (ed.) (Indiana University Press, 1970).

5. Paul Celan to Robert Beaugarde: cited in *Dimension* VII, 3 (Austin, Texas, 1974), p. 337.

6. A. Sinyavsky, *A Voice from the Chorus*, translated by Kyril Fitzlyon and Max Hayward (Farrar Straus & Giroux, 1976) p. 130, and p. 322 for the passage quoted in section 7, below.

7. Loren Eiseley, *The Unexpected Universe* (Harcourt Brace, 1969) p. 146.

8. Osip Mandelstam, 'The Word and Culture' (1921), translated by Sidney Monas, in *Selected Essays*, p. 52.

# Ideas about Voice in Poetry

1. *Voice of a narrator*: this is not only to be heard as we hear it in, say, Emily Brontë, Henry James, E. M. Forster, L.-F.Céline, or Thomas Mann. There is an oral narrative about a Trickster, among the Panamanian Kuna people, in which slight coughs punctuate the telling; these coughs are markers — of suspense, emphasis, and tempo (Joel Sherzer, *Kuna Ways of Speaking*, University of Texas Press, 1983).

2. Walter Benjamin, *Reflections* (Harcourt Brace/Helen Wolff, 1978) p. 92 and p. 327 for reference in section 7.

3. Osip Mandelstam, from 'The Word and Culture' op. cit., p. 52.

4. *Hölderlin*: for the passage quoted from 'Griechenland', see *Selected Poems of Friedrich Hölderlin and Eduard Mörike*, Christopher Middleton (ed.) (University of Chicago Press, 1972) p. 121.

5. Roman Jakobson, 'On the Verbal Art of William Blake and Other Poet-Painters,' *Linguistic Inquiry*, 1, 1, 1970.

6. Gustav Sobin, *Celebration of the Sound Through* (New York, Montemora Foundation 1982) p. 21 (unnumbered).

7. Leo Spitzer, 'The "Ode on a Grecian Urn"', or Content vs Metagrammar,' in his *Essays on English and American Literature* (Princeton University Press, 1962).

# Reflections on a Viking Prow, 1–2

*Details of slides and texts illustrating the lecture as which this essay began*: SB = reproduced from *Schrift und Bild*, catalogue, Frankfurt am Main, Typos Verlag, for Staatliche Kunsthalle, Baden-Baden, 1963; CP = reproduced from *Concrete Poetry: a world view*, edited by Mary Ellen Solt, Bloomington, Indiana University Press, 1968.

1. Prow of Oseberg Viking ship before restoration.
2. Early Stone Age amber figurines (National Museum of Denmark).
3. Late Stone Age flint dagger imitating form of bronze dagger, from Funen, Denmark (1800–1500 BC).
4. Christ Divine Wisdom (painting, Byzantine Museum, Athens — Christ holding Bible open in his left hand).
5. Two figure-painted playing cards, with ideogram texts, from a set used for poetic guessing games. Early 12th c. Japan (University of Durham, Gulbenkian Museum).
6. Persian calligraphy, proverb in shape of a bird, AD 1872 (SB).
7. Kufic script (visual-lexical calligraphy) (SB).
8. Hans Hartung, *Encre de chine*, 1952 (calligraphy as abstract picture) (SB).
9. Codex Alexandrinus. Greek script on vellum, 5th c. AD (British Museum).
10. Vassily Kandinsky, *Rows of Symbols*, 1931 (painting, Kunstsammlung, Basel).
11. Wally Barker, *Brown Watercolor*, 1961. (SB).
12. I.C. Hiltensperger (master calligrapher), *Labyrinth*, early 18th c. (calligraphy in rotation) (SB).
13. Ferdinand Kriwet, *Rundscheibe Nr.5*, 1962 (print in rotation) (SB).
14. Paul Klee, *Er küsse mich*, 1921 (picture-text from Song of Songs (SB).
15. Paul Klee, *Ad marginem*, 1930–36 (isolated letters in painting, Kunstsammlung, Basel).
16. Paul Klee, *Anfang eines Gedichtes*, 1938 (scattered childish letters assembling) (SB).
17. Carlfriedrich Claus, *Paracelsische Denklandschaft*, 1962 (imaginary language picture-text) (SB).
18. Kasimir Malevitch, *Englishman in Moscow*, 1913–14 (Russian letters as elements in design, painting, Amsterdam) (SB).

19. Iliazd (Ilya Zdanevitch), page from *Ledentu, le phare* (play), 1923 (Russian typographic invention) (SB).
20. Jiří Kolář, *Le poème évident*, 1967 (picture/wording collage) (CP).
21. Ian Hamilton Finlay, *Wave/Rock*, 1966 (printed words sand-blasted into glass, photo by Jonathan Williams) (CP).
22. Franz Mon, *Abstraktion*, 1963 (shredded letters) (SB).
23. Rilke, autograph of last Orpheus Sonnet, 1923.
24. Facteur Cheval, interior wall of his Palais Idéal, with inscription (Hauterives, SE France, c.1910).

*Texts*

1. Arthur Rimbaud, 'Marine' (from *Les Illuminations*, c.1872–74).
2. Gerard Manley Hopkins, journal for 11 July, 1866.
3. Eduard Mörike, 'Auf eine Lampe' (1846), 'Im Park' (Spring 1847).
4. Rudyard Kipling, from *Letters of Travel* (The Canadian Pacific, 1892).
5. Rainer Maria Rilke, 'Römische Fontäne' (July 1906), 'Der Ball' (July 1907).
6. William Carlos Williams, 'The Term', *Spring and All*, XXI, 'Poem' ('As the cat . . .') (1920s).
7. Poem by e. e. cummings.

*References in the text*

1. George Kubler, *The Shape of Time* (Yale University Press, 1962).
2. Walter Benjamin, 'Das Kunstwerk im Zeitalter seiner tech-nischen Reproduzierbarkeit' (1935), in *Illuminationen* (Frankfurt am Main: Suhrkamp Verlag, 1961).
3. George Konrad, *The Case Worker* (Harcourt Brace, 1974) p. 18; cf. p. 86 — 'In the phantasmagoric world of good and evil, . . . in that ambiguous heedless world of ideas that has no more relevance to the massive ambiguity of human affairs than an impotent old man to the backside of a whore, I have stood with the judges for as long as I can remember, but . . . far from wholeheartedly.'
4. On Kurosawa: Dennis Giles, 'Kurosawa's Heroes', in *Arion* (new series), 2 (1975) 2.
5. Gerard Manley Hopkins, *Poems and Prose*, W. H. Gardner (ed.) (Penguin, 1953) 'Oak tree', p. 110; 'bluebell' pp. 122–3; 'growing', p. 129 (see below).

6. Rudyard Kipling, *Letters of Travel, 1892–1913* (Scribner, 1920) esp. pp. 30–31, e.g., 'The mountain torrent is a boss of palest emerald ice against the dazzle of the snow; the pine stumps are capped and hooded with gigantic mushrooms of snow . . .'

7. On some poems about things, see N. M. Willard, 'A Poetry of Things: Williams, Rilke, Ponge' in *Comparative Literature*, 17, 1965. An admirable but little known essay on things and poems — which I had not read before writing mine, is Gregor Sebba's 'Das Kunstwerk als Kosmion' in *Politische Ordnung und menschliche Existenz: Festgabe für Eric Voegelin*, Alois Dempf, Hannah Arendt, and Friedrich Engel-Jacobi (eds.) (Munich: C. H. Beck, 1962).

8. Rilke on Amenophis IV, in Magda von Hattingberg, *Rilke und Benvenuta* (Vienna, 1947) p. 282.

9. *Sacramental value*: see David Jones, 'Art and Sacrament' in his *Epoch and Artist* (Faber, 1959).

10. Saint Augustine, quoted by Meister Eckhart, in *The Spear of Gold* H. A. Reinhold (ed.) (Burns Oates, 1947) p. 60.

11. Goethe, *Italienische Reise* Hamburger Ausgabe, XI (1950 and 1957) pp. 93 and 211. The Mayer-Auden translation of the 9 October passage is weak (and wrong), so I have not adopted it. I modify for accuracy their translation of the later passage: *Italian Journey*, translated by W. H. Auden and Elizabeth Mayer (Collins, 1962) pp. 84 and 202.

12. Martin Heidegger, 'The Thing' in *Poetry, Language, Thought*, translated by Albert Hofstadter (New York: Harper & Row, 1971), p. 176. Heidegger oddly ignores the Sanskrit word *vastu*, which is polysemous, meaning 'abiding essence', 'subject of concern', 'object', 'property'. See Sir Monier Monier-Williams, *Sanskrit-English Dictionary.* (Oxford: Clarendon Press, 1899) p. 932. The word vástu (accented *a*) means 'becoming light', 'dawning', 'morning'. Is it possible that this sense coincides with the 'abiding essence' of vástú (equal accent)? Did the latter's sense, as 'object', arise by analogy out of 'abiding essence', but at a later date? The words might be related, within a preliterate, pre-selfconscious semantics of 'disclosure', so that at a certain stage in the evolution of consciousness a thing could be experienced as an opening on being, a dawn of being. This sense seems to be preserved in Greek *phainomenon*, and is tacit even in German *Erscheinung*.

13. Julian Jaynes, *The Origin of Consciousness in the Breakdown of the Bicameral Mind.* (Houghton Mifflin, 1976).

14. Yurok saying: Sandra Corrie Newman, quoting Rea Barber, in
    *Indian Basket Weaving* (Flagstaff: Northland Press, 1974) p. 25.

# Syntax and Signification in Hölderlin's 'Andenken'

1. *Orpingelik*: the quotations are genuine, the reference is lost.
2. Irving Wohlfarth, 'Walter Benjamin's Image of Interpretation' in
   *New German Critique*, 17 (1979) p. 85.
3. Georges Poulet, *Studies in Human Time* (Harper Torchbooks, 1959)
   p. 12, and (for section 8, below) p. 25.
4. J. G. Hamann, *Sibyllinische Blätter des Magus*, R. Unger (ed.) (Jena:
   1905) p. 102. Hamann's ideas exercised a powerful influence on
   the "Sturm und Drang"generation and were still widespread when
   Hölderlin was a student at Tübingen. Even Hegel, fellow-student
   and friend of Hölderlin's, thought highly of him.
5. Elias Canetti, *Aufzeichnungen 1942–48*. (Munich: Carl Hanser
   Verlag, 1965) p. 101. Cf. Rudolf Kassner's imaginary dialogue,
   'Der größte Mensch oder die heilige Zahl' — Seneca there speaks
   parabolically of non-Roman peoples in Asia Minor and Syria:
   'Not all people are Romans, and there are peoples who value
   knowledge of sacred numbers more highly than possession of the
   entire earth. For this reason, it seems to me, they are closer to the
   animals and plants than we are, and the secret of the relation
   between beings, of which we are told only by the fables of the poets,
   is more clearly revealed in them than in us, and beauty for them is
   not so much a mere stimulus or attraction toward that which is
   external and foreign to us and which we have to appropriate . . .
   Whereas our language has spread over the whole earth to
   announce our laws, theirs will spread from the roofs of their houses
   and from their river boats, to touch the dome of heaven and fade in
   the silence of the stars, out of which silence it once came' (*Die
   Mythen der Seele*. (Leipzig, 1927) pp. 83–84. Cf. sections 2 and 3 of
   'Ideas about Voice in Poetry' above.)
6. Wallace Stevens, 'Notes Toward a Supreme Fiction, VIII' in
   *Selected Poems* (Faber, 1953) p. 126.
7. Martin Heidegger, *Erläuterungen zu Hölderlins Gedichten* (Frankfurt
   am Main: Klostermann Verlag, 1951) pp. 75, f.

8. Aristotle, quoted by Nancy Milford, as epigraph to her 'De Memoria' in *The Writer on Her Work*, Janet Sternburg, (ed.) (W. W. Norton, 1980) p. 33.
9. W. H. Auden, *Collected Shorter Poems* (Faber, 1950) p. 175.

# Mallarmé: 'Le Tombeau de Charles Baudelaire'

For quotations from Mallarmé I have generally used Keith Bosley's translations: *The Poems* (Penguin, 1977). On one point I differ: 'la disparition élocutoire du poète' need not mean 'the disappearance of the poet as a speaker'. 'Elocutory disappearance' means that the poet, in the act of speech, disappears — his voice becomes otherwise.

1. Donald Carne-Ross, *op. cit.*, pp. 144–5.
2. For Tynianov, see either Jurii N. Tynianov, *Das Problem der Verssprache*, *passim*, (Munich, 1977) or the less adequate English translation, *The Problem of Verse Language*, edited and translated by Michael Harvey and Brent Harvey (Ann Arbor: Ardis, 1981).
3. Hölderlin's 'Über den Unterschied der Dichtarten' consists of notes for an essay he never wrote — but the discourse, though obscure, is continuous. I hazard, in note 4 below, an extract in translation. (Mapping relations between three distinct tonalities, heroic, naive, and ideal — or abstract and contemplative — in the poem) 'The tragic poem, heroic on the surface, has an ideal base tone, and at the foundation of all such works there must be a single spiritual (or intellectual) vision. This vision can only be that unity with everything that lives, a unity not felt, it is true, by more limited sensibilities, a unity only intuited in the loftiest aspirations, but which can be cognized by the intellect, and which is predicated upon the impossibility of any absolute separation and isolation. The unity is most easily expressed by our saying that actual separation, and with it all that is material and transient, likewise the connection, and with it all that is actually spiritual and permanent, the Objective as such, as well as the Subjective as such, are only a state (*Zustand*) of the Original Union, a state in which that Union finds itself, because it had to emerge out of itself, on account of the stasis (*Stillstand*), which could not occur in it, because the kind of unification that does occur in it should not

always remain the same, as regards material reality, because the parts of the One (*des Einigen*) should not always remain at a constant distance from or proximity to one another, in order that everything should encounter everything and each receive its whole right, its complete measure of life, and that each part in the progression should be as complete as the Whole, the Whole in the progression be as distinct as the parts, that the Whole might gain in content, the parts in inwardness, the Whole in life, the parts in vivacity, the Whole come to feel itself more in the progression, the parts in the progression be more fulfilled in themselves; for it is an eternal law that the Whole in which all substance is stored (*das gehaltreiche Ganze*) does not in its Oneness feel itself with the distinctness and vivacity — this sensuous oneness — with which its parts — also a whole, only connected more loosely — feel themselves, so that one can say that if and when the vivacity, distinctness, unity of the parts, once their Wholeness feels itself, transcend the limit of the parts and become Suffering — as absolute as possible in its decisiveness and isolation — only then does the Whole feel itself, *in these parts*, as vivaciously and distinctly as the parts do in a more tranquil, yet also moved state — in their more limited Wholeness. Tranquil and moved, for instance, as is the lyrical (more individual) mood: for here the individual world in its most complete and perfect life and purest unity, strives to dissolve itself, and at that point where this world individualizes itself, in that part into which its parts converge, it seems to evaporate in the inmost feeling, yet, then and there, as a person who feels and the feeling itself are about to separate, the more individual Unity comes to be present most vivaciously and distinctly, and it resonates . . .'

# Some Old Hats from the History of Imagination

This essay was to some extent provoked by a distinct loathing of 'imagination' current among German writers arriving on the scene during the later 1970s. My witness was the poet Jürgen Theobaldy. Distrust of any 'large' language or language of high colour — as well as a rejection, in principle, of metaphoric wording — may be quite understandable within the German literary context. At this point I would like to refer to Andrei Sinyavsky's thoughts on the great 'realist' Leskov's statement: 'I am afraid I shall be quite unable to draw his portrait [that of a character] for the simple reason that I see him all too well and clear.' Sinyavsky comments: 'This phrase is a declaration of war on all *deliberate* attempts to be 'life-like' and sums up in a few words the essence of the truly creative mind which in practice always concerns itself with the unfamiliar — it is this that rouses the imagination and spurs it on. 'Truth to life' only makes it shy away. A thing too familiar does not surprise and therefore need not be copied. Art always first turns reality into something exotic, and only then starts making a representation of it' (*A Voice from the Chorus*, pp. 116–17).

Long before Shklovsky and Jakobson hit on the idea of 'de-familiarization' in the early 1920s, Keats had thought of 'custom' as a power atrophying 'original minds who do not think of it' (letter to Reynolds, 19 February 1818). Writing to his brother Thomas on 3 July 1818, Keats commiserated with Burns: 'how sad it is when a luxurious imagination is obliged, in self-defence, to deaden its delicacy in vulgarity and in things attainable, that it may not have the leisure to go mad after things that are not.'

1. Robert C. Solomon, *History and Human Nature: a review of European philosophy and culture 1750–1850* (Harcourt Brace, 1979).

# Neighing in the Wind

1. Ralph Freedman, *Hermann Hesse: a pilgrim of crisis* (Jonathan Cape; Pantheon Books, 1979).
2. *Flow and touch of proto-images*: Cf. my essay 'Hermann Hesse's *Morgenlandfahrt*' (1957), in *'Bolshevism in Art' and Other Expository Writings* (Carcanet Press, 1978).
3. *Dovzhenko*: quoted from his journals, *The Poet as Filmmaker* (MIT Press, 1973) pp. 140–1.

# Index

(Page numbers are not given for names and subjects when these are coextensive with particular essays. Thus the page numbers for Hölderlin or Lyrical Imagination fall outside the 'Andenken' and 'Old Hats' essays.)